Kathle...

What would I do

without you!!

Much love

Donna

x
x

12/4/2017

About the Author

Barrie was born in Bournemouth, and had theatrical leanings at an early age. After National Service he came to London and trained at several theatres and tours. His first play 'Teddy Boy' toured in the fifties and his own coffee house was opened in 1960 at The Seven Dials in Soho. It became famous, and infamous, for the many characters it attracted. Amongst its many customers were Quentin Crisp, Simon and Garfunkel, Paul Simon, Lindsey Kemp, Wayne Sleep and many, many more!

From 1972 he became well known as a theatrical agent as well as presenting many children's musicals on tour. He also presented star concerts such as The Jessie Matthews Show at the Shaftsbury Theatre in the West End and Jim Bailey at The London Palladium. He has presented over fifty concerts with John Hanson, Frankie Howerd, Bob Monkhouse and many others.

Lately he has toured his one man show and numerous 'Songbooks', mostly 'West End to Broadway', 'The Cole Porter Story', and others.

He has written children's musicals which have toured the UK and had his own gossip column in the late 'Plays and Players' magazine.

He recently had his first novel published and is writing more projects. At the age of eighty-five he looks back over the years and tries to recapture the many excitements, victories and memories he has enjoyed.

A TICKET TO THE CARNIVAL

FOR KEITH HOPKINS
With thanks for his long friendship,
help and kindness.

Barrie Stacey

A TICKET TO THE CARNIVAL

AUSTIN & MACAULEY

A CIP catalogue record for this title is
available from the British Library.

ISBN 978 1 84963 135 8

www.austinmacauley.com

First Published (2012)
Austin & Macauley Publishers Ltd.
25 Canada Square
Canary Wharf
London
E14 5LB

Printed & Bound in Great Britain

Acknowledgements

VALERIE LEE, for her early help in researching and compiling this book

BRENDA GWYN-WILLIAMS and PHIL PENFOLD for their help and work in preparation

NEILS WENKENS for his interest and good advice

ANGELA GRAHAM-JONES for her extensive work in the compilation and detailing

JOHN GARTLAND for his editing of the work

CHRISTOPHER WATERS for his early help and advice

Foreword

By QUENTIN CRISP

I am delighted at being asked to provide a foreword for *A Ticket To The Carnival*. It is my opinion that everyone should write one book, and that this should be the story of his life because the only thing that any man has to offer the world, that no one else can give, is himself.

Indeed, this is the current trend in literature. At one time fiction was more popular than fact because readers hoped that a novel might be more sensational. They were right then, but now the age of discretion is past. There is no longer anything that cannot be said, but have no fear. Mr Stacey can be trusted to tell all in a manner that will entertain everybody whilst wounding no-one.

I first met him when I began to frequent his coffee bar named 'The As You Like It'. This establishment was the last outpost of the vie de boheme which had once so colourfully flourished in nearby Soho. It was usually called 'The As' by its habitués who were too lazy to utter consecutive words at any one time. They were mostly young people who were about to write a novel that would shake the world, or who had very nearly been offered a part in a play that would run forever, or whose paintings had almost been accepted by a London gallery.

I was amazed to watch Mr Stacey serve those customers with scrupulous correctness while, at the same time, scourging them with the valour of his tongue. Grammarians have forbidden us to describe anything as 'more unique', but at least we can safely say that Mr Stacey was unique in a way that was spectacular and never failing.

As time went by, he seemed to feel that his boundless

energy was not being used to the fullest extent by selling food; he took to trafficking in people, though I have no doubt that he found them as hard to handle and more perishable. I became part of his stock in trade and ingenuity in whisking me round Britain to various provincial theatres. I came to regard him as a most unusual blend of brisk efficiency and unobtrusive kindness.

Because he is such an uncommon man, everybody who knows him has his own, often repeated, Barrie Stacey story to tell. Now we shall know how many of these tales are true.

QUENTIN CRISP

Foreword

By RUSSELL GRANT

Having read Quentin Crisp's glorious foreword in Barrie's book *A Ticket To The Carnival*, I cannot possibly compete nor indeed emulate him, so I shall just be me.

Barrie is unique. In fact, very unique, the most unique of his genre. Some say he is one of the few British eccentrics. I would say most surely (he would say, 'Don't call me Shirley!') and he is certainly one of the few British entrepreneurs who diligently, honestly, selflessly and constructively helps actors young and old to ply their trade, some say art. The art comes as a result of what trade they are plying and for whom, and that is where Mr Stacey comes in with aplomb.

During the strange anti-climax of the 1970s following the climax of the 1960s, Barrie kept so many people in theatre work by staging all kinds of faerie tales. As this fine gent is a combination of Bottom and Oberon, who else but he and his own kind of Fol de Rols could bring that kind of childhood magic to the stage?

I have never known dear Barrie to be depressed or down. He radiates an enthusiastic keenness in whatever he does, like a kind of Mr Micawber in more ironic sense. He offers sympathy only when it is very necessary, he never chastises or scolds but makes you feel the most important person he knows even if you are only the fifth Munchkin on the right. Actually, I was mayor of the Munchkins and doubled as the Wizard himself; he always starred me in the most interesting and challenging of roles, lifted by the intoxicating music of Aman.

So to you all I say 'Hallelujah!' for Barrie Stacey. A goodly man, friend, boss and mother (he called us all daughters), he has only ever used his Scorpio powers in the most serene and creative ways, never to destroy.

I thank him on behalf of myself and all those who owe the debt of gratitude that can only be paid in part by grabbing rare opportunities like this to express lifelong thoughts in words.

RUSSELL GRANT

Contents

Chapter 1

Another Recruit for the Rat-race

Sex, I have always understood, is a three letter word, loosely translated it means – 'You, me and When?' But to a backward teenager – I wasn't allowed to read the *News of the World* until I was three years old, it was something that the other chap enjoyed. It wasn't on the school curriculum then, although there were some snatches of it in the shower and more than a hint on the football field. A couple of would-be 'Lolitas' flaunted around the school spreading the message, and this was my first realisation of the truth in the claim that SEX is here to stay. They really had two things going for them even then, these gentle maidens, but it all passed me by from where I sat, way back in the forties.

I do not propose to dwell too much on where I first appeared and why. For the first part it would probably be very boring, and secondly, I can remember little about it anyway.

I was born in Bournemouth; Boscombe to be precise, quite near a lovely old movie house call 'The Astoria', where the superb organist, Ena Baga, thumped her instrument for the patrons for a decade, and the best seats were one shilling and ninepence. It was at a time when this lovely resort was known as 'The Queen of the South', not only for the fine long stretches of sandy beach, which are surely some of the finest in Europe, but for the gorgeous scenery. It is true that Neville Heath cut up a few willing widows in the bushes at Branksome Chine during Lent, but women were always an unpredictably funny bunch, and this incident did not dampen the enthusiasm of the holiday makers. They poured into the town even more to enjoy its many delights.

The town of Bournemouth was always stylish, with Westover Road very chic, and the hotels a mecca for floozies with ambition. Colonels with an insatiable appetite for a fruity desert were to be seen in abundance, though the old story that there's 'many a good tune to be played on an old fiddle' is perhaps open to doubt. So often a few strings were found to be missing!

My mother was a receptionist at the old Vale Royal Hotel, which overlooked the pier at Bournemouth. It was a hostelry that ran a coterie of chambermaids that would have delighted Paul Raymond. Mother moved to nearby Christchurch when I had forsaken rattles for something more erotic, and we stayed in this lovely old town famous for its Priory church and the gentle waters of the Avon. The King's Arms Hotel was the town's pride and joy, and anyone who was anyone, on staying their night in Christchurch would put up at this excellent inn. The local salmon was superb, and the Old English tea rooms by the Priory served excellent Earl Grey tea and large profiteroles oozing with the most delicious fresh cream. They were devoured with relish by young parsons who took tea at these rooms to get away from the choirboys.

I was the second baby to arrive to Phyllis Rosalind Stacey. The first was stillborn, and I was therefore the novelty – and probably still am. For a time I enjoyed the attention and fuss of being the first of a quartet. A first baby is something akin to a first lover, an event remembered lifelong.

My mother was a quiet, sweet lady, with a strikingly beautiful profile. She was very much in the Gladys Cooper mould, and in later years was not unlike the Prime Minister of today, Mrs Thatcher, save for the fact that she would never have lived over a greengrocer's shop. Mother came from Dorchester, where she started life with her sister, Rene, who did infinitely better in the marriage stakes than my mother and buried three husbands with great rapidity. This left her a widow of substance. She was really rather plain, and one recalls the words of wisdom mothers tell handsome sons – look for the plain wife and enjoy a quiet life. We saw little of Rene in our lives, and it was not until almost the end of my mother's time on earth that she turned up out of the blue. My grandmother, on my mother's side, was a ramrod of a woman, tall and erect as a colonel at Sandhurst. She declined to bring up her two daughters at all, and lived to the ripe old age of ninety-two, with the tradesmen forever in awe of her whiplash tongue and temper. I called on her once when in my teens and told the housekeeper my name. She came back to the front door with much speed to announce that my grandmother would only see friends in the afternoon.

Mother was brought up by her uncle, a charming gentleman with a rotund face framed by silver whiskers. He doted on Phyllis, bringing her up like his own daughter. Mother enjoyed an idyllic childhood until poor uncle was left a widower, and mother lost a devoted friend. Uncle was then seduced by a divorcee with expertise, who had a daughter the same age as Phyllis, and quickly ousted my poor mum and installed her own offspring as the favourite of the house. My uncle had little to say in the matter, and, after a couple of seasons with this hag of a widow, kicked the bucket, and was cremated without more ado. This left the 'Lady in Red' to enjoy herself with the loot uncle left behind, providing, as it did, much more gilt on her gingerbread. The merry widow was last seen leaving for Hong Kong in company with a very dapper Army officer.

My mother's uncle was mayor of Dorchester several times. He was a dear man. Mother suffered badly after his demise, both with grief and the changed circumstances of her life. Finding herself without an allowance, she had joined the staff of Lloyds Bank in the high street of Dorchester and later moved to the Vale Royal Hotel in Bournemouth. Mother loved hotel life and all that went with it. The 'Continental' was all the rage, even if you had two left feet, and perhaps put Arthur Murray on the road to fame and fortune. At that time Denise Robbins, Ethel M Dell and Ursula Bloom were the three writers heavily in favour. This early dynamic trio gave the chambermaids and shop girls exactly what they wanted... romance with a capital R.

Alas, most of us are suckers for a pretty face, and mother was no exception. My father worked in a more lowly capacity at the Vale Royal. Being a painter by trade and work being slow, he took temporary jobs whilst waiting to wield the paintbrush. This brought him to the hotel and Phyllis Hawkins. He took one look at Phyllis, who was being courted by the young and dashing heir to a grocery chain, and fell madly in love, wooing her with a ferocity that would have astonished Casanova. My mother was fascinated by this blond youth. Edwin Oswald Stacey had a pale and freckly complexion, with staggering blue eyes and a wide, generous mouth. Whether it was father's good looks or his motor cycle that made mother a goner I never knew. But we all know the charisma of that machine – one has only to remember Marlon Brando and Even Marie Saint in *The Wild Ones* to recognise this.

With my father looking like a young Lawrence of Arabia and my mother a little like Gladys Cooper in her teens, they were, indeed, a fetching pair. Mother was just as taken with Edwin Stacey as he was with her. Perhaps it was no surprise to the other staff when she left her job, prospects, family and, sad to say, the heir to the grocery chain. He could have been so useful to me in later years, and save me numerous trips to the pawnbroker. As mother's family had hardly been orthodox, perhaps this did not seem so surprising after all, the cook at the Vale related. For didn't her own mother refuse to bring up her offspring, and her father die at an early age. Whether he preferred heaven to his wife's superiority was never revealed. My grandmother rarely got out of bed after reaching the age of sixty years, except for a monthly excursion into Dorchester to reassure the tradespeople that she was alive and kicking. With her tailored clothes and imposing stature she must have resembled Edna Mary Oliver as crossed with Marjorie Main. The illustrious Quentin Crisp once remarked that 'Marriage is a mistake' and I really think he may have stumbled upon something here.

Phyllis Rosalind, with her hair shingled, superb bone structure gracing her face, with large deep-set eyes and warm smile, would have charmed Cleopatra's asp. She sold herself down the river, I fear, when she wed her young painter. For 'Happiness was not a thing called Joe', or even Ted, and after the initial period when bride and groom live in a fantasy world of sex and dreams, she became a slave without pay. Her life was possibly over by the time she was thirty-five. She loved children, which was just as well, as she gave birth to four boys during the early years of her marriage. We all rescued her to some degree from the pure despair that engulfed her later years.

My father loved babies and spent hours playing with them, but children were another matter. As soon as kindergarten was imminent and rattles were thrown away it was a different story. His affection evaporated overnight after the age of five, and it was mother who fulfilled the duties of both parents from then on. Father had a large jealous streak in his personality, and my mother only had to speak to the postman and she was thought to be having the greatest affair since Lily Langtry and Edward VII. Not an easy situation for anyone, and certainly most trying for a young woman embarking on marriage for the first time. Father was a vain man, and no matter what the state of the family purse, which was precarious most of the time, he still had his superbly tailored suits and shirts, not to mention an excellent selection of headgear. His speedboat was moored near the Christchurch Quay, while his membership at the sailing club was almost a must. He excelled in hunting, shooting and fishing, was a crack shot with a rifle, and was a hard act to follow.

Davey Crocket held no charm for me. I was about as handy in father's outdoor pursuits as a fashion model on safari. My brother John, a six footer and all man, was much more the type. Father could cope with John, and he became very popular for a short period until he rebelled and disagreed with my father, which was fatal. Father was quite sure he was God. There are so many about! At least in our particular province what he said was law. My second brother, Roy, was a quiet boy and kept to his own world, quite oblivious to any rows or tantrums within the family. He became a printer and has developed an almost Jewish knack for making money. Would that I could cultivate this skill. I must have gone to the wrong Sunday school.

The youngest of our family was yet another boy, David. He went blind at nine months with a very rare infection when an epidemic swept the town and over eighteen children lost their sight. My mother never really got over this blow, although she taught David well and his I.Q. was years ahead of his age. He was a leading chess player at eighteen, and was travelling to the races at nineteen and backing the right nags too. A little thing like blindness was not going to hamper him unduly.

Mother was a story-teller and spent many happy hours reading us the classics and well-loved fairy stories, so we were all extremely well read. Her diction and delivery were excellent, and a treasured memory is of the dulcet tones of her reading well into the evening. It fills my mind, now, so many years afterwards.

As the years passed, my mother and father had less and less in common, though my mother somehow found a spirit and courage to spar with my father and stop him having everything his own way. Indeed, occasionally their bouts of disagreement would have done justice to the 'Virginia Woolf' of Edward Albee. The marriage slowly disintegrated.

Father's meanness was unbelievable. He was as tight as a crab's backside, and made Molly Picon seem generous. I remember, when we were grown up, the sum of half a crown being tendered as a Christmas present. It was a good job I was not depending on pater to get me through college – in my case, an elementary school! He was an exacting and cruel master. My mother was left with a miserable and lonely existence, shackled to a man who was without compassion. She was, however, Victorian in her outlook, and believed when she had made her bed she would lie on it, and lie on it she did. She died some twenty-nine years ago and we all lost a true friend.

My father was stunned by the loss, and, although we got a little closer to him after her death, and did our best to make his life a little easier, he opted to dive into the freezing waters of the River Stour in the middle of a wintry night twenty-five years ago, which made the Christchurch news headlines and some television news for several evenings. All very sad. It is said that guilt can cast a shadow, and it could be that father wished to redeem his self-respect with his action.

The only thing in his favour as far as I was concerned was that he encouraged me in the arts. When, at the tender age of five, I would be singing in cafés and at concerts for a few bob, he would rehearse me relentlessly at home to make sure I knew what I was doing. This was probably to ensure that I would not make him look a Charlie in front of his friends. I had a strong, resounding voice, very suited to music hall, and knew how to use the pretty baby face looks that the Gods had given me. Just think what life could have been had I been born to Madame Rose and partnered her lovely daughter, Baby June. Shades of 'Let Me Entertain You' indeed.

I had one childhood companion called Claire Ricketts, who shared in all my early escapades and follies. Together we would act out all the scenes we saw at the local picture house in the Bargate. The picture house got films a little after Bournemouth, but it did not matter at all, and we would both see the film around twice, while our respective mothers went about their shopping. If our fathers felt we had been good they would reward us with a pennyworth of toffees. What an age ago it all seems when we pay a couple of quid for a packet of sweets now. This meant we would be at the pictures by one thirty, and probably come out at five thirty, with sometimes Saturday morning at ten o'clock as an added bonus. My knowledge of films has always been extremely good and I can, on a good day, rival Bob Monkhouse and Denis Norden in a movie quiz.

Claire opted for a married life, but I always felt she would have been so good in show business. She had a touch of Shirley Temple about her and indeed was almost as good as the silver screen's darling, thereby reserving a place on the good ship Lollipop. Her sound practical common sense and a flair for what would make money, would have been invaluable later on in my world of presenting shows. She was a great friend and shared many of my ups and downs in the rat race of the theatre and the world of greasepaint.

By the age of seven I had managed to develop mastoids which hung around longer than was healthy, and then anaemia came and went. Our local Dr Kildare absolutely loved me, and the bills from this carry-on ravaged the household for several years, and again did not endear me to my father. This was when it was decided I should go and live at intervals with my Aunt Ethel, who occupied a lovely house in Porchester Road, near the Central Station at Bournemouth. So there I was, just out of the knickerbocker stage, and already it was common gossip I was no 'Huckleberry Finn' tomboy figure, but then I could claim I was no 'Little Lord Fauntleroy' either.

Aunt Ethel was something else again. She made Mary Boland seem ordinary. She came from a large brood, thirteen in all. In those days there were not the distractions in the evenings that we have now, and large families were the rule rather than the exception. She was almost the eldest, only superseded by one, Bessie. Because of this they could not stand the sight of one another, not even wearing sun glasses, either drunk or sober, and sent each other up at each and every available moment for the rest of their lives. My father was the youngest of the brood, and as soon as he was in long pants he was sent to help quell the unrest in Ireland as a boy soldier. He should not have wasted his time, as the same thing is still going on in the land of the shamrock. Was there ever a country that has taken so long to make the peace?

Ethel had brought up my father with her son, Ralph, the product of her marriage to Uncle William. She had been engaged in the employment of William Harding, an architect of the highest reputation, in Bournemouth, which was in the county of Hampshire, but now Dorset, while still only in her late teens. Before many summers were out she married William, whom she truly loved. With at least forty years between them, this was quite an achievement. He adored her and she him and she managed to make him blissfully happy until the day he died, at the ripe old age of ninety-two. She was therefore left comfortably off. With a young son, and quickly made her mark in the social side of that prosperous seaside town.

Ralph was as different from my father as chalk from cheese. A tall, plump boy, he had a real country face, ruddy cheeks with a high, distinguished forehead. His hair decided to

27

emigrate from the early age of twenty-five, never to return. My father's made a similar retreat when she was twenty-seven, but we managed to find a solution of herbs, hope and witchcraft which we piled on his bald pate, and this did indeed grow a few hairs for a number of years. Ralph, however, has always been as bald as the proverbial badger.

What Aunt Ethel and her brothers missed in schooling, as grand-daddy was never one for the learning bit, they made up for down on the farm.

"Life is a banquet," said the witty mother of Gypsy Rose Lee. "May God be with you, but take a hatchet along, just in case."

I concur that life can be a fabulous education, and down on the farm that isn't all hay!

Aunt Ethel was a striking lass, and on the plump side, as any self-respecting country lass should be. She was a dress size fourteen before puberty, with a mass of auburn hair framing a large, jolly face. Her complexion was ruddy, which was not helpful in the ladies' powder room at downtown soirees, but her gigantic sense of humour carried her through and endeared her to the male species. She dressed very well for a woman of her girth, and had great style. She hated being seen without a hat, even in the bathroom, and on occasion her wardrobe would have excited Royalty. She sought the rewards of middle class society, and made it her goal to get there without delay. What she didn't know she learned – and quickly.

Uncle William had been married previously to a spinster of the parish. She bore him a daughter, Bella, who was eccentric, erratic and a true follower of Martita Hunt. She spent her last years living in the grounds of Wimborne Minster. Such was her devotion to the bells. In addition, she talked at length to many of the 'dear departed' sleeping silently in the summer air.

It was to this equivalent to Auntie Mame that I was sent to spend my formative years. Hey ho!

*****

Bournemouth in those days was revered by the rich, the lucky and the aspiring. It was unspoiled by the day trippers and foreign students who have latterly besieged the town and become a yearly malady. After all, fornicating on the beach was hardly a feature of the brochures for Bournemouth at that time. It boasted many hotels for the wealthy, the lonely and the plain randy. 'Bobby's was a centre for teatime, and did a brisk trade in the afternoons in the sun lounge where tea and toast were dispensed with cream cakes and meringues. Lobster teas, Henry Hall and Harry Roy and his band were all that one could ask for. Alfredo, (actually Fred Brown from nearby Westbourne) with his band, played ditties of the day, and the girls dreamed, through the haze of a 'Du Maurier', smoked in a long cigarette holder, of Nice... Monte Carlo... and Monterey. Summer romance was definitely in then, probably due to the books of Barbara Cartland. The waitresses had been at Bobby's since Mafeking, and probably before, and knew their art backwards. They also knew their customers backwards and could tell an enquiring soul the pedigree and progress of their customers without any hesitation at all. The liftman was another wonderful character; small in stature, but so rich in knowledge. He always insisted that Dolly Gray, of First World War fame, was a tart, and this knowledge I accepted without question. At eight years old this was my scene. No wonder I came to be precocious. Every other day (every day would have been far too common), I was instructed to approach the bandleader at Bobby's, our friend Alfredo. Usually between waltzes I would deliver a note from Aunt Ethel. What the note said I never found out. I questioned Aunt Ethel as to why she wrote him a note with such regularity and she replied: "If I told you – you would know." So I was never any the wiser.

Ethel was quick witted and vivacious and I adored her. 'Red sails in the Sunset' was definitely a tune she could dance to. Each day when we left the sun lounge after being fortified by tea and cakes, we emptied the sugar bowl into her large handbag without a murmur and sailed off for another shopping spree along the Westover Road. The sugar cubes were not for table consumption, but for the cocker spaniel waiting patiently at home.

The younger, swinging set, were to be seen at the Pavilion, where tea dances were all the rage. The famous bands of the period seen at one time or another were AMBROSE, MANTIVANI, LEW STONE, HARRY ROY and JOE LOSS. They all loved Bournemouth. There was also a marvellous operatic singer in a wheelchair who sang regularly at teatime in Bobby's. I can remember her magnificent voice till this day.

My aunt was a great success at the theatre, the ballet, the bridge parties and the flower shows, especially the flower shows! I was also always in attendance when she visited the hairdresser, a poor tradesman who usually only lasted a few weeks before she became besotted with another coiffeur whose expertise and personal charm warranted a try. How she would have loved Warren Beatty à la 'Shampoo'. My aunt followed the affairs of Royalty like a bloodhound does the scent. She elected to have a minor operation at her home in the late thirties, attended by a local quack so gorgeous that she almost had three relapses by choice. She developed an unbelievable temperature at this time when the Prince of Wales kissed England goodbye and took off to marry Mrs Simpson. She was so disturbed she fell out of bed and had to have all her stitches reworked. Her scrapbook on the royal scene would have filled a large corner in Christina Foyles' famous bookshop. She was never at a loss for a quick retort, and when asked at the opera if she was the Mayoress, she replied, as quick as a boomerang, "I am afraid I am not this year but I have every hope to be next." Clearly she was not a lass to end up between two slices of bread.

Her cooking prowess was in the top class, and equal, she was assured by many friends, to the best that Mrs Simpson could provide. This was an accolade indeed, as the universe was assured in countless books that Mrs Simpson's dinner parties were the most sought after in Paris, the grub as choice as the gossip. Like most cooks Ethel ate with a voracious appetite, and was of the opinion that expert cooking was simply a matter of common sense.

In the evening we would sing songs of her day and mine,

and end with a few hymns for luck. She was a marvellous gardener and worked as hard as any labourer, keeping the grounds at Porchester Road ablaze with every kind of flower and bloom. I felt it helped her keep one strand from her humble beginning. She was though, in many ways, something of a snob, and this was brought home to me vividly on more than one occasion whilst staying with her. We had a part-time gardener called Mr Smith, an unusual name, that! I would, on the days when he was with us, take his lunch on a tray to the greenhouse at the foot of the garden. He wasn't a bad old stick, but I do remember he usually smelt of Guinness. After all, we were constantly told of the goodness it could achieve; so good luck to him. He was allowed in the house only at holiday time or on Christmas Day for a glass of sherry. I learned with horror a little later on that he was actually Ethel's old man, and my grandfather. She was adamant when approached on the subject. He had, she felt, done nothing for her and her achievements in life, apart from his early biological contribution, and she had no intention of letting him mess up her chances in local society.

Ethel's other fault was borrowing. She hated to return anything she had borrowed – a fault she shared with many a politician. When she was loaned a commodity, it had gone for good. For anyone, except Bella, her step-daughter, this would have been final. Bella loaned her a sewing machine during a bout of spring cleaning and preparing new curtains for the household. The return of this noble machine was very much overdue, but return it she would not. It was obviously against her principles. However, not to be thwarted, Bella found a young actor, somewhere between parts in *Hamlet* and *The Trial of Mary Dugan*, willing to play a quick cameo part for a few bob. She paid him to engage Ethel in polite conversation at the front door while she ran up the garden path to the back door with the speed of a greyhound. There, in spite of being a frail old girl of five feet, she grabbed the desired machine and made for the roadway where a taxi awaited. Such endeavours were, I fear, necessary if one was to retain what was rightfully one's own.

Ethel would never have the tradesmen calling before ten in the morning or after three in the afternoon, for that was when our happy hour commenced in the drawing room. She did not get on with my brothers at all, and even once mistook my brother John for the butcher's boy. This destroyed forever any relationship they might have enjoyed. She arranged good marriages for at least one of her nieces, and her sister bought a pub at Corfe Mullen called 'The Coventry Arms', so the passion for booze was satisfied. The boys in the family did not do anything like as well.

Later, my father decided it was time for me to return home. A dreadful war broke out between Edwin (Ted) Stacey and his elder sister, and she was forced to set about finding another playmate for her social adventures in that most beautiful of resorts. Life at home was in complete contrast to my world with Aunt Ethel. I was thrown from a comfortable middle class existence to the rigours of the working class where it was brought home forcibly to me that bread was short (the coin, not the loaf), and it was arranged that I would deliver morning and evening newspapers to do my bit. Father also insisted that I help with his weekend decorating schedule in the house nearby. I came down to earth with a resounding thud. I dared not disobey, but I hated it with a venom not seen since Evelyn Laye scorned Jessie Matthews. I did, however, like delivering the papers in the early morning air. It suited my tendency to dream, and taught me much about the value of money.

I felt not a little personal resentment after arriving home from Aunt Ethel's. It was a little like asking Joan Collins to leave *Dynasty* and go for a season with 'Eastenders'. Joan Crawford could probably have managed it more easily, but then she had plenty of experience with down trade in 'Mildred Pierce'.

Ethel was livid that she was being dictated to by her baby brother, whom she had cared for since infancy. It was intolerable, monstrous! And the fact that he had achieved so little in life was even worse. For after all, where the hell would he have been without her, she asked; and bringing his four sons into the world on a wing and a prayer was hardly good planning. I had much to occupy me, but it did seem like a good case of jealousy. My father's strange mentality was often difficult to understand, extremely hard to forgive, and bloody annoying to swallow. He had already scotched my plans to pass my examinations and go to secondary school by arranging so much work in the evenings and weekends that I had no time at all to study or do homework. Even so, I came out on the borderline, and the State would have paid half my fees if the family paid the other half. Fat chance of that, and back to the paper round. Father maintained that I would learn more earning a few bob for the kitty than sitting at a desk in the secondary school. As life is often a great education he may have been a little in the right.

The entire affair was so savage on Aunt Ethel's nervous system that she ate a whole box of marshmallows at one sitting.

My mother was not too pleased, either. A little learning might be a dangerous thing, but if you have not grasped how many beans made five what chance had you? Luckily, I had, and the lack of education was never too noticeable.

Mother wanted me to go for banking. "Try something safe," as she put it. If only I had, how much richer I might have been. And so far away from the tempting delights of life upon the wicked stage.

"You'll never be strong enough to go careering off up and down the country in the theatre," she emphasised. "And consider the class of people." She knew the proprietor of a guest house who had almost the entire cast of *Charley's Aunt* staying one wet and windy week. The girl who played the juvenile lead vanished one day with the fish knives and forks. The only thing in her favour was that she did it on a Friday.

"A life on the boards, my son," Mother reasoned, "is not a good idea." She had not been impressed with my early efforts as a child singer, reasoning that it was no life for a child. She went on further to remark that even if I had the talent, and she wasn't too sure about that, either, it was a risky business. You can say that again. Cheek, bravado and a quick tongue, quite apart from a pretty face, might not be enough.

"All fur and no knickers... that's what I think about theatre people."

And I fear, there are multitudes that would agree with my mother. "Take theatricals away from the pubs and the breweries would be broke within a week." Savage stuff, maybe... If there was an answer to that, I certainly could not find it.

Mother also knew I was unhappy, and she tried, in her own way, to make it up to me. But with three children to tend and support, with all my brothers so much younger than myself, and a difficult husband to cope with, what could the poor woman do? She already worked in the mornings to earn a few shillings, so there was little time to try and sort out the problems of number one son, even if she could. A warm and passionate soul, and a mother par excellence, should only do her utmost, and sometimes that was not enough to save the ship. She knew it, and I knew it, and we both accepted it. When I had a personal decision to make I would go to her and ask her advice. She would not tell me what to do, but what she would do if she were me, which was something else again, and sound wisdom.

My father was still most elegant, thanks to Burton's, with an occasional trip to Dunn's emporium, and was dressed eight to the nines on weekday evenings and nine to the nines on Sundays, when he took his leisure at the club. He seemed to divide his spare time between fishing (he was very lucky with mackerel), boating, and drinking. If he took me out in his boat, I did everything wrong so rapidly and well, that it was a wonder that the bloody thing did not capsize. I had no rapture for the sea and I was certainly no Esther Williams either, and that was that. Father was a man's man, and although much has been made of that statement, in his case it was appropriate. He was most attractive to women, though barmaids seemed to head his fan club. They always had at least a couple of things going for them and he liked to think he had the knack to still pull the birds. He was, after all, still in his middle forties, which is nothing when assessing sex appeal in a man. A woman of similar age would probably be between the dressing

34

gown stage, or contemplating a quick 'lift' job on her face. But the male species is a different cup of tea, and so was my old man.

At home, rows were the rule rather than the exception, and over anything from the food not being cooked to his taste, to a mundane point of a bill not being paid. Sometimes it was like living on top of a volcano. We all breathed a sigh of relief when eventually he toddled off to one of his many evening pursuits leaving us to sit and listen to Henry Hall's guest night with mother.

During the war father was sent to make munitions. An old kidney failure had exempted him from the military, and he was detailed to nearby Blandford Camp. He lived in and we were all left in peace. Supper was out best meal of the day, and I went to great lengths to bring home something that would entrance my mother who had been so long deprived of many of the delicacies she had known in her youth. Sometimes it was a well preserved hare, a little lobster, or some smoked salmon. So many delights that she loved married live had denied her, whilst her early upbringing had dictated her tastes.

With paper rounds, walking dogs for lazy owners and other little bits of activity. I was pulling in funds which helped my mother considerably. Father occasionally descended on the house without warning, accusing my mother of having a wild affair with the milkman which was so ridiculous, as mother had no inclination for 'below stairs' intrigues, let alone a bold assignation. Anyway if you have seen the milkman you would have taken the veil. True, some old birds got free cream, but times were desperate and standards slip in an emergency. In those days the tally man had the field very much to himself, and housewives were more than willing to do a spot on the side to help out in this turbulent time.

"Sex is here to stay!" the great Mae West was heard to tell the congregation during a period in Lent... and I feel she knew what she was talking about. Father was jealous of mother with an almost childlike sulkiness, and of everything living. He longed to catch mother in a compromising situation with someone or something, just to give him justification for his mental cruelty and neglect. Alas, alack, mother had had more than enough of men for a lifetime, even though it was only 'Life with Father', and instead she kept on reading Ethel M Dell. A magnificent mother, she was never keen on being a slave to domesticity, and occasionally my father would lambast her if things were not absolutely meticulous in the home. He would pop in out of the blue whilst he should be away making munitions, but mother always had the 'up' on him. She was more than a little telepathic and therefore knew when he was likely to turn up. She must have been a saint, or at the very least a Sunday School teacher. Of that I am sure, for no one had a cleaner slate. But it was a sad and lonely union, all that remained from a passionate love.

The Americans had arrived in Christchurch for the first time, and coloured men were suddenly seen in the area. Indeed, our next door neighbour would never have known about such gentlemen had it not been for her devotion to Margaret Mitchell's *Gone with the Wind*. The presence of this different skin caused much consternation, and not a little nervousness. But, on the other hand, for the more liberal minded, many a liaison commenced, and girls were seen with their skirts around their bottom and high heels in evidence as they trotted arm in arm with the Yanks to the pubs and places of amusement. After a while Messrs H Samuel started re-ordering to replenish their stocks, as vast amounts of jewellery and rings started to appear on the necks and fingers of wenches in the area. More than one girl sported a fur coat she unfortunately could not do up! One married woman of my acquaintance, whose husband was absent, killing Germans, drugged her small children every night at seven and entertained the US army madly for the rest of the night. The jeeps parked outside her hostelry made the 'Stage Door Canteen' car park look redundant.

The sensation of the season was when a local wench produced a pair of piccaninnies. This gave her a lot of explaining to do, and gave the midwife a stroke.

The radio was essential to keep the spirits up in this time of turmoil, and was a very inexpensive way to keep entertained. Even the *Radio Times* was still only three pence. Favourites of the day were the aforementioned Henry Hall and the BBC Dance Orchestra, with singers such as Betty Driver, who was now a favourite with viewers of *Coronation Street*. She left us only recently for the heavens about and drew tons of publicity in the newspapers, which was her due. There was American singer Evelyn Dall, who sang about her man, Johnny Zero. That was when she worked with Ambrose, long before he became the 'Svengali' to Kathy Kirby. There were Alan Breeze, Paddie O'Neill (before she married Alfred Marks), Sam Browne, Dorothy Careless and her sister Beryl Davis, who sang like blackbirds with Geraldo. Then there were excellent bands like Lew Stone to keep spirits up and the outrageous Harry Roy. He would sing 'Somebody stole my gal' and my mother would retort "I don't wonder!" She loathed him.

Fred Waring and his Pennsylvanians and the lovely Hildegarde brightened up Sundays from Radio Luxembourg; and there was always *Dick Barton, Special Agent* for the kiddies, and *Monday Night at Eight*, for grandma.

Bars of chocolate were but a penny piece, and my favourite was Mackintosh's 'Quex' bar, great value for just one penny. The Sunday joint was something like four shillings, and a large cake with icing, one and sixpence. Hey ho, where did all the bargains go? It all seems so long ago – it was!

I was beginning to get restless, but was still helping to make ends meet for my mother, and I spent the occasional weekend with Aunt Ethel, but things were never quite the same as of yore. True, she would still show me the latest additions to her wardrobe, and give a run down on her latest associates in the swinging world of society, but things had changed. We had lost the orchestration somewhere along the way since we had been a double act. We were both clear that the harmony had become stale, and I made sure that everyone was aware that I was much older. Before thirty one ups one's actual age to become more worldly, and then reverses the process after thirty-one.

It reminds me of the lovely story of Marlene Dietrich.

Marlene was having a portrait session with a photographer she had used ten years earlier. She had been well pleased with his results which encouraged her to have a new session some ten years later.

"How dare you turn out such mediocrity," she stormed, "your earlier pictures were fabulous."

"Miss Dietrich," the poor man replied. "You must remember I am ten years older." At least here was one man who knew how to handle a star.

The war had not touched Aunt Ethel, and the larder was as packed as of yore, with every kind of delicacy. I remember some weekends we journeyed to Wimborne and took tea with stepdaughter Bella, now more in love with the bells of Wimborne Minster than ever. How Quasimodo would have loved the scene! Bella ran a little tea shop almost in the Minster precincts.

Mr Jolly, the butcher, was obviously on the very best of terms with my aunt, and we always returned with a joint large enough to feed the whole of the Luton Girls' Choir. I can vividly recall my aunt's devotion to the Salvation Army, though she never joined the cause herself. I fear the bonnets would never have suited her. However she was mesmerised by uniforms, and as she adored playing 'Lady Bountiful', regularly dropped them a fiver. This she threw daintily onto the tambourine.

After my short visits to Aunt Ethel I always returned to my mother, who struggled on in her own way, and when her larder was far from adequate, her camouflage was so clever one never really noticed.

I was befriended by Mr and Mrs Clark in the Bargate, a smashing and devoted couple, who ran the newspaper shop from which I delivered the words of the press to the multitude. Apart from my pay, the tips were mammoth, especially at Christmas, and I managed to seduce the housewives into diving into their purses regularly. At many places along the road, there was a plate of cakes and a hot mug of tea to keep me happy. Alice and Arthur Clark were made for each other, so rare outside the movies, and were lovers until the end of time, and then some. Alice too, was a great supporter of the Salvation Army, as was her sister, and for a time her mother was a member. I can still remember taking tea with the Clarks on Sunday at the time the Salvation Army band and singers came round the Bargate before Sunday service. It was as much a part of Sunday as the *News of the world*, though on a slightly different plane.

The Clarks were kindness itself. They adored my mother and tried so hard to make life more fun for both of us.

My father returned home when the guns stopped firing and rows once again tore the house apart. He had even less time for all of us children now that we had allowed ourselves to grow. Not that mother retaliated much, and the unhappy tension prevailed. Father returned to local work and spent the savings he had built up at Blandford Camp by buying a taxi and plying trade in the town. Daddy, oddly enough, although he did not understand me any more than he would have done an aborigine, wanted to encourage my artistic side. He knew I could sing, and had a quick and amusing brain on a good day. I could also write a legible hand, in spite of my basic education.

During school Kathleen, a warm and friendly teacher, discovered me, at eight years of age, and took me to her heart. This was to the chagrin of the other pupils who thought me teacher's pet, and all that jazz. But Kathleen taught me religiously and well, and did much to make sure I read many books and works to improve my outlook and my education. She took me to the theatre, to stylish tearooms, and we became close and devoted friends. She came to the house to seek permission to take me out, and developed a great friendship with my mother. This pleased me no end, with Kathleen taking tea with us once a week, braving any outbursts of bad humour which might develop from my father. Kathleen was a bright, shortish woman, with lovely curly hair, a round, warm face and she possessed great warmth with a tremendous sense of humour. She died many years ago and left me a large sum to help me on my way. Patience she had in abundance. This was fortunate when faced with between forty and fifty pupils to a class. Such patience has stood teachers in good stead from 'Mr

Chips' to Miss Moffat' in 'The Corn is Green'. She loved Arthur Askey as much as Art did his 'Busy Bee'. The Western Brothers were also great favourites, and she would go and see every concert they gave within fifty miles of her home, regardless of expense. I miss her still.

My mother had a few close friends who did much to sustain her in times of despair. With David, my blind brother, to bring up and care for, such times came often. Eventually, when David was due to go away to a training school for the blind, there was a very grey day indeed. Mother, who had taught her youngest child everything he knew, so well that she probably missed her true vocation, was naturally distraught over the parting. She was losing her baby who had been part of her existence for so long, and was unsure of how David would cope in the harsh world of training he was shortly to encounter. It was an area which was unfamiliar to him. He was, after all, only seven years of age.

Her anxiety was an omen, for David had many trying years of endeavouring to learn a profession in that world of twilight, but eventually, after failing desperately to become a shoe repairer or to make baskets, tasks that other blind children seemed to accomplish with skill, it was realised that David would never make the grade in this way. Instead, his tutors used his natural personality, wit and intelligence and made him host at the college where he was training when visitors and tutors came. He showed them around with aplomb, and became a great success. He finally left college and was established as a 'hello' boy, the telephonist par excellence which he is to this day. He was the only blind person I have heard of to visit the races unaccompanied in his teens. His knowledge of the turf is colossal and his fervour for the sport second to none.

And so with David gone, mother was left with an empty house of echoes, and she immediately took on more outside work. Father was busier, having acquired a larger taxi service, and mother gradually took over the running of this by booking appointments and keeping tabs on the book work. Her only reward, alas, was cursing and rudeness. At Christmas, when taxis were much in demand, the family house was a battlefield, and it was a wonder at all that we ever got to the Christmas pudding. In the outside world, father got on with people fairly well, and no one could guess the life sentence his wife was serving for taking the nuptials. One sage claims that 'to come to know a person' one should always live with them first. How true.

We had discussion, my brother and I, about the possibility of mother leaving father. With the departure of David, and my brothers old enough to paddle their own canoes, I persuaded her this was a course worthy of thought. She was only in middle age, which some, including Miss Brodie, say is your prime. There could be much to be savoured in life for such a woman, given opportunities. But, time and again, she would get near to taking the plunge, and then suddenly lost heart and retreat into the small terrace house she called her home. Later, when I had taken root in Earl's Court, we did get her to leave father and come to London for a couple of weeks. But she was in anguish most of the time, and when he came to find her, he put up such a performance that had he been entered for an Oscar he would have won hands down. The man could act the pants off many a professional actor, and that was a fact.

After sixteen, I began to plan an escape. I had taken to the hills for a few hours one evening when everything had really got too much, but after nightfall I thought better of it when Ovaltine was nigh, so I flew back home. Thereafter I worked and saved like a Jewish tailor and amassed quite a sum, after I had paid my share to mother. I was working towards the day when I could leave and discover the wonders and disillusionments of show business.

The Boscombe Hippodrome was an oasis for me and I was regularly seen in the Gods. There, for a few well-earned coins, I could savour good and bad theatre or more correctly, variety and vaudeville. I even persuaded my mother to come on some occasions, and gave her a well-earned treat. Revues were more numerous than variety bills, and mother was adamant that variety was much preferred for, as she said, "If a revue is bad, it is bad all the way through. But, if one act is poor on a variety bill, the next act might be good."

The Hippodrome was owned by Mr J B Butterworth, a man who had acquired a chain of such premises up and down the country. He made Boscombe his headquarters, for he had also ventured into hotels, and owned a superb one almost down by the sea shore.

The Boscombe Hippodrome presented all the favourites of the period, including Donald Peers (of *The Babbling Brook*), the Western Brothers, Suzette Tarri (everyone's favourite char), Jeanne de Casilas (Why no one has ever taken up the idea of an act on the telephone again I shall never know!), and Beryl Orde, the excellent impressionist. She was to the down-market trade what Florence Desmond was to the upper. Denise Vane was a strip artiste who was billed as 'The English girl from Paris, in dances indescribably daring'. She took off the veils, probably seven, to Egyptian music, whilst pretending to be a statue. I heard recently she still dwells in Chelsea and is a seamstress of the highest order.

Harry Worth was a 'vent' in those days, and Frank Randle came down south once a year to delight everyone with his 'Randle's Scandals', so hot you could get scorched! 'Jane' of the *Daily Mirror* also showed a bit of thigh. Teddy Brown was an expansive talent on the xylophone; Billy Whittaker and Mimi Law (the latter and her brother, the well known impresario, Jerry Jerome, were the original Bisto kids) also toured in their own revues for a year and a day and made a fair living. Great pros in every sense of the word. There was Charlie Shadwell and the BBC Dance Orchestra, Billy Cotton and his Band. Then there was Roy Harper and his Wonder Horse, Hylda Baker (directed in so many revues by Mildred Challenger, referred to later on as 'Bonzo', after she became an agent), Ronné Coyles for much of his youth, Nosmo King and Hubert, Renee Houston and Donald Stewart and Old Mother Riley and her daughter, Kitty. There was a hot time had by all when Renee and Old Mother Riley co-starred on the same bill. Betting on who won the No.1 dressing room could be unbelievable. There was Ernie Lotinga and his 'Josser' character, Charlie Junz and his piano, another star of the period on the halls, the list was endless... I remember with delight so many lovely evenings we enjoyed for a few bob at the music hall of yesteryear.

Such was my life whilst reaching puberty – was anyone as late as I? – and after my days with Aunt Ethel, I was merely marking time before I could bite into the more promising world of adventure, tinsel and... seduction. There surely never was or is more of an education than life upon the wicked stage.

Chapter 2

Starlets in Battledress

Service, national or below stairs, has never been one of my supreme goals. Nevertheless, my papers arrived on my eighteenth birthday along with some diverting cards congratulating me on reaching puberty. Either they were running short of victims in the campaign against the Führer or fate has decreed it was time I left my little wooden hut in Hampshire (now Dorset) and got my backside up to Redford Barracks in Edinburgh. This indeed I did, one freezing morning in November. I was cold and just a little bit frightened. After all, I had seen some very nasty incidents with rookies in the movies. I flew off to the station in a tremendous state of emotional upheaval and hysterics, then had to come all the way back again as I had left my suit coat off. Mother was crying inconsolably, and I kissed her and went. Somehow I sensed that this was the end of my childhood, and indeed my membership of the family. I think at that moment my mother knew it too. How true this turned out to be. Shades of Betty Hutton or Tyrone Power running off from the home base in 'Incendiary Blonde' and 'Blood and Sand' respectively, though my fame and fortune were still to prove elusive. Perhaps what you don't have you can't miss.

My first impression of Edinburgh at six-thirty in the morning was hazy, and I was still snivelling. The long journey had given me time to think, and home sickness, even for a home that had been so constricting, had reared its head. It was something new to me and completely baffling. But gradually my confidence or whatever you want to call it came to the fore.

There were dozens of other poor devils in the same situation as I, and even the mighty have been known to shed a tear on a sad day. Ignorant as a novice being caught in the nunnery gardens, I had not realised that I had been posted to the Horse Guards. The thought of having to mount a horse, control it and myself, almost gave me a seizure. What it did for the unfortunate horse cannot be repeated. After a while the Sergeant got the message I was not for the Horse Guards. It was doubtful if I would have been accepted for *Dad's Army*, let alone the Royal Engineers. If there was a candidate for comedy, I was surely it. I turned right when everyone else turned left. My salute to arms would have made Sergeant York die. At target practice I was really up the creek. Of the few times when the recoil of the rifle didn't completely throw me, I managed to fire on everyone else's target but my own. This caused some consternation among the officers in charge, and chaos to my fellow soldiers also firing.

When marks were awarded, they were all at sea. Absolute wonderment reigned, and we had to shoot at the target all over again. I handled a rifle like Butterfly McQueen handled the civil war in *Gone With The Wind*. When the sergeant said "Shit!" he didn't mean the toilet!

Twice a week we marched with our packs on our backs round the villages, the hamlets, the hills and the dales, probably to see how far it was. The official explanation was that the ramble was supposed to toughen us up and get us used to carrying our packs and battle equipment in case we were summoned to the front of the Charge of the Light Brigade... All that really happened was that it poured with rain and poured some more, and we were absolutely soaked. On our return the local damsels and a few whores sent us up rigid, though not physically. They whistled enough to attract Rin Tin Tin, and we all waddled in as if we were wearing high heels to the local barn dance. We didn't need Lifebuoy to shift the sweat, we needed the whole damn soap works.

Mother sent me cakes and goodies twice a week – it was before Mr Kipling got his fingers in the oven – and she also sent great jars of honey. After all, why should Barbara Cartland have a monopoly on the stuff? Mother's parcels helped, for I always seemed to have an appetite twice the norm. The honey I took with me to the dining mess and heaped the bees' goodness on the army bread. The sergeant, who bore a striking resemblance to Marjorie Main, chanced to see the honey one day and screamed, "Look what mummy's little boy has today!" The cackling that ensued would have done justice to a farmyard and I swore that I would get that sergeant, one way or another. And the day wasn't that far off.

Some weeks later, the sergeant was highly inebriated, whilst on duty. Wincarnis and Vodka is not recommended before lunch, and he had lost the chit for a thousand rations. I was always a master at forgery, so I signed the Commanding Officer's signature on a similar chit. From that day on, because I saved his neck, I had that creep in my pocket. Though I did have my problems... I never drew any pay for many a week, having always lost either my beret, my bayonet, water bottle or eating utensils – and sometimes all of them together. The Pay Officer would merely smile and say, "had a busy week, have we?" and I was dismissed without a sou...

I even mislaid my rifle on a snowy down on manoeuvres one day during training, and was most truly sorry when the sergeant on that particular safari got his balls chewed off. He was only twenty-five and could not be expected to cope with a virgin like this one. The only thing I had not lost was my virginity and God knows that was threatened often enough by a lusty corporal with an appetite for a bit of bum. He, after a skinful of beer in the NAFFI, would mutter, "I'll fuck the arse off you!" To this I would appear astonished and say, "Fancy that!" and take off quickly before he could reply further. After all, f'ing is not everything, as the vicar said to the actress when he failed to rise to the occasion.

We were allowed out occasionally to go into town to meet some birdies or see a movie. Being released like a flock of caged pigeons, the evils of sex were illustrated to us, and there were several inspections of private parts which some seemed to enjoy with abandon. We even survived that.

The soldiers that were assigned to our platoon were not a bad lot. Apart from the usual 'conning' that always goes on when novices appear, and a steady stream of vigorous cursing, all was well. My mother had spent a long hour telling me that when everyone is in uniform there is no knowing who is a 'goodie' or 'baddie'. I discovered there is no indication when they are stark naked either! There were five of us apart from the rest, four youths and myself, and we all came from the New Forest. Mike was from my home town of Christchurch, Rupert was from New Milton and John from Southampton. Then there was Peter. Peter gave camp a new meaning and if that word originally referred to a tent, this child was a marquee. If he was accused of swaying when he walked, it all came naturally and nothing was false. The four of us, apart from Peter, behaved as quietly as possible, but on 'the night of the pyjamas' we really took the biscuit. The first night we put them on, I mean the pyjamas, the entire room had hysteria, and comments flew around like confetti, while invitation flowed as quickly as wine at a Jewish wedding, for a corner of our beds. Anything more poofy than pyjamas could not be imagined.

"Do you think it was something we said?" screamed Peter, fingering his curly hair like a nervous handmaiden. The fact that he had silk pyjamas on was enough to set off a major riot, let alone a hut full of rookies. All very disturbing.

I soon became a star turn. The corporal had his own little room in the corner of our hut, which was his consolation prize for having one stripe on his arm. He came in one night as drunk as a skunk, fell over my rifle and into the tea bucket, waking the whole room, and he cursed me to the heavens and beyond. This made me the flavour of the month, as the target for his wrath, and I could do no wrong for quite a time with my mates. So much could be achieved if you possessed a sense of humour.

In my opinion, Edinburgh was and still is a queen of a town. It is beautiful, steeped in tradition and style, its manners would do credit to a finishing school. It is a city where if you asked the way they would take you there, not merely show you which direction. All of us rookies had some damn good times in the six weeks we were at Edinburgh. I remember on one occasion we met Forsythe, Seaman and Farrell, a well-known American vaudeville act. They had given a concert for the troops and they took six of us out for a meal afterwards. They were a super act and kind, caring people. Little did I know that

47

my next visit to Edinburgh would be as an impresario (such a posh word) to arrange presentation of my first pantomime at the Brunton Hall Theatre, Musselburgh, just a few miles out of Edinburgh. But more of that later.

My stay in the Horse Guards would not even excite John Wayne, let alone the military higher echelon. After all, I never did learn to sit a horse well, let alone canter, so they decided to post me to the Royal Engineers, who hung out at the bleak Fulwood Barracks in Preston. It was a stark and dismal dump where we became sappers for our sins. The Guard House, just inside the main gate, made *Birdman of Alcatraz* seem like a *Weekend in Havana*. The man on guard, a cross between Lon Chaney and Boris Karloff (or so it seemed that evening) was most forbidding. The place scared the life out of some of us, and petrified me. But everything seems better in daylight, and after a few hours' sleep, we seemed to take everything more in our stride. The Royal Engineers were after all a noble regiment, but hardly ready for the likes of me. Apart from the military training, the building of Bailey Bridges of all dimensions was the high spot of the training schedule. In all seriousness, the bridges were splendid and went on to save many a life and expedition as the war broadened. We all owe a debt of thanks to Mr Bailey, who obviously was not related to Billy Bailey who would never come home.

After what seemed to be an eternity, although actually only five weeks, we were sent on night manoeuvres, to build a Bailey Bridge over some obscure river near Preston, Lancashire. I fell into the water at a most inopportune moment, taking with me some rather important nuts and bolts, and the panel fell on a few fingers. After being hauled out with a tadpole or two up my bum, I spent the rest of the night with a high temperature, in the Officers' tent. I was no fool, even then. My mates had several things to say about my 'Esther Williams' take off, none of them complimentary, especially from those who had felt the weight of the section of Bailey Bridge which had fallen. "F'king idiot" and "he knew what he was doing!" filtered through across the darkened waters. It was really felt I could be better employed elsewhere, a fact that an astute captain obviously accepted. I was posted without delay to a military establishment in Halifax, where I would stay for a month's training on a special course for military clerks. I became a pen-pusher. This was one instance where the military casting officer was dead on.

In Halifax I learned to type with only two fingers, and my speeds would have excited many a stenographer. I have always been grateful to that particular captain who assigned me to the clerks course. Being able to type saved me a fortune, once I took to scriptwriting.

When the course was finished, I had a speed to worry Joan Crawford, everyone's favourite secretary in the forties. As the sun sank in the Yorkshire skies, I said farewell to Halifax and was again on the move. This time, I was posted to Fishguard, to serve a Major Moore and his staff in the field. The field turned out to be a muddy one, with a regiment of rabbits, not to mention other creatures of the marsh. Fishguard, I recall, was a fishing town in Wales, where one could board a boat to Ireland. Here I had a bit of luck for Major Moore's deputy was a captain of my acquaintance. He was from my home town and I had delivered his morning papers on my round when a newspaper boy. He knew me and I knew him. What better grounds for an understanding or two. He, in turn, was very glad to see someone from his own neck of the woods. Though, once knowing my track record in the services, whether he would be so keen on me later on was another matter. At this particular moment he was of the opinion that I could only add something to life at that time in the mud which was Fishguard.

So here I was as the Company Clerk, and I managed to live, work and sleep in the company office, which was a long, low, wooden hut with a fire bunker in the centre. There were desks for about five clerks on either side. I was dragged in as escort for the many individuals who were charged with misdemeanours, some trivial, some devastating; and I would stand there whilst the poor devils screamed their innocence or guilt. When there was nothing left to say, they'd meekly receive the sentence. Major Moore was lenient to the point of softness, longing to read his manual on rose growing rather than gaze on these rapscallions. The major was strictly upper class material. His moustache and accent would have graced any officers' mess from Whitehall to Poona. Even his horse neighed 'pukka'. But he was none the worse for that. At first he viewed me with a rather suspicious eye, probably not believing what he saw the first time. But as time went on he appreciated my efforts in his office. I really liked Major Moore.

Evan, the corporal of the office in this Palace of Varieties, was having it away with a WAAF, who was delightful. She made us all laugh and she loved to dance, preferably with a man, and especially the tango. Some said she could even make love to the tango, but I could not swear to go as far as that. Spike Jones and his city Slickers maybe. What she and Evan got up to was under wraps, for each spoke in their native Welsh, which was a great pity for us, and not at all informative.

By this time I had built up a gramophone collection which had everything from Fred Waring and his Pennsylvanians to Phil Harris and 'Woodman, spare that tree. The favourite girls were the Andrews sisters, Vera Lynn, Anne Shelton, and a lass I still think was one of the finest vocalists of all time, Frances Langford. Her version of 'I'm in the Mood for Love' would turn on a eunuch.

At Fishguard in the field, I started to collect a menagerie. Occasionally there were four dogs, two cats, a horse and a pig and sometimes a goat for good measure. The dogs were called 'Spot', 'Butch', 'Rover' and 'Lily' according to their markings or sexual preferences. The cats were called 'Maud' and 'Elsie', both mothers, though neither had husbands that I knew of. The cows were more difficult for me to name or to recall, but I think they went by the legends of 'Cow', 'Gate' and 'Express'. The horse was 'Flick' after the Twentieth Century Fox movie which was popular at that time. The pig was 'Percy'. The whole lot would have delighted Walt Disney, and they did not do so badly with the regiment at Fishguard. They all had an act and were willing to travel. They came and slept in the Company Office at night, and no greater friends had any man.

Dawn was a reveille to the animals and me. Many people swear that history is made at night, but I beg to differ. Nothing is quite as nice as doing your own thing in the morning. All the animals would march out of the office as dawn broke, and then the business of the day was under way. The scene would have done credit to Noah's Ark, not to mention Gerry Cottle's circus.

I remember we were disturbed one evening, when everyone was dozing off, but a sapper who had consumed a drink too many and came stumbling into the office by mistake. 'Flick' the stallion, peed on him from a great height, and the man beat a hasty retreat. Visitors had to know the password at that time of night.

I think the Officers knew we had a circus of our own, but as in the early morning light they were usually shaving and preparing for breakfast, or possibly even toddling back into camp after a hot night between the sheets with a local lass, nothing was said. The Major had a poodle in tow and got me to shampoo her and a few other strays on Sunday afternoons outside the office in a huge bath tub; so his lips were sealed from the start. If it was alright with the leader of the band, I did not expect any protestations from the mere musicians.

Around this time I started growing whiskers, a feat I have done ever since. The Major stopped short one morning on inspection parade and uttered, "Stacey! You have whiskers!" I knew I had to join the razor ranks that morning.

The boys knew I could sing and I did some singing later on in the camp entertainment programmes. I must be careful with my choice of words. We could boast some very talented artistes in the regiment such as pianists who would have graced any music hall extremely well, and some Welsh lads, who could sing well enough for a 'Number Two' company of the D'oyly Carte. It has always puzzled me why the Welsh and Australians have such superb singing voices, but it is a fact. Could it be something they ate for breakfast that we don't know about? The entire troupe would make 'Privates on Parade' and 'It ain't half Hot, Mum' envious to say the least.

The Picture House at Fishguard was a very popular place of entertainment. It was small and intimate... you can say *that* again! One had to book well in advance to see the sumptuous double features they would be showing. It was the hub of social contact, and everyone who was anyone, and even the unsure, packed the place to see Marilyn Monroe, Betty Grable, Alice Faye or John Wayne. If you were seen with a girl or boy at any of these immensely social performances, the gossip column next morning at the camp was ablaze as to who was laying whom. If you weren't with anyone you were either a nun or had the pox. That never happened in a Rank house.

We were being groomed at Fishguard to go to the Far East, which excited some and paralysed others. But most people like a bit of Chinese, if not the Orient; though a bit of Jap proved to be another matter.

Eventually we were denied this adventure, and again I was on the move.

I was posted this time to an estate in a village called Wellesbourne, which is halfway between Leamington Spa and Stratford-upon-Avon. I had a bicycle with me at the time and spent many happy hours cycling home down the country lanes singing the ditties of the day such as 'Don't Fence Me In'. The estate at Wellesbourne where we were going to serve King and Country was called Walton Hall. A few years later Danny la Rue bought the place with its extensive grounds for a hotel, but alas, after a lengthy period, lost a cool million on the venture. As it was very successful for a number of years, some skulduggery could be suspected.

Wellesbourne was really noticeable for the fact that it had

nine pubs and six shops, not to mention knocking ones, and about as many residents. It was here I came to be known as one of that celebrated brigade of renegades, a NAAFI cowboy. For the uninitiated, this is a soldier who lays around either on the canteen kitchen table or on one of the NAAFI girls. He is a regular devotee to one or several NAAFI girls; if really lucky, the manageress of the NAAFI, so he then becomes one of their establishment.

The girls were the salt of the earth and worked liked Trojans, both on duty and otherwise, to make the ranks feel at home (not that the officers were deprived, either). There was a particular NAAFI manageress whose name I recall was Alice, a pioneer woman, plump, with breasts that would excite a monk. She managed the NAAFI at Wellesbourne with distinction. Her nickname was the 'Countess Alice', which indeed she was. She had married an impoverished Polish airman, with a title, but little else. This poor chap had met his match while over the North Sea in a Spitfire, and departed for parts unknown when they had been wed but three years.

Alice did much for me in a short space of time and no doubt I was not the only one. She possessed a warm nature, and was utterly kind. I remember her vividly to this day and wonder where she is. Other girls in the NAAFI were gems, especially Peggy. She married and went to Plymouth, and from there travelled to the Far East and is there still. Mrs Heims was also a lovely manageress, with a heart as large as the universe. She retired and went to live in Southbourne, Bournemouth and I would love to hear from her again.

The surroundings of Walton Hall at Wellesbourne were magical. It possessed some lovely streams and gardens. The settings, come to think of it, are not dissimilar to Buxton in Derbyshire, where I presented many star concerts in later years. It was at Wellesbourne that I first knew the meaning of 'field' lavatories. You could sit on the loo, hold a conversation, and read the *News of the World* all at the same time. In winter, it was not quite as comfortable, for a cold wind round your assets can be a deterrent. It was surprising whom you met while sitting on the loo, and many friendships blossomed this way.

After a spell at Wellesbourne, I was sent, yet again, on my merry way. This time to Westward Ho! Playground of Sir Francis Drake, where the military had taken over a holiday camp. It was here I was to end my service. It was situated on a hill overlooking the sea. Lundy Island was quite visible and the whole location was perfect as a military camp, and almost as blissful as a holiday one. I have wondered often whether Jimmy Perry, the television author and producer, ever stayed there, as it fits the locale for the popular 'Hi-De-Hi' series to a tee.

Dances were still held in the camp ballroom, and often in the evenings we made good friends with willing dancing partners. It was here I met such buddies as Sheila Allen, Kay Morrish (Rowe), Betty Way and many others. These local girls came and gave us super evenings. This whole outfit was a company of Combined Operations, and that was now my new regiment. The group had civilian employees, and that is where Sheila and Kay came in. We were all billeted in a large and spacious house called Torridge, overlooking the beach at Westward Ho! The House, being built on the cliffs, overlooked the whole scene and gave a breathtaking view of the locale. The beach went on for miles, spacious and very similar to the one which Sarah Miles enjoyed when chasing Robert Mitchum in 'Ryan's Daughter' a few years ago.

In those days I was nicknamed General Slim, for I was as thin as a razor blade, but not nearly as sharp. My boss was a Major Wheatcroft who came from the famous gardening family (I seemed to collect majors with a horticultural bent). He was very amicable, stuttered badly, and really was no trouble at all. The Second-in-Command was a different kettle of fish. His name was Geoffrey Taylor, and he was as brilliant as he was young. He came from Sheffield, and was a foremost expert in demolitions. He was impatient, demanding, and had a temper to match Hurricane Higgins. He drank very strong tea, and was an absolute swine to work for. I was, at first, scared to death of the man. His anger could be violent, and on several occasions he tore the door knob off and threw it at whoever was in the company office. This was either to see if we were awake, or just to warn us he was not amused.

Every time Geoffrey Taylor sent for me I literally shook like jelly. He knew this and built on it. Finally I found my voice and gave him an answer. I wanted to say 'get stuffed' which he would have understood, but I got somewhere near it and after that we got on like a house on fire, and respected one another's position.

I shared an office with the Sergeant Major, a portly gentleman, who had been in the Army since birth, and we hit it off immediately. We toiled for sixteen to eighteen hours a day. It was a very busy unit, and Geoffrey Taylor worked very odd hours being the primary expert on demolitions for miles. I was happy to go along with this, and seemed to have worked long and odd hours ever since. I worked the switchboard some evenings in the Combined Operations outpost and quickly mastered the many wires that made up the board, with five main lines and four dozen extensions. After two days I could have stood in for Judy Holliday in 'The Bells are Ringing', so capable was I!

My job at Westward Ho! was to look after three officers and one hundred men in the Combined Operations outfit. I loved the job and the people. I had responsibility, and could make the whole job really slick, which I hope I did. From this came in-roads again into the theatre and the world of show business.

Bideford, a town a few miles from Westward Ho! was a lovely sleepy Devonshire centre, bordered by Northam, Appledore and Fremington. I met a lady who was employed as a governess, called Vera Norman. I had often seen her walking past Torridge House, while I was busy on the switchboard. From the child in the pram which accompanied her, I concluded she was a local mother and housewife, which was far from the case. Vera had something of a Wendy Hiller look about her, tall, with a striking, determined face, and a wealth of stamina. The child she had gurgling in the pram at the time, later became an excellent ballet dancer and is now touring the world. Vera had a passion for the drama, and was one of the leading actresses for the local amateur dramatic society, which boasted a very high standard. It featured not a few professional artistes who either had left the profession or were living down in Devon because of the war. Vera urged me to participate and I enjoyed the warm companionship and artistry I found in this company. Later on, many of the younger members became professional and I have often had the pleasure of meeting them in town.

I got engaged to a local dairyman's daughter, a buxom lass with a superb voice. She sang 'high C' at any time of day, but alas, my eyes gradually turned from this would-be Jeanette MacDonald, to her mother, who could hit a 'top C' with even greater force than her daughter. It was not that I had a 'kink' for operatic hens, it just happened that way. The union was short-lived.

The local cinema in Bideford, the Regal, ran a repertory company in the summer which was very popular with the visitors the lovely town attracted. Many artistes who had appeared there later made it to the gravy train. Ronald Leigh-Hunt, Sheila Hancock, the late Alec Ross and Vanda Godsell, to name a few.

It was when I was at Westward Ho! that I first met my idol, Jessie Matthews, who was starring in 'Castle in the Air' by Alan Melville at the now vanished Theatre Royal, Exeter. Her co-star was Jack Buchanan, and the third lead was Constance Carpenter, who later on replaced Gertrude Lawrence when she fell fatally ill on Broadway playing the lead in 'The King and I'.

I travelled to Exeter, saw the show and Jessie came down and signed a picture for me. She was singing 'Bewitched, Bothered and Bewildered' in her dressing room. She had recently recorded this, but at this stage in her career she was rapidly moving towards the doldrums, so the title was sadly appropriate.

The months I spent with the Combined Operations at Westward Ho! were some of the happiest times I have ever enjoyed, and I will always look back on this period of my life with great warmth and affection.

Chapter 3

My Arrival in London

At long last I had completed my military training, for want of a better word, and returned to the real world to think about what I was going to do. There followed a period of re-adjustment and deliberation.

Bournemouth at this time had rediscovered its youth, and was blossoming out anew. Students were starting to come from France and other countries, and people in general, having been demobbed, were out to enjoy themselves. We had a large high tea-cum-dinner club in Westover Road, and the famous Joe Loss and his Band were resident there, with vocalists such as Howard Jones and Rose Brennan, who were delighting the patrons. Other equally famous bands followed, and it was the start of Bournemouth kicking away the image of a town that was a cemetery for the old, the frail and the indisposed.

My home life was far from amicable. My parents, I fear, did not understand me. Aunt Ethel was very ill and was not able, in any way to sustain the special relationship we had hitherto enjoyed. She spoke my language and I had learned to speak hers, but what use is a speciality without a stage? It was inevitable that as my home held no delights for me, in spite of my mother doing her best to keep me in good spirits, I had to earn some cash. Obviously, there must be something, somewhere, that I could do to further my insatiable ambition to make a career for myself.

What to do and how to do it was the sixty-four thousand dollar question. My thoughts inevitably turned to London. After all, Dick Whittington knew bugger all when he took to the high road. At least, I was a little wiser than that. And at twenty-one, the world could be your oyster, if maybe not your pearl. But I was aware that London can be as lonely to the stranger as a farmhouse in the Orkneys.

Summing up, I had long known I was not a talented actor. It was true I could sing, but so could the blackbirds. And what you can get away with as a child performer hardly goes down well, when you are a tall and pimply adolescent, unless your audience is full of devotees of youth or you are Justin Bieber. So what else was new? Back home a friendly neighbour who had known me all her life, wrote to her sister, Mabel in Kilburn, introducing me, and asking this good lady if I could stay with her until I picked up some threads in the big city.

Mabel was a large, buxom woman, tall as a mountain, with a beakish nose, and the strength of a navvy. We took to each other right away, the only proviso was that I let Mabel do most of the talking. I always took care also to never challenge her knowledgeable opinions. She provided good, wholesome fare, like any farmer's daughter, and you always knew what was on the menu by the day of the week. She was married to a musician called Bert, who looked a little like Harry Worth on a good day. He had played bass in the orchestra on every theatrical tour in every pit in the country, or so you presumed after speaking to him for less than an hour. He knew every big name, theatre, and almost all the tricks of the trade. He was certain that everyone was conning everyone else, and sometimes I do not think that he was far wrong.

Mabel and Bert led separate lives which inevitably happens in so many marriages, and she went on her merry way whatever he said or did. Bert warned me each and every day of the toughness of the business, and the fate of silly sods like myself who would be putty in the hands of those conniving thespians. Bert had done it all, seen it all, and was vastly witty and entertaining. He had given up the business these past ten years and aimed to enjoy life. This he managed to do as long as he kept out of his wife's way. He resided on the first floor in the large front room, which was the best room in the house, and there spent his days reminiscing and reading, sleeping and having a quiet tipple to pass the time away. He went for long walks with the cocker spaniel, at least twice a day, and then returned to tell all who would listen, how the world should be run.

Mabel and Bert had two children, an intelligent and handsome girl, who did extremely well in the world of commerce before she got the marriage bug and flew, in wedded bliss, to the country to mate. The boy, Maurice, after the onslaught of the bombing, took to his bed and died of tuberculosis. The house was a sprawling one, and had three floors. Some of the rooms were never used or touched, and this, I felt, was a shame with so many homeless or looking for a place. Nowadays the road is crowded with residents from every corner of the earth, and like much of Kilburn, a white persona can sometimes be very hard to find. I had the room on the first floor back, and was extremely comfortable, though for a time it was feared I had the makings of tuberculosis. I had to spend long evenings in bed, which I did, reading every book I could get my hands on. I was not advanced enough for anything else. Happily, the tuberculosis turned out to be a false alarm, and I soon went back to my usual schedule of early mornings and late nights. So, at least I had a roof over my head and was right around the corner from the movie palace, the Gaumont State. It was one of the biggest in the world at that time and even now. Later I was to present my first large scale variety show there as a concert promoter. To every provincial child, London was the mecca, the font, the ultimate. The capital was as vast as the home lot at Universal Studios in Hollywood multiplied by ten thousand, but the two had something in common. Street upon street, especially in the Kilburn area, seemed to resemble each other. If you had seen one you had seen them all.

I was amazed there could be trees and foliage in the Charing Cross Road, that Hyde Park was as big as some of the small towns I had known. The pace of the city was at once impressive, exciting and disturbing. Being a stranger and constantly losing the way while rushing from one interview for possible work to another, I came to look on the friendly tube station as a signpost back to my lodgings. No matter where I wandered during those first few weeks, the tube got me safely back and saved my bacon. London buses were something again. They seemed to have no particular timetable, and were terribly perplexing as to which direction they were going. When you had waited an eternity, a whole flock of the bloody things sailed by, perhaps all going on the same route like a waggon train and all boasting the same route number. Consequently the first bus was full, and the ones following practically empty. I have never understood this and probably never will, and I doubt if anyone else does either. Taxis are an inseparable part of the London scene, though I was constantly surprised that drivers did not get off their bottoms and open the taxi door for you. Obviously this was taking things too far. It was no matter if you were carrying a 'Dorothy' bag or a ton of luggage, they still sat in their cabin like God Almighty – quite a different breed from cabbies in New York.

One got over the fact that one could pass the whole day not recognising a soul. This comes as a surprise after living à la 'Peyton Place', where if you saw a person you did not know, warranted an investigation. One lived on cups of tea in reasonable cafés, and the whole length of Shaftsbury Avenue was a scene of complete wonderment and intrigue. I could never get over the fact that those theatres were all packed each evening by theatregoers, all new, different, and caring. Later on, when I was a little more familiar with the city life and Shaftsbury Avenue and its many faces, I came to realise that not always were the theatres packed each evening, nor did the masses care if they were not. Nevertheless, it was a fact that London theatre land could lead the world, and on many occasions actually did, not excluding Broadway.

London was a city of excitement, but the sum of a hundred pounds I had arrived with was fast fading, and the opportunity to earn a few bob was rapidly becoming a necessity.

Mabel encouraged me in her own warm way, while her old man, Bert, tried to discourage me from going anywhere near the world of greasepaint. "Riddled with Nancy boys," he would scream.

Like every other stage-struck person, I scanned 'The Stage' newspaper frantically to find an advertisement to fit this newcomer of unknown talent. Regardless of what I had done as a juvenile, I was on my own again now that I had become a big boy. However, I had a whole heap of drive and courage and was undaunted. I was in London at last and the city was full of opportunity, fame and success. I only had to hold arms outstretched and I might, on a good day, touch a little sparkle that would set me on my way.

Sure enough, in this very issue of 'The Stage', a typist with theatrical knowledge was required in Victoria. Not a starring role, not even a walk-on, but a chance to earn a salary. I almost ran in case I was too late. For, with only a few pounds left, it was a job or the streets, and I was not experienced in the ways of the flesh, be it for boy or girl. The wages of sin would not be considerable to such a novice. A job it had to be. I found the office in a tatty back street, over a naff caff, nearer the House of Commons than the Victoria Palace. I climbed the dreary stairs that were almost too worn to carry the burden of human feet, but were still trying to cope as if they hated to give up. Upon my arrival, I was ushered into a musty and untidy office to meet the proprietress, one Catherine Billinghurst. This was my first bit of luck, as it turned out. She was in her middle forties, short and wore glasses, hair curling at the nape of her neck. Her complexion was very pink, helped with a powder of a similar shade, and her well-cut blouse, was buttoned at the neck by a cameo brooch.

She sat in a tall rocking chair and looked at me with laughing, friendly eyes. Her high-heeled shoes left me ablaze with curiosity. I told her I was new to London, which I am sure she could see in a jiffy. I was, I said, hoping to re-enter the theatrical profession, and I was at this time running out of cash and needed to work. She smiled, and asked if I thought I could cope with an exacting job, typing scripts all day. I replied, "If it pays the rent, I can cope, but I do not intend to make a career of it." She threw back her head and laughed.

"Let's see if you can type first, shall we?"

I was shown into the main office where five strange faces peered at me as if I was from outer space. Catherine put a foolscap page in front of me, then a typewriter which had seen better days. She bade me commence. I typed like a thing possessed, and with scarcely an error, finished the page and handed it back to her. She inhaled her cigarette then ran her eyes over my work.

"That's satisfactory," she replied. "You can start today. But I cannot afford much."

"How much?" I enquired.

"Ten pounds and a rise after four weeks if you are a good boy."

My God, I thought, it was a start!

"I'll take it," I said gratefully, and began my first chapter as a citizen of London Town.

*****

Catherine Billinghurst had previously been an agent in Gerrard Street, which is in the heart of the metropolis, a street with many connections. It had the 'Boulogne', a nightclub of some interest, many song publishers and a motley selection of restaurants. Top of these, which catered for chorus boys, and ladies in waiting, was 'Le Gran', a coffee house which was run by two French spinsters and supported by streams of thespians, extras and never-was merchants. On Saturday it was used as a meeting place for young men who fancied a new date for the weekend. Perhaps the spinsters noticed. Of course they did! And if they did, they said a 'Fa la la…' and discussed the weather. Not a trace of the Chinoiserie, which now governs the street. That's pure 'Flower Drum Song' with a sprinkle of Pearl S buck.

But in the year of grace in question it was totally theatrical, and 'La Billinghurst' set up as an agent. She really missed her vocation when, three years later, she moved to the Dacre Street site where I had my interview. She bought the typing bureau from an ageing spinster who had decided to go to the meadows, and from that moment on, the agency side of the business took a back seat and the typing made the money. She found Dorothy Tutin and declared she would be a star when the poor girl was just a two liner. She also told the world that Peter Ustinov would be a genius – and he was.

Catherine's PA was a lovely girl called Madge Livermore,

who worked like a busy bee all hours of the clock and was a real treasure. Madge was a slight, thin young woman who ran everywhere as if it was a sin to walk. She was very upper class, but had learnt to cope with staff who were definitely down market material, and she was not a snob. She dressed simply but well, and had a small well defined face with slightly bucked teeth. She always wore pearls whatever the day, and could be, I felt, between thirty-five and forty. She wielded the whip regarding work and would have pleased the overseer of a chain gang with her devotion to massive output. I always felt she was the typical lass who lived with an older married man and was content to sit in the shadows and devour any titbits he might throw her, rather than enter the controversial club of marriage. That way she could have her career which she loved and also a lover. Could there have ever been such a caring and supportive mistress?

Miss Baxendale, a jolly, plump lady, with a large bottom, with her hair always permanently waved. Her dress was strictly in the manner of the milliner's assistants in the world of H G Wells's 'Kipps'.

Her glasses, without which she was as blind as a bat, dangled on a piece of black elastic. This effect was something akin to Larry Grayson's spectacles many years later. She had been in the office in Dacre Street for an eternity and was left over from the previous management before Catherine bought the business. She resented the intrusion, the gaiety and the dubious potential of the new workers, and told all the customers, most of them from the Ark, that 'Things ain't what they used t'be!" this was a term worth quoting, for around this time Joan Littlewood backed Lionel Bart who had written his first theatrical 'trifle'. This bore that title, and introduced Yootha Joyce (as the 'brass' upstairs) Barbara Windsor, and Toni Palmer to an unsuspecting world. Miss Baxendale became 'Miss Bax' and also became my friend. I found she had a passion for Maurice Chevalier. "Dear Maurice," she used to say, "so misunderstood." She brought her lunch in every day in an enormous bag and nibbled at odd times when she felt the urge. She was constantly discovered sitting on the lavatory reading the *News of the World* for lengthy periods, with her knickers around her ankles. As there was only one loo, anticipated at that, and with no lock, it meant you could not often respond immediately when nature called. She was a lovely old salt and it was many a Thursday she loaned me ten bob to cope until the treasury handbag appeared on Friday afternoon.

Mr Parkinson worked the duplicating machine, and was more temperamental than Joan Turner and Kathy Kirby together. He was tall, with thinning hair and a long moustache. He had served in the forces with Catherine Billinghurst and answered to her commands with almost a salute and a willingness to serve.

"Parkinson," she would say, "it is time to have a beer." He would smile like a walrus at feeding time, his wide face beaming for the prospect of a well-earned drink, but also that he was included with his boss on the visit to a nearby pub. His long, droopy moustache almost bristled with appreciation. He was as thin as could be, and his head was almost bald, save for a strip of hair refusing to disappear from the top of his pate.

They departed to the Golden Lion for the happy hour and quenched their considerable thirst. He was to 'La Billinghurst' what Erich von Stroheim had been to Norma Desmond in 'Sunset Boulevard'.

Catherine Billinghurst had one son, Giles, who suddenly arrived when she was about forty-eight years of age, much to the astonishment of everyone, not least to herself. He is already showing much promise as a writer and an actor. With a mother like Catherine I should not expect anything else.

And so it was I became a theatrical typist in this small office in Dacre Street, Westminster. I worked long and hard, from seven in the morning until eight or nine in the evening for ten quid a week. Catherine did, after a while, give me another couple of pounds, but it was still very hard toiling. However, I was grateful, as I could pay my way at Kilburn with Mabel without stress, and get acclimatised to London and show business in general.

A friend of mine, John Lyons, chanced to see in an office

opposite Charing Cross Hospital, that a flat was available in Earl's Court. Through John I acquired a top floor pad in Nevern Place. It was owned by a Swedish man of almost seventy, and the second bedroom was reserved for his son, a Flight Sergeant, who was still in the RAF. The rent was four guineas a week, a most attractive sum. Although the furniture was a little reminiscent of early Priestley, it was home. I was very happy there for five years. It had a large lounge, bedroom, kitchen and bathroom, and was bliss in the summer with the open windows collecting the cool breeze. In the winter it was as cold as a polar bear's bum.

I can remember one unusually cold snap while I lived at Nevern Place, my hot water bottle in the morning sported ice instead of water. Mabel was not quite sure I was ready for such a bold step as acquiring a flat of my own. But I was, and all turned out well.

The beauty of the office was that if I got a modelling promotion or a short term television job, I could always return to Catherine's and take up where I had left off. In those days it was not too easy, as employers always looked upon theatricals with very mixed views.

During my stay with Catherine I was, on occasion, loaned out to various clients to type manuscripts and books. This I loved, and some of the personalities included the great Shakespearian actor Robert Speight, Stanley Miller, the playwright, who later did all the Somerset Maugham translations for television, and a great favourite of mine, Laura Whetter.

Laura turned out love stories like a sausage machine, pork, of course, and her books enraptured her publishers, Ward and Lock. When I turned up for dictation, she was on her forty-sixth book. She was a tiny woman, no more than five feet, with a warm, crinkly face, a trifle plain, but she had a divine turn of phrase and I adored her. She cared nothing for clothes and was often mistaken for the char woman.

On this particular day she opened the door and beckoned me into the lounge with the words, "Sit down on the Ivor Novello." In my innocence, it took a moment or two to realise what she was talking about. After coffee we started on her book. She walked up and down without a moment's hesitation for at last four hours, never tripping or stumbling for a second. She never repeated herself and the story she was telling ran as if on wheels. I was astounded!

Laura had two children, one was obsessed that she would be the next Ingrid Bergman, a fact fate was to deny emphatically, and a boy. Neither had the charm, grace or talent of their mother, and they faded into obscurity as quickly as the mist upon the meadow. Laura was married to P L Mannock, a popular and respected critic of the day, who wrote for the *Daily Herald*.

At two p.m. my lunch was brought in and my employer vanished to the dining room until about four o'clock, when I would wake her up with a tap on the shoulder. She would stir herself from her slumbers, which were made all the more enjoyable by a sizeable gin, downed with her lunch omelette. We then returned to her book, her heroine, and the latest whisper of romance that eventually would reach the pages.

Laura died a few years later and I never did see her again. What a super lady she was.

*****

Another job I acquired was to answer fan mail, and this brought me into contact with Sir Laurence Olivier. I was to answer mail for both Sir Laurence and his wife, Vivien Leigh. Alas, I was only to see Sir Laurence twice and Miss Leigh never.

However, I did have some other goodies. Irene Manning was a visiting American who needed some clerical help. She was known briefly over here as an operatic hen when she made 'The Desert Song', which must have been filmed more times than 'A Star is Born'. She was very glamorous and exotic.

Sonnie Hale had many scripts typed by our agency. He seemed to write as quickly as most people aged. He was a very nondescript person, unbelievably tatty, and I could not comprehend that he was married to Jessie Matthews with whom I was to work, and whom I adored, many years later. His talents hardly helped Miss Matthews in her career, but at this time he was presenting something of his own under the nom-de-plume of Robert Monro. The play was called 'A Nest of Robins' and he had persuaded his wife to co-star. It was a story of an actress and her husband, and was completely forgettable as a script. Jessie made it work out of town, but unfortunately her considerable temper came to the fore when it was scheduled to come into the Garrick Theatre, near Leicester Square. I think she must have kicked her ex-husband out and told him to get lost. Perhaps he should have done this during their film days together at Gaumont British.

One day it was discovered that a decent copy of Sandy Wilson's great success 'The Boy Friend' could not be found. As the show had opened in the West End to great acclaim, and an ever greater advance at the box office, it was decided by the American impresario, Cy Feur, who was co-presenting the show in the United States, that copies must be found right away. So I was despatched to the Savoy Hotel to the suite of Mr Feur, to get the show down on paper again as it was written. Sandy Wilson and I toiled for several days to do just that. Cy Feur came and went with great rapidity. The only constructive thing he said was, "If you want anything, kid, ring for the genie." And ring for the genie we did. After a long and laborious morning working with Sandy Wilson, we ordered a gallon of gin and tonic and two of the largest fillets of fish ever seen. MacFisheries would have gone into a frenzy over such a pair of creatures. With a sumptuous trifle and whipped cream, which must have been whipped by a gladiator, to follow, all washed down with the gin, the script was finished, and a fine day was had by all. We were almost too sloshed to get out of the place.

Sandy Wilson was a joy. He was talented, and then just on the crest of a wave. His 'Buccaneer' which was to follow, was thought by many to be his best work – and later on 'Valmouth' arrived. 'Valmouth' was camp when camp was coffee, and it is a national scandal that it has never reappeared in the West End. The recent arrival at Chichester Festival Theatre seems to have gone awry, which is both perplexing and sad. Fenella Fielding is long overdue for a return in a good piece. I saw her a long time ago in a Simon Gray play 'Chapter Seventeen' – such a waste of a first-rate actress. The play was described as a black comedy. It was certainly black. I could not make head nor tail of it, and it folded after nine weeks on the road, in spite of a splendid cast and an author with a sound reputation. I do feel that if you cannot understand a play it has really not got much going for it.

It was a long time before I was to meet Sandy Wilson again, although I did speak many times to his manager, Joan Rees, a dragon-like lady who protected Sandy with the roar and aggressiveness of a tigress. She left us all, having been hit by a truck while on her way to the hairdresser. She was great fun and, if I may say so, rather over fond of her liquor. That I am sure she would have been the first person to admit. With her death Sandy must have lost a great friend and colleague.

Sandy Wilson's output in recent years has reduced, which is a great pity, but at least Sandy gave Julie Andrews her first chance. Sadly, this is also the case with Julian Slade.

So it was that I was earning a modest salary to keep the wolf from the door. Gradually, I began to pick up the strains of life in the wicked city, and the incessant hum of activity which was show business.

*****

I had started writing a script whilst residing with the buxom Mabel in Kilburn. She encouraged me no end. I was even allowed to use the ground floor front room as a study, which was praise indeed, as it had not been used for many a moon. I started taking elocution lessons with a tutor in West Hampstead, but a stone's throw from my digs in Kilburn. Just the second synagogue from the left. The tutor agreed to take me for two lessons a week on the rudiments of how to talk wisely and well. By now I had a slight Hampshire accent intermingled with a strong Devonshire one which I had picked up during my long sojourn in that beautiful county. The tutor was straight from the world of San Toy. She dressed in velvet kimonos, was divine, and great fun. Surely she should have played 'Judith Bliss' in Noel Coward's period soufflé 'Hay Fever?'

Perhaps she even had. She was petite, with grey, carefully waved hair, crinkly eyes that smiled easily, and she conducted the lessons with something of the archness of 'Madame Dubonnet' in 'The Boy Friend'. One would never overstep the mark with this particular madame.

I found learning slow, but worked and worked, then worked some more. After six months of visits I was far better than I expected, but not as good as I could have been. However, I always felt that this was not time wasted or money misspent, for I could say, "Round the Rugged Rocks went Rose," like a veteran.

I remember the good lady really rocked me on my second visit, when she asked me to post her bookie's cheque on the way home. It was a Sunday morning! She was a splendid elocution mistress, having coached Binnie Hale and many others to the pitch of stardom. Such a person would, I had imagined, have kept her enthusiasm for the nags strictly for a weekday. But, obviously, what was good enough for Wilfred Hyde White was certainly good enough for her.

At the end of six months she introduced me to a noted director, whose name I shall not mention. Whether he was coming for lunch or possibly to pick up some hot tips for the racecourse I could not hazard a guess. He advised me and the good lady that I should keep the speaking voice that the good Lord had given me.

"You are stuck with it," he said, "but I find it highly individual and not at all unattractive."

We all had a glass of sherry and a dry biscuit, and I felt that all was not lost. Whether or not the director meant what he said I shall never know.

I was now writing with a passion at any interval I found was free, and before long had a script ready which I called 'Smoke rings'. It was a little drama about the danger of dawdling with a reefer. Far better stick to a 'Du Maurier' of a common Woodbine. It was put on by a true stalwart of the theatre, a certain Mr Chaudry.

Mr Chaudry was all of six feet tall, black and a gentleman in every way. He was also a true patron of the arts. He ruled the little Irving Theatre in Leicester Square, surrounded by movie houses of great magnitude. Alas, the Irving is no longer a theatre club, but a picture gallery downstairs and an Indian restaurant upstairs. Mr Chaudry in the 'Smoke Rings' period, was assisted by a white mistress who looked like a cross between Freda Jackson in 'No Room at the Inn' and Kathleen Harrison after she had joined the Huggetts. More than that I cannot say.

A straight play was staged at the Irving Theatre each evening, except on Mondays, and this was followed by a wild night revue at eleven o'clock. In between, you could have Indian curry, very hot, or numerous other quick, spicy dishes.

'Smoke Rings' did make a little ripple in the press, greatly helped by Catherine Billinghurst, who had now taken a great interest in all I was doing. So the play was not a total loss. Catherine seemed to know the whole of Fleet Street like the back of her hand, which was very useful when trying to catch their attention to mention an unknown writer. She knew how to write for the demands of the theatre, and her comments were invaluable. She helped me much in those days and I remember her excellent counselling still.

The leading lady in 'Smoke Rings' was a young actress called Pamela. It was her first time on stage, but she was a natural. A young woman of Catholic beliefs, she would go to confession at eleven a.m. on Sunday, but then be back in bed 'screwing like a carpenter' by one p.m. Which always made me think about the Catholic religion with just a little scepticism.

I left Catherine's employment shortly after this and stayed on at the Irving Theatre as an assistant stage manager. After 'Smoke Rings' had not caused a forest fire. Mr Chaudry was staging a new play by a young actor, Owen Holder, whom everyone thought was going to be a very important playwright indeed. About this time he was caught up at the lovely

Haymarket Theatre in a splendid play by N C Hunter entitled, 'Waters of the Moon'. The cast, never to be equalled, included Dame Edith Evans, Dame Sybil Thorndike, Kathleen Harrison, who became a Dame soon afterwards, and Harold Scott. They were supported by Wendy Hiller, also now a Dame (perhaps the show should have been called 'There is Nothing Like a Dame') and it ran almost as long as Variety Bandbox, the radio success.

A lovely tale emerged at this time regarding Dame Edith. Whether it was true or not I have no idea. It is said that Edith was having a nap, as was her wont, on a chaise longue in her dressing room, fanned by Dame Sybil at her head. The stage manager flew in, almost bursting a gut, and screamed that the Duchess of Kent had arrived and wished to see Dame Edith. Rumour has it that same Sybil whispered something to the Queen of the English Theatre, to which Dame Edith reacted by opening one eye and uttering, "You can tell the duchess of Kent from me that I do not wish to see her!" She then closed her eyes and continued her nap.

I worshipped Dame Edith from afar, and alas, never met her. My favourite quote of hers has always been that one when she was confronted by a young man requesting an audience. She replied with feeling, "Young man, are you mad – or merely insane?"

I stayed on at the Irving for a mere three pounds a week, but supplemented this a little with perks from the late night revue artistes. There was much love and devotion at that time for the theatre and the business in general. People would clamour to work for low wages in this neck of the woods, and I defended my job with the wrath of a warrior. Would that many artistes in the theatre of today who claim to love their profession and craft as much were prepared to work as hard for so little.

A play or two followed, then a saucy revue. Each evening we ran the straight play and then had to pack the entire set away into the basement before the revue could start. One Sunday, the dress rehearsal started at nine in the morning until three the following morning, until the leading lady said, with a snort, "Well, chaps..." (she was a bit like that) "I don't know what you idiots plan to do. Me? I'm pissing off home!"

Think of that today, a rehearsal of 18 hours, in terms of unions, committees and all the pow-wows regarding overtime, feeding time, and probably toilet paper subsistence.

At this time smaller nightclubs were attracting some excellent talent, and people like Fenella Fielding, Digby Wolfe, Johnny Brandon, Joan Heal and Anna Quayle were making their presence felt. Johnny Brandon was going great guns in those days, and later turned up in a revue with Joan Heal called 'Maid to Measure' at the Cambridge Theatre which brought Jessie Matthews back to the West End, co-starring with a most unlikely pair, Tommy Fields and an American, Lew Parker. It was not a tailored success, but worth everything to see Miss Matthews back in the West End again.

The Stork Room later gave way to the Pigalle in Piccadilly, where Sammy Davis Junior stormed London, and later Betty Hutton came, saw and conquered for a while, though it was rumoured that her bar bill at the end of the nine weeks season at this venue, outstripped her salary for the entire run. She also introduced a new husband at her opening, who unfortunately had got the chop by the time it closed.

Around this time I was touring in a fringe touring company in that excellent Garson Kanin play 'Born Yesterday'. This toured for a few weeks and was perhaps the only part, except for a male Hedda Hopper, to fit my dubious talents as an actor. I loved the part and it did me, we got on well.

At this time also, London was experiencing a new mushrooming of theatre clubs. While we now have the fringe, the theatre clubs were on a much larger scale, and kept to a proscenium production rather than a theatre in the round. These club theatres were flourishing and providing useful platforms for new actors, writers and directors. The New Lindsey was in full swing, and I was delighted when I was invited to see a 'run through' of a new musical by Robb Stewart called 'Chrysanthemum'. I thought it delightful then and still do now. It had a superb cast, including the wonderful Valerie Tandy, now sadly no longer with us, and an Australian of note, Colin

Croft. Later, this musical ran for a short time on Shaftesbury Avenue with Pat Kirkwood. Pat, a true star, has not had the breaks in later years. Perhaps she prefers the social life to one in the theatre. Who knows? The show, anyway, was a poor imitation of the New Lindsey production.

At the Chepstow Theatre Club, a charming little revue was running with Edna Freyer singing 'I'm in love with the man on the knitting pattern book'. And Ted Gatty revealing a ditty about a mermaid (with Gatty naturally as the Mermaid) which ended up something like this:

Come and be done by the Gypsy Queen,
Come and be done by an old has-been,
I'll tell you, young man, very confidentially,
That a Mermaid is *most* unsatisfactory!

Another excellent juvenile at that time was Bunny Eastoe, who was around much later in Mark Furness's male revue, 'Why not, Bangkok', which was really more cock than bang. Nevertheless, great fun.

There was an abundance of superb revues and musicals at this time, all performed with great style and class, with good, catchy tunes, inventive dancing, and a huge sense of fun. Recently musicals have gone more and more dramatic; for me, I prefer the former strain.

After my stint at the Irving Theatre, I was beginning to realise I had to earn much more for the best things in life. I had enjoyed typing scripts which had taught me so much, but I was eager to get started in something much more worthwhile in the world of greasepaint. Then, fate took a hand when I returned to work for Catherine Billinghurst. A temporary typist arrived to join us who was to show the way to an added income and many new, interesting contacts.

Chapter 4

Coffee Days in the Haymarket

It was dawning on me, after even my short time in London, that a part time job had prospects.

With the arrival of the new 'temp' in the office, things started to look up. He was stout, tall and his sense of humour was as catching as the pox on Navy Day. Terry was intelligent and interesting and we all liked him immediately. He said what I already knew, that typing scripts merely provides bread and board. The butter and jam were noticeably absent. But not for long. Terry told me about his evening job, and that he would do his best to get me 'in'. Meanwhile, he would read us some of his poetry at lunchtime. That while we devoured spam rolls most days, and cottage pies and chips on Fridays. Such fare we shovelled down our throats at the Lyons Corner House for the inclusive price of two shillings and three pence.

Terry had a little goatee beard which just covered his chin, and he looked a little like Cedric of the 'Three Monarchs' fame. He had the most outrageous laugh (apart from my own) in show business. He was as good as his word, and arranged an interview for me at his evening employment, which turned out to be a new coffee house situated in the Haymarket, next to the Carlton Cinema. It was the largest coffee house in London, except for the Boulevard in Wigmore Street. On a good night, with as many standing as sitting, it could accommodate several hundreds. The hardworking Terry was already installed on the coffee machine. His laughter soared up to the ceiling with the stream from the machine and created an atmosphere of infectious merriment.

There was a constant queue almost all of the opening hours at this most popular rendezvous, which necessitated three assistants on the coffee counter. One person warmed the milk, one poured the coffee and the other served and took the money.

I was interviewed, if that is the right word, by one Gabrielle. She was a large lady of around forty, and the wife of a Parisian taxi driver, who, I believe, got lost with the traffic, as we never saw him. Madame Gabrielle was the reigning manageress. She wore her black hair in a 'Louise Brooks' fringe and was known to everyone, staff and customers alike, as 'Richard the Third'. Gabrielle and I took to each other immediately, and we remained great friends.

Her immediate superior was Dinks. Dinks was as thin as a rake, around forty, and was the director, supervisor and boss. She created the policy, ran the place and invariably came up regularly with new ideas for raising the cash receipts. She took me on as a relief for half a crown an hour, plus supper, and I was there in the first instance for a fortnight. Following this, I was redundant for at least three days. Dinks had helped create a chain of coffee houses in the West End; the initial one had already attracted a certain section of café society at the Coffee House, in Northumberland Avenue. There, the arty, the farty, the crafty and the bold, ate their granary bread, and each other! Dinks was truly a woman of the world. She worked as hard as ten men, spoke hardly at all, but had a dry sense of humour, if pressed. She tolerated no one who slacked, but after four hours of hard slog she would beckon me and together we would descend to the staff room and drink strong tea by the gallon.

I ought to say at this point that the Coffee House was nothing from the outside, for it had a very tiny entrance, almost like a long passage, which one passed through. It had mirrors on each side, and the hallway opened out onto the main floor with its tables and fixed chairs all around. There was an outer space for eating and a more complex inner space with a grass carpeting and a 'flying' fountain. Water came down through a shute in the middle of the restaurant. The place could seat something like two hundred at one time. The food bay, fronted for service on two sides with a glass counter, was manned by two assistants. The menu was salads of many varieties, excellent home-made cakes and sandwiches with various fillings. Coffee, tea, fruit juices and the like were obtained at the farther end of the outer restaurant. Downstairs was a massive kitchen, a rest room and eating room for staff, and a large office.

Trade by day was in the style of 'Cadena' or 'Karrdomah' eating house; in the evening it bordered on Bohemian, Camp and theatrical. It was trendy and fun and enjoyed a thriving and healthy trade.

Dinks and Gabrielle did shifts in turn, and the staff worked with a devotion that was commendable. Anyone lazy did not last a day. Dinks wore a white coat at lunchtimes as we all did, and was indistinguishable to the customer from the rest of us. It was assumed that she was an ordinary lackey, which could be unfortunate. An example worth quoting is the day a customer was clearly lining up to issue a complaint and Dinks stepped forward.

"Madam, can I help you?"

"I want to see the supervisor," the woman yelled.

"I am the supervisor," replied dinks.

"Then I want the manageress."

"I am the manageress!"

"Then I want... the director!"

There was a slight pause. The old woman was clearly out for blood.

"I am the director," Dinks replied. "So why don't you... fuck off."

*****

After my first week at the Coffee House, Dinks and Gabrielle decided to visit the West Country, either for Devon cream, or more devious delights. They left me completely in charge of the thirty-five staff, and I did the morning, afternoon and evening shift. After I got over the initial shock, I worked my ass off and we did good business. Now the staff were really international. On the washing machine, before he made it to the privileged post of coffee maker, was Colin Wilson of *The Outsider* fame. He looked like a young professor, with a pale skin, long, tall frame, and he wore large, horn-rimmed glasses.

His hair was thinning although only in his twenties. He was an avid reader and absorbed much material in between his duties on the washing up and coffee preparations. At night the constant reading continued, that is, if he was not off duty and doing something infinitely more interesting. Usually Friday, when women washed their hair with that deceptive preparation known as 'Amami' and dreamed they were Kay Francis, was his night off.

Colin had one fault, and certainly not a gentlemanly one at that. Whoever shared his bed was categorised for all the world the next morning, and her rating at the Coffee House was announced for eternity by the ungallant youth. So many of us were recommended to the Foreign Legion for less. If Mr Wilson was sowing his wild oats he must have planted a field. He married shortly after he became a front rank novelist, but only when an irate father took the horse whip to him after he had undone a lady too many. He and a young lady took to the hills as man and wife and lived happily ever after. Colin's book *The Outsider* put him definitely on the inside, and from that moment on he never looked back. He is an established literary figure in the world of books.

On the food counter was Wally Cooper, known to all as 'Poppy'. Wally had been a striptease dancer (more 'tease' than 'strip') at the Kit Kat Club in Beirut for long seasons. He then came back to the land of his birth to decide whether he should have the operation. During this period he came to us and I installed him on the food counter. He spoke in a soft, high pitched voice, had peroxide hair and a white complexion, and he looked something like David Bowie before he took the vows.

Wally was a superb salesman and he had a wonderful sense of humour. He never seemed to have lovers, but was always in readiness. He had a small party one night at this flat in Earl's Court. I recall that it was just after two in the morning that a scuffle was heard outside the front door. 'Queer bashing' was a constant sport in the area. I lived several streets away, but it was clear that I would have to stay the night, for the toughs were not fussy whom they clobbered, whether it was queen, princess, butch or normal. Lights were gradually put out and the eight or so party guests were despatched to various rooms in the house. I crept into Wally's double bed and started to doze. Just as I was in the land of Nod, Wally jumped out of bed, exclaiming, "Christ! The jewels!" From this I assumed invasion was imminent, as he whipped a jewel box from a drawer in his dressing table, then returned to bed with the famous box wrapped in a pair of knickers.

I haven't seen Wally since then, but believe he eventually made it to the 'chopping board' out East and now looks like 'Blanche Du Bois' on a good day.

Incidentally, his pal, Phil, known at the time as 'Petal' to the masses, was six feet two inches high, and looked like the tall half of Revnell and West. He waited on tables, especially the ones harbouring something male, butch and hopeful, clearing the dishes. He was very sparing on dialogue. He had been in the Navy, a little after Nelson, and whether it was Navy cake or the rations that got him down, we will never know. Whatever, he came ashore on a mermaid, a buoy not being close at hand.

After a lengthy period of playing roulette with a number of gentlemen, he got married – just to prove he could – and produced several smashing children. He was a superb character and a very good worker.

April Ashley was also on the staff. She usually did table clearing. She was then still a man, and devastating. If, as was said, Tyrone Power was the prettiest man in the world, April came a close second. April was not with us for long. His friend, Tallulah, came and took him off to Earl's Court, where they later worked in a supermarket. I read April's book once and it seemed all was well. I am happy that she eventually found what she was looking for.

Lord Wolfenden's son was also on the staff. A cool boy; it was difficult to tell whether he was 'Arthur' or 'Martha', even to our most excellent detection. It had just been announced, as a result of his father's famous report, that males could make it in the hay with other males. So, he was a source of interest, the son rather than the father. More interest was displayed by the girls, incidentally, than the boys.

Others of our Imperial staff at the Coffee House who passed their chicken days making a few shillings were, Jeremy Kingston, now the editor of a famous magazine, Adrienne Corri, who will surely still look twenty-five when she draws the old age pension, and half the students of the drama schools and the medical colleges. Girls were in the majority on the day staff, but the division with boys was equal at night.

Lindsay Kemp was probably the only member of staff I ever fired. He was caught eating a chicken – the feathered variety – in the kitchen, but his crime was that he left half of the unfortunate bird. Lindsay was so outrageous even in those days. Small and tubby, with a pixie face and, at most times, a little make-up to help the day along. His mother, I recall, was a handsome woman who wore large hats and arrived either on her way to the Cadena – or as she returned. Obviously, she had difficulty in understanding her talented son. But, brother! If she had only known what was in store for her! Lindsay, in those days, had not discovered the full effect of rouge, mascara, and all the other delights he later adopted.

But he stood out even then as a candidate for Mardi Gras or the Chelsea Art Balls. I have met Lindsay many times on my travels, and occasionally on his. I have been dazzled each time by his rare and special genius. Ronne Coyles was another fabulous character in the Coffee House days. Ronne had been a child performer on the halls when they were great, and this was so through to the forties. Ronne came on the scene when the halls as we knew them were closing, left, right and centre. He was a brilliant salesman, and his work with Wally Cooper on the food counter at the Haymarket would have put Gert and Daisy to shame. Ronne joined us later to help open the 'As You Like It' Coffee House in Monmouth Street. Soon after, I persuaded him to return to the stage, where he has done extremely well, and established himself both as a classical pantomime dame, a revue artist of note, and an impresario, to boot.

He met a sea captain while serving strawberry gateaux in the Coffee House, and they struck up an immediate friendship which has been invaluable. Bob managed Ronnie's career for years but alas died some time ago.

The moral of this tale is do not neglect the strawberry gateaux, for you never can tell! So the great Bernard Shaw once said.

Much has been reported about the Coffee House. By day it could truthfully be said that it was something like an updated Lyons Corner House, but by night remarkably like 'La Cage Aux Folles'. Business crowded in from the time that the door opened. Coffee trade, then lunch, then afternoon tea, was enjoyed by the famous, the hoping to be famous, and the fading. It could also be truthfully said that after seven in the evening trade was constant, and you can take that any way you like. Its clientele was definitely outrageous, and when twilight fell, it was every man for himself.

I managed to run the place on very lucrative lines, so that when Gabrielle and Dinks returned from their Devonshire sojourn, takings were up. In fact, everything was up, and the management were more than pleased with the results. The two ladies were obviously relieved that their choice of manager had been correct. They knew that if further offers of a trip abroad or elsewhere occurred, they could vanish with the knowledge that all would be well, with the tills ringing their particular brand of music to keep the shareholders happy, but I could never stay still that long.

It was at this juncture that I started booking piano players to lull the clientele into wonderland, and these boys came on around 7pm and played until 10 o'clock. The customers were entranced, as the pianists were excellent and handpicked. Basil Moss, an actor of repute, and constantly in the employment of the BBC television, was the first in a long line of piano players. The staff were also delighted and, all in all, music made our particular world go round even more brightly at the Coffee House.

Things, however, suddenly took an unexpected turn. One Monday evening I was offered a lift by a harridan working at the Coffee House, and after we finished work for the day, set off in a tired old van, which looked worse than we did at that time of night. I was curled up in the back of the van, almost dozing, with several others. I remember going through Knightsbridge... and on to South Kensington. The driver of this unremarkable vehicle chose, for some reason, to collide with a taxi close to Saint Stephen's Hospital. The van overturned and refused to release me. Whether I was chasing the lead in a remake of Joan Crawford's 'A Woman's Face', or just a victim of a slight case of misjudgement we will never know. Suffice to say that I was dragged along the road on my face for twenty yards or so. I woke up with a stream of language coming from my lips, which amazed the Casualty Department of the hospital. It amazed me as much later when Matron visited me in Ward 3A and referred to some of the salty language I had delivered to the staff.

"I have never in all my life..." she said (and who was I to doubt her, as the two nurses winked at each other) "heard such appalling language."

"Bloody hell, you must have done!" I retorted!" But she would have none of it.

I apologised profusely, mumbled something about not knowing what had come over me, but it was too late, the damage had been done. After casualty, I was wheeled down the corridor by two giant men to Ward 3A, and tipped into the first bed. In the morning I awoke slowly and carefully, running my fingers over my body to see that everything was there. It was. I had two legs and everything seemed to be in place. My shoulders and elbows were paining me greatly, but perhaps it was all just a bad movie, and I'd wake up well. I shouted I must leave as the lunchtime customers would be arriving – meaning the Haymarket Coffee House. Alas, the sister, with the largest breasts since Sabrina, arrived and thrust a mirror in my face, a face which resembled a map of Birmingham. I retired to think again and to commiserate with myself. I was in for a few bad weeks, but the nurses were marvellous.

The press gave me a few lines, so I got a little more attention than the other patients. This was mostly due to the fact that my play 'Teddy Boy', my first full length play to hit the circuit, was touring the provinces. This made me a little more newsworthy; maybe news was a little thin on the ground that day.

I was besieged with visitors, friends, and some enemies who obviously wanted to see if I was near to meeting my Maker. I thought of the story of the ageing actress looking into an ornate mirror and saying over and over again, "But I *am* beautiful!" Alas, I could not muster such a positive attitude and collapsed on the pillows convinced I would see the sun setting on my fortunes.

The stay in hospital put me back quite a bit. At the time of the accident I was hugging a script which belonged to Jeremy Kingston, a young writer, working with us at the Coffee House. A few months later when it was cleaned up (the cover of the script, not the work) I sent it to Betty Box, the film producer, who in time shelled out a bag of gold to buy it and make a film of it. Jeremy was delighted, working as he was to make a few bob to get him through college. Things such as grants were unheard of in that day and age.

When I finally got out of St Stephen's, to go home for two weeks to Christchurch, the hordes of visitors I played to had taxed even the caring staff of the hospital. In Christchurch my mother built me up with constant Bovril and a thousand baked custards. After this period I flew back to town, and recommenced work at the Coffee House, both arms in plaster, and an ankle likewise. I looked like a battle scarred victim from 'Gone With The Wind'. But cream was needed in my coffee, and as I had always used my hands either for typing, or more heavenly pursuits, my fingers were supple enough to collect and count the cash. So I was worth every penny I was paid. By contrast, I always think of the Madame of the Knocking Shop collecting monies from a client, and insisting the notes be left in the vase on the mantelpiece. She never liked to touch the notes by hand.

*****

London was now beginning to get more 'with-it', in the fields of pop, rock and disco; and the world, especially the young, was taking more and more interest in the British. As well they might.

After the excitement of my play going on tour – more of this later – the management of the Coffee House in the Haymarket decided, without a word of warning, on a change of policy. This, in its own way, did me a favour. It was time for a change. The bistro was gradually building up a 'gay' reputation, which was not at all surprising, since it employed many workers of a distinctly camp nature.

I recall one evening a middle-aged matron, fresh from the opera, coming in wearing more jewels than Tiffany's could boast. With a swish of furs she declared, even before she had ordered two hot chocolates, and in a tone reminiscent of Hermoine Gingold, "I say, Rupert! This place is littered with queers!"

As her escort was wearing even more make-up than a tart before the fleet came in, Rupert burnt his tongue with the hot chocolate before he fell off his high stool. The poor, sad old matron had obviously not used her deviation detector when she discovered Rupert. We all knew then that her hot chocolate was in vain, and that she would end up between lilac sheets alone and neglected.

So, with the Coffee House a veritable faggot palace when dusk descended, a place where one could pick up a partner or possibly the pox – all for the price of a coffee and a doughnut, it dawned on me that it was not quite the launching pad for a young man with potential. The management panicked, governed as they were by a squad of City types who still thought that gay was merry. They threw caution to the winds. Notices were posted asking 'undesirables' to go elsewhere for their coffee and crumpet, or words to that effect. So the gay trade took umbrage. You can imagine the powder room talk about this development, when the fairies started reviewing the situation. Walls have changed colour for a lesser crisis!

The coloured fraternity swore it meant them, and as I had many coloured staff, loyal friends who worked steadily and well in the kitchen, I was very upset. The ladies of the oldest profession said, "Sod them!" in their best accents, gathered their Dolly bags and found somewhere else to buy their coffees and ply their trade. The main stream of customers muttered that "something very strange' was going on!

So no one did any business.

It came to pass that all the staff at that time were moved to other branches, except for possibly one or two, who needed to show the newcomers the ropes. At this time numerous places were opening up all over town, catering exclusively for the male clientele with a distinctly gay bent. Some of that clientele were old practioners, and some were possibly 'Arthur and Martha's' (youngsters who had not really made up their mind as to which direction they were going). Prominent among these new bistros or clubs was the 'A' and 'B' off Frith Street. The 'Festival Club', located up an alleyway at the back of the Coliseum, was run by a smashing Canadian called Ted, and the 'Mousehole' in Swallow Street. This opened late and closed early, and collected more hoi-poloi than the rest put together. Here, the mice did more than eat the cheese, and many a merger involving a chorus boy and the gentry was brought about over a mug of coffee.

The legitimate clubs opposite in Swallow Street were livid with the 'Mousehole' as they pronounced it degraded the environment of their posh niteries. Many a squall was occasioned by commissionaires from these establishments abusing the carriage trade arriving at the 'Mousehole' for a titbit.

Meanwhile, back at the 'Haymarket', those staff who insisted on wearing mascara for all occasions were sent on their merry way. Gabrielle was transferred to the small coffee house in Northumberland Avenue, where she stayed for a year and a day before moving on.

Dinks started to plot the new order for the establishment in Fleet Street. The organisation had made a bomb with just four branches, Trafalgar Square, the Haymarket, Holborn and Fleet Street. Their shares were sky high, and the business a gold mine. Clever Dinks had tucked away as many shares as her handbag would hold, and, after a late sojourn when the company took over the Roundhouse at Chalk Farm, she eventually flew off to the Lake District where she started raising chickens with pedigrees, and is still there to this very day. I long to charter a canoe and visit her in her surroundings. Alas, my theatrical train has never stopped near her, so I await that pleasure.

Having seen the whole situation become less promising, I hurried to my solicitor to speed up the damages from the van accident. I needed the money to move. I could have taken the affair to court, but really had nothing to wear, I was not in the Mae West league when she promenaded down the centre court in 'I'm No Angel', wiggling her bottom at the magistrate and saying, "How'm I doin', Judge?" Being still relatively shy, I opted to take the grand they offered and get on with the business of living.

So ended an era the like of which London has not seen since that day.

Chapter 5

Getting a Show on the Road

In the middle of my stay at the Coffee House, I chanced to meet a budding impresario, Malcolm Knight. He was an actor who specialised in playing adolescent parts, chiefly because he looked around fourteen, no matter what the day. Melvyn Hayes had already cornered much of this particular market with good acting roles in such films as 'No Trees in the Street'. James Kenney had earned good notices with his title role in 'Cosh Baby' at the Comedy Theatre in town. It seemed that little baby-faced toughs were definitely in.

I had started writing a play which was based on a working-class family; a sort of sub-Coronation Street. However, it was not long before this popular soap opera reared its head.

Malcolm Knight was a short, skinny lad, who appeared here and there in small parts in plays and television, which was not nearly enough to satisfy his ego. So he was looking to improve his lot and find himself a starring role. It so happened that my play was originally entitled, 'Street Children' and had such a part. It was the story of a working-class couple, with three kids, one going to the dogs, one going the way of the flesh, and one going nowhere. Mum was a working-class lass and Dad a factory worker, when he wasn't at the dog track. It was hardly riveting stuff, but it was honest, taut, and earned me some good notices as it played the number one theatre circuit in those days.

Malcolm Knight read it and ran a fever. Here was a part he could play and perhaps make him a star. It had the substance and stature that he longed for and was, after all, the lead. Perfect. He raked up a backer, a nice, coloured gent, who lived over a laundry just opposite Harrods, I ask myself so many years after... but there was. The coloured gent obviously knew nothing about show business or its intricacies. He was a silent partner in more ways than one, as he hardly ever spoke. He preferred to look and listen, which suited Mr Knight, who spoke for all and sundry.

We gathered together an assorted crew of actors and were fortunate enough to secure Garfield Morgan to play the chap next door and direct this diverse piece.

Garfield was a smashing person, a damned good actor, and the whole thing was raised three notches by having him with us. Another lovely character lady, Lucy Craig, played the mother, and she was a delight. With the necessary money available from the backer for the play, the rehearsals commenced. Now, I never agree to having an author anywhere near a rehearsal. They are a danger to themselves, let along the play in question, and should be locked up in a tower until a pardon is granted. If the play is awful, they should stay there for good.

The new title for the play was 'Teddy Boy' and it rehearsed during an undertakers' strike in the late spring of 1956. During this time three other junior masterpieces were on the music hall circuit. The idea was to try out straight plays of rather bold content to keep the theatregoing public from straying. Variety and vaudeville was practically dead, or at least unconscious, and the oncoming impact of television was really beginning to be felt.

All the plays did was titillate a little, but the trend did not take root and the public quickly tired of this novelty. To linger over the raunchy titles was like running a season of films from Monogram and Republic Pictures' greatest successes. Perhaps I should have revived 'The Revolt of Mamie Stover' starring Fiona Richmond.

We usually opened the four week season of high drama on the circuit with 'Teddy Boy', followed by 'A Girl Like Sadie' courtesy of David Kirk Productions, with 'Daughter of Desire' and 'Women are my Business' coming up in the rear. After all, anything seemed to go in this sort of theatre. It was totally different from ventures like 'Love on the Dole', a very fine play that always seemed to be booked on the music halls. David Kirk, an impresario of note, who had kept the flag flying on the touring circuit with first class plays all these years, presented shows in this period, and David and I often look back at life in that period with affection and humour.

Janet Munro caught the public's attention in 'Daughter of Desire', which wasn't all that bad. She went on to make a name for herself in spite of the title, before she died so prematurely.

Pat Dean starred in ''Women are my Business'. She was better known as Patricia Phoenix, star of 'Coronation Street'. Sad to say Pat left us too, but her star will always shine brightly. Also in the cast of the same play, as an actor, was my good friend, John Chilvers. Later on he became the administrator of the Grand Theatre, Swansea. He ran the theatre on a shoestring and struggled manfully to keep the doors open with no subsidy, when all the factors were against him. Then the local council came to his rescue, and the theatre blossomed anew without the constant struggle of trying to make ends meet. John was awarded the MBE for his efforts of a few years ago.

I had an interlude in Act One of 'Teddy Boy', at the end of Scene Two where the floosy of the piece, the bold daughter of the family, seized her chance to get to base with the attractive young husband next door. While his wife was out at the launderette she gave him her version of the kiss of life. This led to a minor seduction which climaxed when her hands were practically on her target and his trousers started to fall down when the curtain fell. What a shame I made my mark in sex opera so early when the world was still not ready.

We arrived in Barnsley on a Sunday afternoon, with the temperature at hot as noonday in Poona. We had arranged to stay with a dear lady about two miles from the theatre. The chief backer was in the best bedroom with his lady love, and the others were scattered around the house. Malcolm Knight and I had to sleep in the front room on two apple boxes, which decided to part like the Red Sea, somewhere near midnight. We both fell onto the floor, the 'Teddy Boy' in red silk pyjamas, and me in my briefs. Such is the lot of a star and author, so don't put your daughter on the stage, Mrs

Worthington, until you have at least checked the sleeping arrangements.

When we arrived at the theatre, 'Mrs What's-er-name' was fresh from cleaning the stalls and the dressing rooms, such as they were. Lo and behold, in the evening she was head cook and bottle washer at the lodgings. Later on still, back at the theatre, she appeared as the usherette. In addition, she was barmaid when they ran short, which was often. She was sixty if she was a day, and must have cleaned up a fortune. No doubt she now runs a bordello in downtown Tunis, given her enterprise, catering for poofs, harlots and randy travellers. A rich life, no doubt.

On the opening night, the audience loved the play and laughed in all the places I hoped they would. I could never write completely serious drama, I have the giggles too much – and too often. The night went so well I was convinced that Noel Coward had a rival. On the second night they laughed at none of these places and I felt a complete failure. On the third night the first night audience must have sent all their friends, because they laughed, once again, in the right places. All was well with my world. Hollywood was undoubtedly mine, and London my oyster in no time at all.

By the fourteenth week of the tour I had earned two hundred and forty pounds in total, and a few good notices. Not much to show my papa from my chosen profession. At Hull the orchestra stayed and watched the play through every performance. Why, I have no idea. But they liked it, and watch it they did.

It is sad that so many of the music halls we played then have bitten the dust, and are now bingo halls or just plain offices or shops. East Ham Palace did the best business, and all in all, it was considered a worthwhile tour.

Malcolm Knight had made a first fling into management, and after a period out of the rat-race, came back to become a busy and prolific theatrical manager thereafter.

*****

To get a play produced today is possibly harder than it was then. If you can interest a literary agent in your work, that is in your favour, and a promise of success. The arduous task of sending scripts to repertory companies and managements is soul destroying, for they scarcely read them, and certainly very few send them back. In the good old days, they more often than not ended up as loo paper. Now that the living has become decidedly more gracious, they probably join the other would-be masterpieces gathering dust on a shelf. Now and again a play is read, produced, and scores a hit, making the author famous and the producer rich. It is this one in a million chance that keeps the dramatist going.

By far the best tip is get to know a television producer, or backer, a manager or his secretary over a cocktail. This, believe it or not, is still a major factor in the business and can be relied upon to at least get your yarn read and reviewed.

Optimism is the keynote in our game, for without it we would all perish and wither away.

Chapter 6

I Find Monmouth Street

After mucking about for several months I finally got one thousand pounds compensation for my accident. This I took instead of haggling, for, knowing my luck, the Judge would have probably demanded I pay the driver of the van some money.

I left the Coffee House when the new regime was introduced, which seemed as good a time as any, and shortly afterwards was to receive a telephone call from Terence de Lacey, a young actor friend who lived in Cardiff. Terry had stayed with me when on the run from a jealous husband a few years previously, and we had worked together at Catherine Billinghurst's where I got him a temporary job. Later he had worked at the Coffee House.

During the time he stayed with me at Nevern Place I was writing furiously on one script or another. Writing to me is like opium to an addict. Terence caught the bug and penned a television play. As luck would have it Terry was very fortunate and sold his play immediately to Harlech Television, now HTV.

The play was quite well received, and it was the general opinion that he should continue writing and make a lot of money. But after a period of reconciliation with a lover, he decided to go into the production world of television, and became a trainee studio manager. Starting at the bottom, he learned the trade when the industry was in its infancy. So by the time Harlech Television became HTV he was experienced and able.

A little while prior to this, Terry, tall, blond, and as handsome as ever, called me and said he had an idea for a film, and would I help him with it? Of course I would. Only three days had passed since I had left the Coffee House, but already

I was restless for something to do. I boarded a train for Cardiff and spent the next six weeks writing a seafaring script with him.

The script, alas, did not make Warner Brothers or the big time. Perhaps with Gregory Peck and the cross-eyes lovely, Virginia Mayo, in a couple of sea epics, the studio had had enough of maritime adventures at that time. 'Jaws' was but a gleam in his father's eye and the 'Onedin Line' was waiting for Peter Gilmore to come of age to play in it. Reluctantly, we had to admit we were beaten.

Back to London I came, and Terry moved on to the television studios. If I had not been a friend of Geoffrey Ferris, I would never have met Terence. Mr Ferris was a plump, jolly young Welshman, who had hit London a little after me, and we became firm friends. Geoffrey was so Welsh he made Ruth Madoc seem like a foreigner. He had been stage-struck for as long as I had, and as he had much talent and enthusiasm he quickly climbed the ladder of success. He has made himself quite a name in theatre production, staging or re-staging such as classics as Lionel Bart's 'Oliver' all over the world. This he followed by a very engaging production of the excellent revue, 'Tomfoolery'.

So with time on my hands, after my seafaring screenplay and my Coffee House days, I went back to appear with a cough and a spit here and there on the 'little box'. A few quickies and sometimes a nice little appearance in 'Emergency Ward Ten' provided some after dinner mints and paid for the milk. A line here and there in several other sagas kept me from sinking into oblivion. I went on to make many episodes of a Biblical romp called 'Paul of Tarsus'. Here, multitudes of us flew around the set at the BBC (it was supposed to be Palestine, but looked more like Rome with its many fallen arches, and that was only the buildings). We were in long robes which on some looked like smocks. If you looked too camp, and I fear many of us did, whiskers and a tatty beard were also stuck on. We pinched each other's bums the moment we were in danger of acting – which wasn't very often.

I said, "Jesus is Love," with dedication one week, and

"God is Love," with equal fervour the next, running the whole gamut of emotion from A to C, with no trouble at all. Like so many pot-boilers, one could pick up the series at any given episode and really not have missed much. It reminded me in later years of the time we were playing the north at the Theatre Royal, Newcastle-Upon-Tyne. I saw Hylda Baker do, and I really mean 'do', a little trifle called 'Busybody'.

This particular evening, which was the opening performance, the play rambled on for four hours, mostly due to the fact that the leading lady carried some of her words around on a pad, and later had the script pinned onto the desk which was back centre on stage. Hylda appeared bored with the whole charade, which was a pity for those who had paid to see her. The late Valentine Dyall, who was a real 'pro' and who was the leading man, struggled valiantly and kept the piece from foundering totally. It was a pity, as I have always had a great respect for Hylda Baker as a music hall artiste. Her timing in variety had been something to applaud. I also remember how splendid she was in a most worthy musical, 'Mr and Mrs' which ran at the Palace and had much to commend it. It only goes to show that one should never take on a job merely for the sake of working. Do justice to it, or, when you get too old to cope, stay offstage.

The Biblical frolics and other little romps paid the rent and kept me going. Also, in the magazine field, another popular and lucrative pastime with me was appearing in the photo glossies, where boy meets girl, loses girl, gets girl, then vanishes, usually with the cameraman. The pay offered was usually a few guineas, which at least kept the creditors off my back. It was during this time that I was approached by an Indian gentleman who, tired of the elephant trade, had started a newspaper for no apparent reason and called it *The London Weekly News*. After reading some of my work, he engaged me to write the show business column, which included reviewing the current stage attractions.

I was in seventh heaven, and would have done the job for peanuts which, as it turned out, was almost all I got. A zany photographer who had made the headlines attempting to snap

Princess Margaret during one of her vacations, was brought in to edit this rag of rags. Ray Bellassario really knew where to use the scissors and where to expand a certain idea, which angle to blow up to please the public and which to delete. He was a real journalist.

The paper was just starting to build its circulation and we had been at it for about six weeks when Sabu, the Indian – I never did know his real name – failed to get WH Smith's and other newsstands to stock the paper. So he went bust in the seventh week and we were again unemployed and hungry.

With money from the car crash, I started thinking about a café of my own. I saw an advertisement in *The Evening News* for a place in Monmouth Street. This crosses the notorious Seven Dials and borders St Martin's Lane, Earlham Street and five others, thereby earning its name. A friend of mine from the Coffee House days, Freddie Lees, came over for high tea and biscuits, to talk over my plans.

Freddie and I had been close buddies and we both adored gossip. But then who doesn't? Freddie liked the sound of the new venture and encouraged me to take it further. Monmouth Street seemed, on inspection, to be a continuous mass of vehicles on their way to Trafalgar Square and other points of interest. Passers-by were inclined to move quickly through it without noticing what shops and wares were to be enjoyed.

"Not good for passing trade," I told myself.

However, premises at a practical price were rare in Monmouth Street and practically everywhere, and as I did not have an inexhaustible supply of money, I could not be too choosy.

I sailed forth to see what bargain could be struck to acquire number eighteen Monmouth Street. When I saw the joint my heart sank. One could say I did not find a pretty sight. I mean the premises and not the daughter of Tommy Farr, the boxer, who seemed to be in charge of the place.

The windows were painted over for a start, whether to protect the public or the inmates I had no idea, but obscured they were. There was a juke box at one end of a long room. This room had enough width for tables wither side, and a pathway down the middle, with window box type of seating along the front of the room and down the sides. The furniture and equipment would have done credit to Quentin Crisp's room in Beaufort Street, Chelsea. The juke box churned out wailing records, while a teenage couple bit chunks out of each other on the tatty seating. At the rear end was an impoverished sort of counter, and to the right a small kitchen, like a shoe box. The kitchen contained a sink, draining board and enough room for a small cutting table. A door opened on to a yard which could accommodate a few bins and nothing else. Obviously much had to be dome before the clientele I desired could be coaxed to enter. But everything is possible, as the film director said to the starlet as she slid down the casting couch.

"You'll have it reorganised in no time," said Freddie. I was not too convinced.

A room on the second floor went with the business, so did a quartet of mice who obviously had an act to rehearse. The rest of the place was inhabited by old residents who had been there since the country said goodbye to Dolly Gray. On the top floor dwelt Monmouth Mary. She was shortish, and of marriageable age, but only just, somewhere between sixty and death. Her hair was flaxen as a Dutch whore in tulip time, and her lipstick was permanently applied upside down in a strange shade of burnt orange, which gave her a quaint sort of Marcel Marceau look. Her face was liberally applied with a Pond's face powder, so popular at the time. She lived with a retired lifeguard who was really a very nice bloke, stout and ruddy-faced, as if he had seen a thousand nights at sea. He was straightforward and sincere in manner, and what he did with Monmouth Mary was indeed a puzzle, for even drunk she was scarcely an enchantress. He had lived with her since Poppy Day 1943.

Mary lived and died for the post. To sort the mail was her destiny in life, and she defended the right religiously. Perhaps her mother had been crossed by a homing pigeon in labour, or else she had an illicit affair when young with a postman that had left a warm, nostalgic memory. Mary had delivered the mail to all floor of this doss house in a checked smock which had seen better days and carpet slippers made by Frisby's which the lifeguard had given her one Christmas. She and I got on well, as long as I did not interfere with the mail.

On the second floor lived a Mr Passadesco, a retired Soho waiter, who once came from Sorrento for a weekend in London and had stayed ever since. In the Blitz he took a seamstress called Bella when she was between stitches, in the shelter. She shared the tiny room with her man and a cat called May. Mr Passadesco slept by day and Bella took over the solitary bed by night, when she returned home from her labours. Mr Passadesco, long since retired, did his own thing to keep himself happy when not sleeping, while Bella toiled with her needle in her emporium elsewhere, sewing sequins on bikinis and costumes.

On the first floor was a German doctor who had ways of making you succumb. He was into boy scouts in a big way. He occupied the front room. A waiter who was frigid was closeted in the back one. What a combination!

None of the residents were pleased at the prospect of a café on the ground floor. But why they should be aggressive to a poor player like myself, after putting up with the garbage that preceded us, I could not fathom. It appeared that for many years the shop was a florists, and when the owner died she made the landlord promise he would never kick out her lodgers. As modern laws developed, one could not kick them out anyway.

The only loo in the house was in the backyard and a troupe of rats had been known to pay their respects occasionally when one was using it. Some say they came from the hotel next door, others that they were left over from the Blitz. Wherever they came from, they had been well-trained.

Monmouth Street had many cafés, and the most revered was the 'Mon Plaisir' opposite, which was run by a French couple in their middle years, and the host's brother. They started doing extremely well in the early sixties until the brother dropped dead – so handy with the undertaker only four doors away. Then the owner fell off a ladder during Lent and could never work again. Madame. And never was there a title so aptly suited, sold the business to a fellow countryman and returned to the land of Piaf and the croissant. The restaurant is still doing well today.

Further down the road was the ill-flavoured and infamous place known as 'The Nucleus'. On the other side were two 'egg and chip' dives with very little character or value. The French hospital was in the middle. It had a sliding door at the back which ran along Monmouth Street, disguised as a panel, so very handy when the doctors smuggled in their lovers in the evening as the clock struck ten. God help you if you had concussion at that hour.

Opposite number eighteen was a second-hand shop of amazing calibre, owned by a Mrs Pusey, who hailed from the land of a shamrock. She was a large, round-faced lady, with wispy grey hair, almost a pioneer type of woman, with a tongue that could wound like a whiplash. Her lined, well-worn face was a panorama of experience. She ruled her family and neighbours with vigour. As she dealt in second-hand furniture and oddments of sorts, the tables outside her shop were loaded with bargains. She kept her money in her long red knickers which she wore each and every day, and if you wanted an adventure you tendered her a five pound note and stood back.

Next door to Mrs Pusey lived an old Irish actor, Bert Lena. Slight and short in stature, he had a long face with a sharp, punch-like nose. He wore tweeds and was the sort of character you would expect to find when touring Ireland and enquiring the way to Glocca Mora. Bert was a good sort and very helpful. Cheery and well meaning, he was a kind neighbour and worked quite consistently in television and films. His best friend was little Jack Wright, who occasionally did some television and commercials for me, when I became an agent much later on. Jack was really a little leprechaun, with his leathery lined face and tiny build. Jack later achieved fame as Benny Hill's sidekick, and looked all the better for it.

On the ground floor of Bert Lena's house was a comedy team known as Walter and Wally. Walter was as big as a house, a giant of a man, with a permanent grin on his face –

and Wally was as thin as a bullrush and flitted around like a dormouse. Small and thin, he was a little like Uriah Heap in 'David Copperfield'. They both were hitting fifty, and cleaned for me at the café for a while. I remember they sent out most unusual Christmas cards which, in the year in question, consisted of an enlarged framed picture of Walter's penis. The caption calmly said 'Pull This for Christmas'.

Mrs Smith resided further along the road, a small, and still pretty little lady, petite and utterly feminine. She lived all alone in the small terraced house. A very good friend in very many ways, not least when she had some furniture to throw out, for she always gave me the first offer. She knew all that went on in Monmouth Street, and between this good lady and Mrs Pusey, nothing escaped detection.

Number fourteen was a bookshop which one could truthfully say was risqué! It was dark and mysterious, and all sorts of literature was exchanged in its chambers. The owner was known to be disagreeable, and if you crossed him on a bad day, it was rumoured he would run you down in his automobile, or sever a toe or possibly a hand with another of his weapons, depending on his mood. A good friend of mine, David was the shop boy, and did his very best to keep the whole affair from plunging into complete notoriety, and helped make the shop pay. The owner was always on business in Liverpool, Birmingham or other major cities, probably dealing with his enemies in his own inimitable way. David went on to better things, and ended up owning a splendid shop in Carnaby Street, until the Indian invasion in that famous area, when he sold out. Whether he could not stand the elephants, or whether he just felt it time to move on, I have no idea.

David had a great capacity for making money. He set up small factories around the London suburbs, where Western cowboy regalia and ammunition belts for would-be warriors were created. Later on, 'G' strings, willie warmers, whips and other specialities joined the output. Sex shops were very much on the up and up, and business was brisk for these products.

Next door but one to the 'As You Like It' Coffee House, actually at the back of number fourteen, was a strip club cum knocking shop. It advertised the suggestion that if you wanted to paint the lady of your choice, before you screwed her, she would model exclusively for you. The girls stood in all manner of slight covering, whatever the weather, and in a variety of poses. All kinds of voyeurs would gather. Some could paint, some could draw, and some, sad to say, could do nothing at all, either standing up or lying down.

After the paint box period, the place closed, either through lack of materials or perhaps because of the shortage of models. It re-opened as an ordinary down-to-earth knocking shop and was maintained by a pert little girlie, Madame Sandra. She was from the north, only twenty-one, and bow-legged to boot. She worked for a pimp, a lover, or a combination of both, but if she failed to take him home twenty pounds a day she was for the high jump. Many was the morning when she came in with a black eye or a livid bruise on her face or elsewhere. Her real name was Rosie, and she was one of eleven children, a little girl lost. She came to London on impulse, was picked up by a cunning operator with a bevy of whores on a string, and joined the collection. She was cool and to the point on matters of business, and as impersonal as an almoner in a centre for sex fiends.

She ate three times a day from our café and the order was always the same: 'Two trifles with cream, two soups and two Coca Colas'. This may seem an inadequate diet, but as she could cope with at least twenty-five customers a day, it could bear looking into.

She gave each customer fifteen minutes, and if they took longer they had to pay double. Her engagement book was crowded, and she usually had between twelve and thirty customers, even on a bad day. I asked her one day what she thought about as she lay there on the tatty bed doing service, and she replied, "Working out how much money I can save from the day to go on a shopping spree down Regent Street." She loved the movie magazines and worshipped film stars. Marilyn Monroe was her favourite, and she imagined, when being laid by every fourth bloke of the day, that she was either Marilyn or Jayne Mansfield, and the customers either John

Wayne or Tony Curtis. She occasionally got a man who turned her on. Then she was happy to give it away for nothing, if she had taken enough to satisfy her pimp.

One day I learned that Sandra was coming up to her twenty-second birthday, and we arranged a small party in our bed sitting room above the café as a birthday treat. A supreme trifle was prepared, so that it was a little out of the ordinary from her usual fare, with accompanying goodies all washed down with champagne. Everyone gave her little presents, and she was so overcome that she cried into the trifle, and almost put the candles out on the birthday cake. Her happiness was short-lived.

Next morning I found a note pushed under the café door, informing me in no uncertain terms, that if I arranged anything like it again, I would have my neck broken. Soon after, Madame Sandra was found, murdered, in the river at Chiswick, at the tender age of twenty-four. She was the second of six prostitutes to come to that sticky end. I wonder if many of her clients ever knew what happened to their little madame?

Around the corner was Ashers, the greengrocers. They supplied most of the cafés in the area with produce, and did a roaring trade with the everyday housewife. Mr Asher was a very short, rotund Jewish gentleman of at least thirteen stone, and his wife was as slight as he was large. She was a little wisp of a woman, probably only four feet in height, but as sharp as a hawk and strong as an ox. She had a splendidly worn 'market' face, glowing with expertise and good business sense, and was a great asset to any business gentleman. They adored each other, but one would never know, as they regularly rowed in the shop and in front of the customers from morning to night.

Allan, their son, also worked in the business and later took over when his parents retired. He was a cheery, bespectacled young man, who kept his cool when all was a battlefield. As the business went from strength to strength, much of this was due to his endeavours. His wife, Adrienne, had never taken to the vegetable business, and had her eyes on the upmarket trade in another line of business, probably the rag trade. She was a most striking wench, and one felt, the moment one met her, that here was a girl to watch, Allan and Adrienne moved to the new Covent Garden when the old one retired. They soon moved on to more salubrious circles.

Mr Portwine, the butcher, was in nearby Earlham Street. His father had fed the soldiers in the Boer War, and half the West End afterwards, and passed the business down through the ages to each son. There was no finer butcher in the universe, and their produce was excellent. Dennis, the son was excellent, took over the shop. He was a wise and curious man, hefty in girth, with a large, florid face. He knew everything of consequence and interest in the street. He was certainly a personality, and his team of assistants, Graham, Jack and others had much to commend them, and not only in the quality of the meat. Many regulars in the area, all within shouting distance of Seven Dials, were seen habitually in this shop, which has seen it all, and said nothing.

Further down Monmouth Street was a tobacconist and sweetshop known to one and all as E de Swart, because that was the name above the shop window. It was actually run by a French woman called Lena, who was known for her eccentric behaviour. Petite in stature, she dressed with a style and quality that has always been associated with the French. She maintained that standard always – chic forever. Although not a terribly young woman, Lena was, I thought, a most attractive one, a trim figure and a most vital face, made up to perfection on a good day. She was certainly a character to remember. It could be agreed, however, that her nerves and temperament left much to be desired. But she got away with it through her utter femininity. She never missed Mass, not even in an epidemic, and one felt she might have harboured a passion for the vicar or that her devotion to religion was so strong she should have gone into a nunnery.

The shop was a little chaotic. The window boasted a display of dummy items of considerable age, each coated in dust. They were only changed if a Royal holiday was declared or a new confectionary salesman was put on the route. On entering the establishment, the customer was assailed by Lena, who swept in from her adjoining sitting room at practically a gallop. If she had more than two customers to serve she went into a rage. It was reputed that she joined the shop as a girl, possibly to save herself from the guillotine, to work for Madame D de Swart, who later collapsed and died during an influenza epidemic. She left the business to Lena. Upstairs was a rooming house, mostly populated by Indians and waiters who were rarely seen. They peeped from behind curtains, which never seemed to be pulled back, except in the twilight. One year I had the front of the 'As You Like It' repainted and given new wood panelling. Not to be outdone, Lena had her front painted in dirty dark green, which did nothing for the chocolates, or trade in general.

Lena asked me how I liked it.

I replied, "Not a lot."

At which she hissed, "I don't care what *you* like. *I* like it!"

After a while Lena was given a posh GLC flat, and I would often see her scurrying along to church and confession. I wonder if she ever yearns for the good old days of the sixties when she ran her sweetshop. I only know she had scented candles at her funeral.

*****

There was a coffee house at the other end of the street, where it bordered with Shaftesbury Avenue, and this was presided over by Madame Rose, a shrivelled-up little woman who was all of four feet eight inches high. She had a large nose, a high forehead and a mass of curly hair. Her age was indeterminable. She moved furtively like a ferret stalking its prey. Her face was work-lined, and she could count on getting a minus for dress sense from anyone adjudicating. She looked a little demented, the kind of person you would expect to be serving in a commercial hotel on the wrong side of Bloomsbury. Her clientele was various, and the food likewise. It was a common occurrence to see Madame Rose dashing up the street screaming, "I've been robbed."

As it was doubtful that anyone would have taken advantage of her person, it was concluded that someone had put a paw in her till – as it was left open more times that a prostitute's legs on Navy Day. So thefts had to be expected, and when the customers did not rob poor Madame Rose, her gigolo did. The poor woman never had a winning day.

After a particularly fraught winter, she sold the shop and it became a milliner's for a few months. Inexpensive little numbers were on view for the shop girl; although in Monmouth Street few shop girls were evident, let alone typists and sales assistants. They all came from farther afield.

A little while later, the premises were sold yet again to an old friend of mine, Jack Hockett. Jack had worked from and with me at the Coffee House in earlier days, and was now forging ahead with one of the most successful ticket agencies in the country. He worked as hard as anyone I have known, and was what I call a quick mover. He was down a street before most people got halfway. A small, slight man, Jack was aided and abetted by his faithful assistant, Peter, and if you ever wanted a ticket for any theatre, major event or concert and have failed elsewhere, the 'Premier Ticket Agency' in Shaftesbury Avenue was the place for you. Jack was a kind and warm creature and as stage-struck as the rest of us.

Goodness knows what happened to Jack.

Opposite our café was the house of Madame Vanessa. She had been a chorus dancer before Miss Bluebell achieved fame, and had appeared in various theatres from Bangkok to Borneo. She loved the hot sun and the humid nights. Vanessa was of plump countenance and walked badly for a dancer, as if her shoes had gone on strike, in protest against the weight they were forced to carry. Her rouge was outrageous, and made her look like Hermoine Gingold after Mardi Gras. A snowstorm of powder covered her face. She never moved without a ton of jewellery, and I was always surprised that two guards from Group Four never accompanied her. She talked slowly, in between puffs of the cigarette, which perched forever between her scarlet lips.

In later years, she had taken to face lifts and heavy make-up, and as the lifts had gone wrong several times and the make-up was far from expertly applied, she would not be missed – even on Halloween.

She came to the 'As You Like It' as soon as we were open, and was almost a founder member. She had appeared at the Kit Kat Club in Beirut, she told us countless times, and Egypt was also a land of numerous suitors for her hand in marriage. Why she had never taken a husband was not explained, but we took her to our hearts without delay. After many years as a Tiller girl and working for troupes such as that of Madame Bluebell, she longed to return to Tangier or Morocco to sit in the sun and reminisce… so much more exciting a location than Monmouth Street in the sixties.

She always seemed to have money, so it was assumed she would never starve. But the poor thing died of malnutrition, and when she was removed from her bed to be taken to the undertakers they found twenty thousand pounds in notes under the mattress.

Sad that she missed those days in the sun in Tangier at the very end, for I think I knew what she was yearning for.

*****

After Freddie Lees had persuaded me that I could make a go of the place, we contacted the advertiser, who had a small and somewhat seedy nightclub in the Charlotte Street area, and made an arrangement of cash down and the rest over a period. After all, I only had a thousand pounds, which wasn't a heavy handbag, even in the 1960s. So this is how the 'As You Like It' came about. I was still living in Earl's Court, and for a month tried commuting. But it was a heavy burden, and with the second floor room available, mice and all, I decided to move, and settle in, Freddie Lees was a great help, and together with Ronne Coyles and a young barman, Peter Almond, we did, indeed, get the place going. Peter was a good worker and had much experience. He had once worked at Buckingham Palace, and what he told us would have made the National newspapers in no time at all.

To create the character of the restaurant was a task indeed, for, by day the patrons were regular and quite respectable, but after twilight it was a totally different scene. I had bought on the 'never-never' some strong oak furniture which gave the place some class. I covered the ageing window and structure with a clear image and all wall seats with an attractive maroon material. The counter was very spruce in blue with a splendid glass top.

Lunchtime patrons were not slow in coming in, a mixture of office workers, 'Tin Pan Alley' types, 'resting' actors and would-be pop stars, plus a whole company of theatricals rehearsing in the area. Staff from the British Museum made up the rest.

The Royal Shakespeare Company often came in during the early period, and I can still remember Glenda Jackson and Virginia Mckenna coming in for lunch and then helping serve all the company when they descended on us in a rush. Sometimes there were at least thirty hungry bodies, breathless to be served. We opened at ten a.m. and closed at two a.m. the following morning.

I tried to obtain everything reasonably priced, and the standard good, so that one could obtain a whole meal for something like six shillings. This could include soup at one shilling and three pence, a mixed salad at three shillings and ninepence, and sweet and coffee. Sandwiches were always in granary bread at one shilling and sixpence, while sweets were unusual for this kind of quick trade, offering Florentines, truffles and mousses. We never gave bills, and everyone paid on their way out, telling us what they had. It was that sort of place. Only one customer in a thousand left without paying.

It was tough going at first and I could see my money melting away, but somehow we managed to keep afloat.

The evening trade did not pick up quickly, but I hired a neon sign, and this did much to get the trade moving. We were also still hampered in the evenings by undesirables – rough trade who frequented the dive further up Monmouth Street which was called 'The Nucleus'. More about that later. I have always maintained that with a sense of humour one can do wonders, and if that fails, using a bit of 'camp' can usually get one out of a sticky situation.

105

We were surrounded by theatres, and I hit on the idea of delivering sandwiches for tea and rehearsals, which caught on like a forest fire. One of our main customers was the Festival Ballet. Out of a permanent home, they were usually domiciled for rehearsals at the Donmar Rehearsal Rooms in Earlham Street. This is now known as the 'Warehouse'. Here, we delivered tea, coffee and a great array of sandwiches, twice a day, and quite a few of the artistes came for lunch as well. So all-in-all the idea of delivering food did much to help the cash flow. I fell in love with Beryl Grey with no trouble at all. A ballerina of considerable fame, she was everything a woman should be, and then some. Tall and chic, with superb black hair worn in a chignon, she possessed the complexion of an angel. Merle Oberon, another favourite of mine, was of similar colouring The almost Eastern face had the appeal of pale porcelain. Beryl reminded me of Barbara Goalen, the model, who was popular at the time.

Beryl Grey usually dressed in black and white or check, with exquisite bows on her blouses and suits, very starched and European, she was a bandbox figure indeed. Beryl had rescued the Festival Ballet from stormy financial waters, and did much to put the company back on its feet. I would have sailed the Seven Seas for her.

*****

The most popular sandwiches for ballet dancers turned out to be banana, and these they ate with glee from morning to night. The big surprise with ballet companies is that most of the men are normal, and not the screaming poofs as the world might lead us to believe. Dedicated and professional artistes to their fingertips, they work and train like racehorses. It is a wonder if they can get anything up after their daily schedule of workouts and rehearsals. Amazing, but Michail Baryshnikov still seems to do all right as the randiest stud on the great white way. He seems to dance all day and… all night! However, we supplied the Festival Ballet with refreshments for several years until they finally found new premises and a home in

Kensington.

When one leaves a successful business, be it a restaurant or a brothel, it is automatically assumed that the clients will follow. How wrong that is. Two weeks after opening the 'As You Like It', we had attracted about twenty of the old customers from the Haymarket Coffee House, and they only stayed to sniff the air. We had to establish ourselves all over again, and we did.

Most customers came in to spend six shillings, which seemed nothing, but then it was the amount of money put aside for lunch. Luncheon vouchers were all the rage, and most of our lunch trade consisted of these Monopoly notes. We scored over the neighbouring cafés and restaurants as our food wasn't all that bad, and it was dead cheap. The menu and the joint were different, and the selection of salads would not have disgraced the Ritz.

The soup started off homemade, but this did not seem to impress people, as long as it was thick and hot and the service quick, so we changed to Knorr Swiss, with a sprinkle of seasoning here and there. No one mentioned the difference. Croutons can camouflage, the most ordinary of soups. I found a little baker, Hungarian by birth, who fled from that land during the Hungarian uprising. He baked some charmers for sweets and delivered with a smile and song. He had an assistant who often stood in for the pastry maker when he had more urgent commitments, a large red headed lad with a permanent cheeky grin and a ready wit. One didn't need much insight to know the boy would not be delivering truffles and Florentines for very long. He went by the name of Colin Bissett, and years later reminded me of the bakery (which was called Palma Patisserie). He soon was a well-known manager in the world of theatre administration and was ruling the Orchard theatre, Dartford, the newest of places of entertainment in the heart of Kent.

Recently he fled to America to pursue his first love, the ballet. He was last seen controlling the Pittsburgh Ballet Company, whose high kicks were the epitome of dancing, both memorable and daring.

Incidentally, he was the leader of the band for the Northern Ballet for a short while, until the rein really got to him. Colin was great fun and God's gift to the wine trade. He is always a star turn himself, with or without an act.

With the help of our Hungarian baker we expanded the selection of homemade trifles, apple pies, almond slices and fresh fruit salad (even the passion fruit was fresh). All were topped with the most delicious real clotted cream, the sort that would make a Devonshire housewife jealous.

On cold winter days I made a goulash or 'Hungarian hash-up' (some pals said cock-up), and this, piping hot, went down a treat. It was followed by a hot apple pie, with extra cloves, so the parts of you to be warmed and cosseted were completely catered for. I always think catering is really a personal creation. Serve what you relish and love. It is the thing to do to survive and become well established. For if you are neither deranged or retarded, your choice must be shared by thousands of others, and your own particular personality is stamped not only on the atmosphere, but on the standards of the food on offer.

Even if I say so myself, I worked hard at my new business. The day started at seven in the morning, when I got up and prepared my pot of strong tea. If the Russians arrived and imposed widespread torture, I fear I would ask for my strong tea before the firing squad. That is one of the few essentials in life.

The milkman usually appeared at the stroke of eight. From then on the day swept past like a magic carpet. The milkman knew the ins and outs of local gossip, and was usually full of spicy bits from the 'Nucleus'. A place of dubious attractions, it was, from the outside, an ordinary coffee house. From the inside it was a 'B' feature, a real George Raft movie. If you were a little corrupt, crooked or violent, you were a member of the 'Nucleus'. Coffee was about the last thing they served, and all the bad boys of the realm, on leaving the clink, the squad or the probation centre, would undoubtedly appear at this house of ill repute within days if their term ending. The police were well aware of this and had their finger on the pulse of this modern equivalent of Fagin's kitchen.

The milkman's favourite tale was of one morning, when he was calling for the milk order, he flew down the stairs and saw a scene that Fellini would have given his eye teeth for. At least six couples were screwing away like express trains, making his delivery of six cartons of double cream a little superfluous.

It was a formation event that even Busby Berkeley had not come up with, way back in the thirties.

After the first three months we were indeed established and the element of downtown café society was being drawn to Monmouth Street. The theatre deliveries mushroomed, and almost every week we were attending to at least four rehearsal companies. We provided the Theatre Royal, Drury Lane, with sandwiches and pastries fit for a king, not to mention the food that the star of 'Hello Dolly!' consumed. Joe Layton, the American producer and choreographer, rang me from New York to make sure I would, with my minions, attend the new production company he was forming at the Drury Lane Theatre. Greater fame hath no sandwich maker. We were compared to similar bistros in Greenwich Village and were voted the victors.

The editor of *See Europe on Five Dollars a Day*, a very popular food guide of the sixties, appeared one busy lunchtime to test our wares and skills. This large gentleman, a little like the late Orson Welles in bulk, ordered two soups, a salad with all my favourite mixes, dominated by cream cheese, and very spicy pineapple, plus a homemade Cornish pastie. Then, obviously still with a burning appetite, he tried my cauliflower and chicory mix, bordered by egg mayonnaise salad, tuna fish and a breathless concoction which included radishes, banana, apple and cherries in its own piquant sauce. He downed it all like a shipwrecked sailor, and washed it down with a jug of iced coffee, before he administered the coup de grace with trifle, cream and a Florentine.

He declared it was all superb and so reasonable that he would recommend us to his magazine without delay. This he did. There's a copy of his review on the next page.

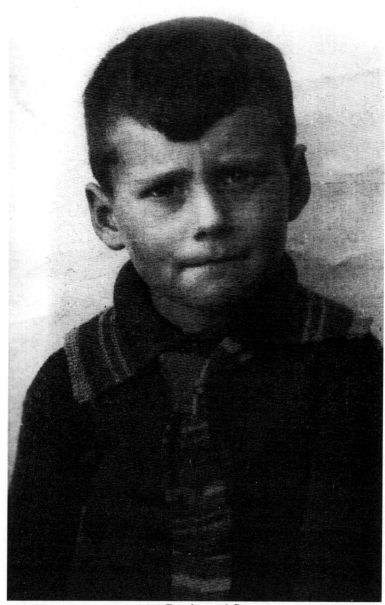
Barrie aged five

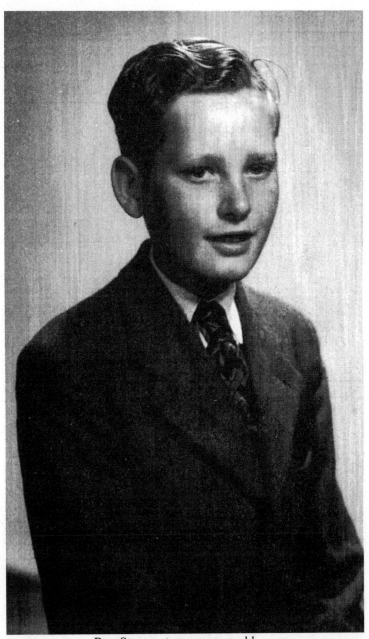
Roy Stacey at seven years old

Mother with John, Roy and David Stacey

Oswald Edwin Stacey (Father) in his twenties

Barrie aged thirty

Dear Aunt Ethel, who taught me much of what I know

Barrie as best man at brother John's wedding

Mother on College outing (Second from right, top row)

A Theatrical Coffee House

The As-You-Like-It Coffee House, 18 Monmouth Street, WC2 (TEM 6220)

Barrie Stacey, a young playwright whose first play 'Teddy Boy', didn't exactly make the big-time, has invested whatever money he salvaged and his enthusiasm into a coffee house where numerous people of the theatre – as well as theatre-goers – go to be served really good coffee and wholesome snacks.

He found a tiny place and decorated it with simple things – but all tell-tale as to his interests and aspirations. The tables and chairs suggest an English-Scandinavian design – light wood and pastel colours. On the walls are enormous caricatures of either dead or retired movie stars. Greta Garbo, Bette Davis and Barbara Stanwyck stare down at you sadly as you munch away at 'granary' (whole-wheat) bread sandwiches.

The coffee house specialises in 30 varieties of salads daily. Granary bread is used in all the sandwiches, and the pastries are freshly baked for the coffee house. For about six shillings (84c), you can have a very English meal of soup, mixed salad, dessert and coffee. Afternoon tea is 2/6 (35c).

From 10.30 till 2 a.m. every night, the coffee house becomes a private supper club, featuring vocalists and guitarists who 'entertain unobtrusively'. But the prices never change, and Mr Stacey is pleased to welcome tourists, if they will inquire about a 'temporary' membership during the day.

The inclusion in this most prestigious of guides brought us countless customers and friends, who would never visit London without coming to see us. It helped no end in those early days when to balance the books one needed a little bit of luck, or a particularly large gin!

Freddie Lees had gone off for another season of vivid portrayals, while Ronne Coyles had also returned to the world of make-believe, and was entrancing patrons in a touring revue. This boasted his accurate and spikey impressions of stars of the ilk of Eartha Kitt, Marilyn Monroe, Peter Lorré and Marlene Dietrich.

We had recently witnessed the arrival of Gunter, a German youth with potential. Gunter was the waiter to end all waiters. But as he was also a star performer, to mention him in the same breath as a serving maid would be sacrilege. He could charm the birds off the trees. The fact that he could move at all in his trousers made him a contortionist of the highest order. He was the only man I knew to wear clothes out from the inside. He had one over-large factor that really was a best seller and made him a star of the lunch movie. You didn't need a lorgnette to spy this factor either. Gunter was bi-sexual, and spent most nights jumping from one bed to another in the same house with Olympic ease. He had boundless energy and was staggeringly good looking. I recall his thick, dark, curly hair, and his wide smile as he moved like some powerful car looking for a part in 'Born Free'. His loyalty to me was a tonic.

I remember many days when an office girl would come in just for a sandwich, and Gunter attended her as if God had created him for nothing else. He got everything backwards when reciting the menu, except his sex appeal. His rendering of the salads on offer was something to be heard. 'Cheese cream' and 'Pineapple and fish tuna' were notable examples.

Anyway, girls who just came in for a sandwich left, after having the 'full treatment', and more likely a kiss, from the prick-teasing Gunter. This man gave bi-sexuality a new meaning, and was as busy as a dragonfly at a hen party. He came in one morning and had us all in hysterics when he said,

119

"Darling, I went to a party last night. And I danced with a man... he was so handsome... so young... and sweetie... so *rich*!"

He was soon making a fortune on his return to Europe. This was to be expected with his quick brain and tenacity.

A good guy who took the world by storm – and unique charm.

*****

I always found the Germans superb workers, and we ran for several seasons with their help. Fritz, another, rather reserved German youth, was the favourite of Madame Vanessa. Fritz reminded her of an old lover when she had toured the world. He came to us on the recommendation of two frauleins I had working for me at the Haymarket Coffee House. He had been a steward on a German boat, *The Hanseatic*, and had met the woman who told him to contact me on arrival. He was slim and dark, with a sly wit and smile, an excellent worker. He built his own public. We teased him mercilessly about the interest of Madame Vanessa, and being shy he was an easy target. We gave him ultimatums such as, "If you have to make love to Vanessa or die, what would you do?" And he would reply, "I would die!"

Hans was another worker who came for a season. Blond as only Germans and Scandinavians can be, tall and well built, he was charm itself and called everyone 'Honey Baby'. He was an actor from Berlin who later on really hit the gravy train and became a very much sought-after artiste in the Fatherland.

We did have some English help. One was Peter Almond, who was footman to Princess Margaret before her Royal Highness gave Lord Snowdon the boot.

As everyone knows, Princess Margaret was a mimic of international standing, and her mimicry had caused much merriment through the years. There was consternation, I am told, when, as a young girl, she imitated her mother's dulcet tones when ordering menus for the Royal household. Thus, when the Queen Mother (Queen at the time) sat down to dinner

– the fare was all wrong. The cook was called to explain her actions. Very perplexing.

Her Royal Highness was also, of course, an excellent pianist with a charming singing voice to match, and had delighted friends with her superb cabaret style and appeal. It is rumoured that the great Greta Garbo once asked her to play for her in Paris, and the Princess obliged with ten verses of 'La Ronde', some of them not ever sung in public before... or since.

It often happens that tourists chanced through our doors in the evenings, not quite knowing what to expect, some still clutching their *See Europe on five Dollars a Day*. A few less hardy creatures took one look at the crowded atmosphere, café residents installed for the night and windows fogged up with everything from smoke to outrageous wit, before beating a hasty retreat. For those that braved the scene, there was much to be enjoyed. Americans in particular seem to be more adventurous than other races. They would come in heavily rouged, mostly the women, with rayments all the colours of the rainbow, and still glowing from the excitement of seeing a truly wonderful stage production at one of our lovely West End theatres. That enjoyed at a price that wouldn't get them a babysitter back home.

Such a woman came flying through the door one particular evening, looking a bit like Spring Byington, on a day off from the 'Andy hardy' series, and said, in a high pitched Washington voice, "Aren't they all darling! I haven't seen anything like this since I was a waitress in Greenwich Village." Whereby her escort, possibly her husband, whispered, "Can't you keep anything to yourself?"

We were recommended in Istanbul, saluted in Tangier and adored in Tokyo. You could tour the whole of Europe and not come across a riveting clientele such as the 'As You Like It' could boast.

Protection money was indeed a regular evil for many establishments at this time, but hardly for small cafés earning a modest income. But our fame had spread, giving us an entirely false financial value and eyes were obviously focused on our growing income. They had to be kidding. We were making just enough money to row the boat, but not enough to be worth stealing.

It happened one night – and not only to Claudette Colbert, thank God. I was just about to close, when a young man came lurching in and asked if he could have a sandwich and some soup. He looked all in and, at three a.m. I wasn't far behind. The look on his face worried me, but I scuttled away to attend to his order.

When I returned he was laid out cold like a dead rabbit across the seating. I raised him slowly, got a cold compress and put it on his feverish brow, and by God, he was feverish, and gradually got him to take some soup. He came round after a while, and I could see he was on the run from someone or something. A gangster confederate who had been 'crossed' was all I needed. He smiled a very weak and wry smile and thanked me for the soup. At least his old woman had taught him some manners. He got up to go, thrust a pound note into my hand, and fell abruptly to the floor with a crash. I picked him up and asked, as he came round, if I should fetch a doctor, silly idiot that I was.

"No way!" he muttered. And then I knew. Nevertheless he was human, a guy in trouble, and not all that bad. No one is ever totally bad, not even Bette Davis. I could see he was not going anywhere, and it was almost three thirty in the morning. I took him upstairs to my room on the second floor, helped him into bed, and then found an impromptu roost for myself on the floor.

Here I should explain that my room with a view on the second floor, had a three quarters bed, which was enough for most couples. Indeed, it had given me much pleasure over the seasons, and now housed our sick friend well enough. With the exception of my two chairs, some other pieces and a screen, the rest of the room was pure tat. A gas stove stood in the far corner.

For four days I nursed my new friend through his fever, popping upstairs, every time trade grew quiet, to tend him. Slowly, but surely, he recovered his strength, and within a week was able to leave. He was a big man, at least six foot, sandy hair and stocky. He was not handsome, he was not plain.

I shall never forget his parting message and his appreciation. From that day I could do no wrong. He became an inseparable friend; not that I saw him often. But for years afterwards, presents of great opulence and style would arrive at Christmas, with hampers fit for a Sheik's larder.

If love were all, and it isn't, this might have been the start of something new. Whatever happened to Ricky, for that was his name, I never did know. He is probably ruling over Casablanca since his namesake (alias Humphrey Bogart) kicked the bucket. Who can tell?

As I was never trained for below stairs duties or as a serving maid, and neither were most of the thespians who came to work for me, I was forced to devise table numbers. Thus, when I was panic stricken – taking orders during rush hours – I would scream "Apple pie for table nine!" and the sweet got to the target. Table nine was our favourite, and on this cloth many introductions were made that would be very important indeed. On this very table I first met Shirley Hafey, a singer cum dancer and occasional actress, who had also been one of the numerous handmaidens who threw petal leaves when Cleopatra entered Rome in the fabled film 'Cleopatra', as created by Twentieth Century Fox. Shirley, who is a Scorpio, has truly a sting in the tail and a temper to match. A most attractive and impressionable wench, she was, and is, a wild and loyal person, and a lady well worth knowing. She had come to me via David Keller, a singing teacher of quality and renown, who practised at nearby Wigmore Hall. The famous and the unknown came to his classes, and he could claim Jess Conrad, Dickie Valentine, Alvin Stardust, Gary Martin and many more amongst his clientele. David had been a singer and actor for many years and the musicals he appeared in were numerous.

They included 'The Pyjama Game', 'Annie Get Your Gun' and 'Carousel'. He was also in Jessie Matthew's last show 'Sauce Tartare' at the Cambridge Theatre. His tales of rows and rivalry between Jessie and Renee Houston would brighten many a rainy afternoon.

He was a prolific talker, and unfortunately had a tendency to hold forth on the state of his health and his general ability to cope, before he started the scales. This did not endear him to the few who did not love him. And it did take up a little of their hour before they commenced the lesson. However, to know David was to love him, and his friendship has been treasured by anyone lucky enough to win it.

David, a large man, with a round, florid face, was heavily built. His smile would welcome you like a beacon the moment you arrived. Apart from the fact that he did not seem to be walking too well (I only knew him in the winter of his life), one would never know he did not enjoy good health.

He had left the stage on his doctor's advice, and set up as a singing teacher. This quickly made him a great success, and gave him the recognition he had never attained as a performer. Aggie Jones, his accompanist and associate, was completely the opposite. Tiny, almost doll-like in appearance, she had a tremendous streak of toughness within. With a bush of fuzzy hair and a twitch of nerves on her cheek when a pupil reached a bum note, she was kind and considerate. They both gave so much in tuition and probably hardly made a penny. Aggie looked for all the world like David's mother, as he was six feet, while she was a diminutive four feet and a quarter inches. They made an intriguing duo.

After the Wigmore Hall Studios closed at the end of a busy day, David and Aggie would toddle to a nearby tavern to quench their tremendous thirsts and review the day's work. It was here I would join them on many an evening and bask in their friendship. Much later on, on such an evening, we would leave, absolutely smashed, to go on our various ways.

David had marvellous connections for those starting in the business. He was able to place most of his pupils in steady and lucrative employment when their scales were far-reaching and true. It was through David that I met my close friend and associate Keith Hopkins, the Welsh singing star, who became the leading man for two seasons at the Little Theatre at Newquay. David had recommended artistes for this venue for many years, and cast and worked for the management. This was Ronnie Brandon and Dickie Pounds, who were household names in the world of summer season entertainment, and had played all the major resorts in their time with spectacular and glamorous productions. They enjoyed every moment at Newquay. Many stars of today started with this talented duo and were given their first chance and taste of teamwork. Roy Hudd, to mention just one, was one of Ronnie and Dickie's early successes.

Ronnie was a short, dapper man, with thinning hair, a ready smile and great charm. He had the ability to make everyone a member of this family. And they really were. Now Dickie, or should I say his wife, was another thing altogether. She was something of a tornado and liked her own way, which was not usually a bad thing. Quick of movement, she was a tiny figure with great impact. Only four feet nine, she looked like a miniature Thora Hird, and wore trousers and shirts, and sometimes a tie. Her hair was always very short and shingled. She quickly moulded a show into shape, and woe betide anyone if they did not go along with her, for she had a tongue which could whiplash a cowboy. She adored Ronnie and he her, and after many years as producers in large towns, they settled in Newquay to end their days in this lovely resort.

With its tiny stage and antiquated equipment, the theatre would have defeated most people, but not Dickie and Ronnie. Even after the modern theatres they had been used to, their seasons at Newquay were still a keynote of entertainment of the highest order.

While touching on Newquay, one must never omit a large, devastating lady who ruled most of the resort for one reason or another, Dorothy Du Pré. She had lived in Newquay since her husband had been advised to move out of London. They settled there and opened a restaurant. When he died, Dorothy sold the business and let out her house in Mountwise to visiting summer pros. This she has done ever since. She also helped to run the bar at the 'Cosy Nook' theatre in Newquay, which is almost by the water's edge. Dorothy knew everything one would wish to know about the place. She had a personality as wide as the Thames, and to stay with her is to move into the world of 'Hellzapoppin'. She lit up at midnight when her 'happy hour' begins, and her warmth was only matched by her generosity and kindness. Many is the night we have watched the dawn come up in her lounge, mainly because we were too sloshed to get up, after having laughed the night away. Dorothy was, by then, sprawled on the floor with nothing but a bra and slip, downing her umpteenth drink and defying the world to murmur a protest!

Dorothy was seventeen stone if she was a day, and tall with it. Her blonde hair was tousled, and her ample bosom usually exposed a little to the fresh air. "If you've got it, flaunt it," she used to say. She could be anything from sixty-five to death, and her faithful companion was a large and ageing cat called 'Wen', who ruled over the house with determination. Dorothy loved life and when she laughed the whole row shook, which is only as it should be. A character so sadly missed in today's world!

*****

I have mentioned a little from the 'As You Like It' but had, in passing, to mention some of these extraordinary characters. Back to table nine.

Through my introduction, Shirley Hafey met Ron Riley. Ron was the spitting image of Ray Bolger, the dancer, and indeed stepped in something of the same way. After meeting Shirley, they formed a dancing act and toured the whole world singing and dancing the songs of Rogers and Hart and Gershwin. Shirley also became one of the queens of the commercials when she was featured in many on the tiny screen. She was seen in several West End plays. Ron has forsaken the world of dance for the role of therapist and is a good friend to this day.

Another interesting introduction occurred on table nine. A young man partook of coffee one day, John Newman, accompanied by another bright boy, John Nickson. Messrs Newman and Nickson were determined to go into theatrical management, and after a truffle or two asked me what I thought. Seeing that I was new to the whirlpool of theatre production, I was scarcely one to advise. But to the theatre they went and now John Newman is in the front rank of impresarios. He has done better than most to keep the wolf from the door and lay up a few jewels for his old age or the revolution, whichever comes first. John Nickson went into publicity and disappeared without a trace, rather like the Irishman who bought a newspaper shop and blew it away!

As the evening trade took shape at the 'As You Like It', the people it attracted, who became founder members, would have drawn Charles Dickens and the late Andy Warhol combined, such was the assortment. They and their companions created the core of the establishment at night. One such member of the clan was the Countess De Vismes. She had mislaid her first name in the mists of time. Doubtless somewhere in the old world the ghosts of her parents still flutter, amazed and bemused by the conduct of their only daughter. Whether she had been christened, and where, only she and Somerset House knew.

The Soho crowd referred to her as either 'The Countess' or 'Eileen', but she was usually referred to as 'The Countess'. She was the Countess De Vesmes, and that was that.

She was rumoured to be a Countess by marriage to a member of the Austrian aristocracy she had met while washing up at the Cumberland Hotel during the Second World War. Her early years must have been stylish and worldly because she was still a woman to be reckoned with. One of her claims to fame was that she was once Augustus John's mistress, and he painted her in colours so rich that the portrait was a hit in society throughout the region. It was a fame that would get her into most clubs, both listed and unlisted.

But now she looked like a close relation to the 'Baby Jane' of Bette Davis in the famous Warner Brothers' film. Her wrinkled face suggested a maze of traffic, heightened by thick make-up which was not from the Max Factor collection. Two sharp, unblinking eyes nestled in pockets of tangled mascara with some long false eye lashes for good measure. We were all aware of her devotion to 'Sadie Thompson' as played by Joan Crawford, by the thick line of scarlet which encased her lips. But even with this slash of mistaken decoration, one could glimpse a stamp of pride that even her tatty fox fur, twisted around her craggy old neck, could not diminish. Her coat of many colours clashed violently with the soft print of her dress, rescued from the bins of yesteryear. When meeting, she perused one rather like a connoisseur inspecting a rare stamp whose pedigree was in doubt. Through it all, she managed more than a hint of intelligence. She was nobody's fool, even on an off day.

Her long nails were the same colour as her vivid lipstick; she ordered a meal with the cultured tones of Dame Edith Evans. Some days she wore a hat that would have excited Ascot, let alone Gertrude Shilling. These were her good days, her salad days, her banqueting days, when she was equal to the world. On a bad day she would choose from a collection of absurd headgear, perhaps a schoolboy's cap or an Egyptian fez (probably given to her by the late and beloved Tommy Cooper). The bad days were to be avoided, days when the Countess was not at home to the world. She was not herself, her back arched and her head was down on her chest. Then she would be perfect to play the old hag in the forest, collecting sticks before meeting 'Cinderella'.

She spoke seven languages on a good day, and a passable English on a bad one. She succumbed to drugs when Chelsea was but a village, and her many 'trips' were of sudden and long duration. She was as tough as steel and as quarrelsome as Irish zealots.

She would wine, dine and sip iced water by the gallon. Late at night in the 'As You Like It', when the clientele changed from courtesan to cannibal, she would be ridiculed by a passing youth, as young will sometimes mock the old. The misguided youth would cheek her with careless taunt and she would sit up, like Queen Christina meeting the Spanish envoy for the first time. To the lad's opening remark, "'Ow are you, old dear?" she would draw herself up to her full height (all five feet six inches, if the weather was right) and decree, "Young man, I am never better than I should be, and may you have everything you want when you want it!" Then she would pass out cold before the soup.

One evening I recall, the Countess was being sent up by a group of businessmen who chanced to pop in for a little supper after a particularly boring conference next door at the Shaftesbury Hotel (now the Mountbatten Hotel). The Countess was eating her Scotch egg, which perched uncertainly on her trifle and cream (to each his own), when the men suddenly became rude towards the Countess, muttering the insult in French. Without a murmur and scarcely raising her heavily weighted eyebrows, she picked them up immediately and cussed them in French, Spanish, German and Latin, with a little Greek thrown in for good measure. They were so stunned they ordered double apple pie all round. A certain sign that things were not always as they seemed.

In the winter the Countess was often in need of a room at the inn. Her rent was paid most irregularly by friends, and the landlord was rarely in the mood for delays.

That particular winter it was cold enough to give a Saint Bernard dog palpitations. The Countess was found by a young policeman in the middle of Neal's Yard, a piece of waste ground behind the shops in Monmouth Street. It was barren there, but nowadays is a growing market of superb vegetarian eating houses. The Countess, obviously in need of a bed that evening, had accepted the invitation from a friendly dustbin and there she slept, upright, with the lid just above her nut, as the cold night air descended, with a little frost for luck. Even the tomcats had decided it was not a night to be out, and the only sign of life was a little game of charades by a quartet of rats who had a big claim to the right of way in Neal's Yard at the time.

There was a full moon that night, which may have meant something. The constable thought the Countess was dead, what little he could see of her. But what woman of quality would die without an audience? The young copper was straight from the mint and investigated the situation. As he shone his torch, the lid of the dustbin rose, to reveal the Countess De Vismes. The

Countess opened one eye, rather like Long John Silver using his patch for the best effect. She stared at the policeman, then, retrieving a straying eyelash that was intent on going absent without leave, she remarked to this junior 'Dixon of Dock Green', "Young man, would you have a light for a lady?"

She drew from her pocket a cigarette holder that was made for 'De Reske', took out a 'Du Maurier' and held it up for ignition. The astonished policeman got out a lighter, his disbelief still suspended, and lit her cigarette. She drew several puffs on it, then brought down the dustbin lid over her head and terminated the audience.

She was last seen in a coffee bar which had tables shaped like coffins, with chairs to march. 'The Macabre' was well named without a doubt, and was situated on the verge of Wardour Street and Berwick Street Market. She deigned to lie down there one wet and windy Sunday, after being totally disappointed by the company present, and fell asleep. One young punk threw coffee over her. Whether to wake her or to amuse his friends, it was never revealed. The Countess, dismayed to be woken before Mass, cried out, "Oh, Christ! It's not snowing again?" then fell into a stupor which lasted until three in the morning when the place closed.

She was admitted, under protest, whether from herself or the hospital staff I have no idea, to a hospital near Chalk Farm, which she promptly christened 'The Snake Pit'.

I visited her several times, and the scene was always the same. She was under the impression she was staying at 'The Negresco' in Nice, and that her suitor was late.

She smoked like Napoleon before battle, and when she set the bedclothes on fire for the third time, a doctor arrived to question her.

"Do you realise you could have set the ward on fire?" he asked.

"What a lovely idea," she replied, and then said, "pass me my monocle, there's a good chap, I wish to read the *Times*."

She was known from Soho to Streatham, from Pimlico to Peckham, and we are the poorer for her demise. The Countess entertained underneath the arches in Villiers Street, which is just to the left of the famous Players Theatre. There, many years before, another superb character actress had begun her professional career, the late Elsa Lanchester.

The Countess was reported dead many times by various customers of the places she frequented, but a good girl is hard to put down, and this one had no intention of dying just yet – she still had a lot of living to do. I often wonder where she finally ended this extraordinary life!

One afternoon, a lady known as 'The Fox' flew in. I should hasten to add she was not a witch, but moved at a very fast pace. 'Fox' by name and cunning by nature, she was no worse a woman for that. She was a tiny lady, no more than four feet ten, but with a large body on short legs. She looked like a knowing concierge, with hair greying at the temples and held back by a large brooch, or on market day, by two slides. She had a large bust and a quick, fertile brain.

On the day in question she danced in, ordered an egg mayonnaise sandwich 'on tick' and said, "Have you heard – the Countess is dead!"

"Oh dear," I replied, stirring the asparagus soup, "she owes me eight pounds fifteen shillings."

'The Fox' attacked her sandwich and muttered, "Then you got away lightly, old dear."

She finished her sandwich and flew out as quickly as she had arrived.

I cannot recall when I first laid eyes on 'The Fox', but she was a regular customer in all the cafés in Soho from five in the evening, and was in the business for anything and everything. She could sniff out a sale or profit quicker than a market trader in Petticoat Lane. If the going was good she stayed at the Shaftesbury Hotel, which never seemed busy, but always did a fair trade with the oddest of clients. If things were slow, she looked around somewhere for a bed, and often ended up on someone's floor.

She once took twenty tramps into Young's Chinese Restaurant in West Street and ordered everything in sight. When the poor travellers were well into the meal (the waiters must have taken the whole scene as something from 'The Inn of the Sixth Happiness') 'The Fox' vanished for a pee, and was never seen again. At least, not at Young's. The waiters were left with twenty men of no fixed abode. It was definitely a stag party, for no lady got into the act when 'The Fox' was starring. Whether they eventually got their dough I never knew.

'The Fox' did walk-ons (a quick performance for film or television without any dialogue) and was open to a good offer, day or night. She frequently journeyed to France on one venture or another, and often returned with riches beyond compare, which usually lasted a week or so. She was known to all, and dodged by many. I liked her pluck and cheek, and we got on extremely well.

Another regular customer was Ernest Page, the horoscope teller. He was a tall, handsome man with a slightly bowed back, and a most impressive beard of grey, which gave him great distinction. He had twinkling blue eyes, bordered by many crinkly lines which added to the hint of humour his figure suggested. He looked rather like a guest at the Last Supper. The black sheep of the family, he became a prophet of modern times, and after leaving a menial job in the City, he took to the roads and never looked back.

He wore his hair long in Biblical style, and was so good looking he could be taken for Jesus Christ, as played by Robert Powell. He was gracious and accommodating, but was always in command of each and every consultation. He set up shop in my café most evenings and would give a reading by appointment for the princely sum of five shillings. He came to the 'As You Like It' with many others, including my good friend Quentin Crisp, when they were forced to leave a faded bistro named 'French's' in nearby Old Compton Street, which indeed had ruled for centuries.

Ernest came on the dot of eight each evening with his case of charts, figures and beliefs, and left at one in the morning, before the last rites of the day were given. Occasionally he came on Sundays, when we were brave enough to open the doors, but Sunday afternoon was never a good day for chart readings. Perhaps all his victims were into the psychiatric couch, or each other, before teatime. He was consulted by the famous and the infamous, the rich and the penniless, the favoured and the neglected. He once told my fortune as a birthday present, but I fear I was not converted, I find the crystal much more fun. But for many, Ernest was the coming Messiah, the prophet par excellence, the advisor to the court. People returned to see him again and again and get his message – all for five shillings.

He ate and drank my victuals for all of eight years and paid me the going price, so I had no quarrel with the gentleman. We once had a fight going on in the restaurant between two punchy sailors who had lost their ship, or each other. The punch up was sudden and devastating. Six tables were overturned before the situation was back in hand. Two dozen customers were dazed by the affair, and some a little frightened. The staff were always as cool as cucumbers in such an event, and minutes after the affray the taped music was going and tables reset to commence business.

Ernest, looking even more like an extra from the court of a Biblical epic, sitting majestically with a little leek soup dressing his beard where it had landed during the upset, stood up as the waters subsided, and ordered a pot of strong tea as if nothing had happened.

I have heard the 'As You Like It' called many things, but maybe the best description was 'a variety agent's waiting room by day, and the court of Cecil B de Mille by night'.

About the same time that we closed the 'As You Like It' Coffee House forever, Ernest Page was hit on the head by a dustbin lid, wielded by a young punk or perhaps a disappointed client, in Hyde Park. He collapsed and died without further ado. No one knows who did it, but what was certain was that Ernest had omitted to predict his own demise, so he just missed the annals of everlasting fame.

*****

In the middle of our run, Monmouth Street became more violent. The cowboys carried real sharp-shooters instead of Robert Mitchum water pistols, and the drug peddlers were an awful menace. The methods of concealment were many, but sooner or later the police and our good selves saw through their disguise. With the element of violence gathering momentum I had to think of a deterrent. Although the mixture of clientele did not attract a lot of youngsters, it alternatively would not always dissuade the toughs from coming in to pester us… and occasionally shock a few customers. The language of these roughs would put a fruit porter to shame. Although many of my regulars did not turn a hair, even a peroxide one, let alone a wig, strangers who perhaps had ventured in from the other world for a bowl of soup and a club sandwich, would not be prepared for such gems of the English language. The scene caused them to raise their eyebrows and their temperature. To regulars, such coarseness would mean nothing, and between cigarette they would murmur, "Up yours!" which was not always a good idea at that time of night.

But the whole scene was worrying me. I had already been approached for protection money, and it occurred to me that the new and threatening customers and the protection demand could somehow be related. This was where my good friend Ricky, that I had nursed earlier, came in. He was the person I could rely on. Ricky controlled the end of Soho of which we were a part, or so we came to realise. He made it quietly known that we were not to be bothered. We escaped protection money demands and were allowed to sail on course through the minefields without further ado. The teenage and rougher elements were, however, still swearing at night and causing some irritation and discomfort. I had to think of something apart from fire, flood and epidemic to dissuade these undesirables.

I suddenly hit on the idea of a club membership after eight o'clock at night.

"It will never work!" muttered seasoned residents, "never in a million years."

I did not intend to be around in a million years, so decided to give my idea a trial. I found a tough ex-soldier who had frightened the Japs in Burma, and arranged for him to act as doorman. A maid was sent to Bourne and Hollingsworth for some material, and soon the front door was framed inside with a lobby of curtain, in readiness for the hour when the password was required.

Alex, the doorman, had great charm, a gentle persuasion, and muscles that would have delighted Marilyn Monroe had she been around. So we did maintain the warmth and allure of the place after all. A small membership fee was taken from the clients and patrons which, in turn, kept Alex with pennies for his efforts.

This worked quite well, and it seemed as if our anxiety was over for the time being. However, we did have one or two incidents. One morning, at two fifteen to be precise – a.m. not p.m. – after playing 'postman's knock' with a few hostesses from next door, a group of us were sitting enjoying a splendid pot of tea. Only those who have toiled as maids or waitresses know that feeling of ecstasy when, after a century on one's feet, the door is finally closed and a cup of tea awaits. This early morning we had drawn back the curtain from the door as the night was hot and humid. Suddenly, without warning, a large penis was thrust through the letterbox and peed all over us as we sipped our strong tea.

"If we can't sodding well join you, we'll piss over you!" echoed a voice from a dispirited young man.

"What a funny thing!" remarked a spinster of the parish who could not sleep and had come in for a chat and a cup of tea. "I've never seen the like!" she said. And she hadn't.

Madame Judith Piepé was a friend and customer. She worked for the disillusioned, the poor, the wilted and the just plain unlucky, not to mention the homeless. She was sort of leader at the St Anne's Annexe in Shaftesbury Avenue for those in need (in need of what was really the question).

Judith was a short, plump Austrian lady, with glowing red cheeks and a large, wild fuzz of dark grey hair. She spoke so slowly and took so long, that if you had a train to catch, it was difficult to hear the end of the story, which was a pity as Judith was always very entertaining. She looked for all the world like the wife of a curate or bishop. The slow, faltering accent betrayed nothing of her stamina and courage, for she had spent several years as the guest of the SS and Gestapo in a concentration camp, and had not been treated in any shape or form the way a lady should be.

On arrival in this country, she spent her days trying to be of service to the representatives of mankind that inhabited Soho and its byways. On her travels she wore a capacious cloak (very similar to that of our old friend who posed in a black robe sipping Sandeman sherry on the popular poster, and frightened the hell out of me for several years when I was a toddler.) Her cloak was worn summer and winter, regardless of the temperature. And as I have just recalled, she took a lifetime to tell you the news of the day, or yesterday, but if you caught the first few sentences you could always return ten minutes later and still get the gist of the conversation, without any problem whatsoever.

One day Judith urged me to go to Islington Town Hall to hear a young singer she had discovered. Talent spotting was one of her many fortes. As she did this quite often, and swore on her life that her latest discovery was the best thing since Sinatra, I did not attach a great deal of importance on this particular day. I can remember it in detail, as it was the first really hot day of summer, and we were fagged out after serving a ferocious lunch, and had put our legs up in the afternoon sun to recover, guzzling iced coffee and lamenting we were not in Spain browning our bodies. Judith, as usual, was decked out in her woollen cloak and dress, and was adamant that we should catch her latest discovery who was appearing at the Town Hall that very evening, and we were to all go along. She predicted that this songbird, who also played the guitar, was going to be the star of stars, nothing could stop him.

She was totally right. Paul Simon went on in front of the little folk of Islington and, later on, the entire universe. He moved with great rapidity from the humble beginnings, acquiring a partner on the way. They became known as Paul Simon and Art Garfunkel. They joined us at the 'As You Like It' whilst waiting for the big break that came so soon after. On many evenings they entertained us with their music and songs, all for free. Later on, we would have paid an enormous price, like all the peasants, to hear them. Madame Piepé fed and bedded them for quite a long time, along with other homeless creatures, and gave them the hospitality of her home. Paul Simon has recently arrived to do a series of concerts in London and elsewhere. Somewhere between seventy and death and his reviews are ecstatic.

One evening she arrived at the café with eight nuns who all trooped up to my bed-sitter where they gulped down quantities of tea and numerous biscuits, and discussed the universe in general and the sinners of the world.

The customers did not bat an eyelid at the procession as it passed through; for all they knew it could be some of the cast from 'The Sound of Music', whose cloisters were nearby.

A friend I made at the café was Pip. He was Egyptian, almost of Royal rank, and came from one of the top families of that country. He loved England, but his family were far from accommodating, chiefly because he would not return to the land of his birth. Therefore he was forced to try and graft a little to help his ailing purse. Pip loved people, and so it was Pip who began helping us when things got very busy at the café. He was desperately slim, like a young, boyish Spanish dander, with sharp, aquiline features, black hair, and something like an eighteen inch waist. He was five feet six inches tall and commanded attention in any company. His real name was Nadim.

As it turned out, he was a tremendous disco dancer, and at the 'Talk of the Town' (now the Hippodrome) he would attract a large crowd of fans who would watch him dance solo and trip the light fantastic. He was truly a very striking man. His English was smooth, if a little fractured when he became excited, and he needed to see people happy and fulfilled. He had been married once when he was sixteen, in the land of the pyramids, but the marriage was annulled, and he came to England to study art, and ended up at the Slade. He travelled to Europe several times a year and spent money, when he had it, as if it was going out of fashion. His father was a self-made man and ended up a magnate of very high standing. His mother was a beautiful Frenchwoman, Pip was her only son and the apple of her eye. To his father, he was merely a melon. In Egypt they like to get their sons married off early to father endless children before they start to wane.

Pip had done his best and was spliced at an early age. The wedding was so opulent that it made Aly Khan's shindig when he married Rita Hayworth look like a 'B' film celebration. Pip travelled extensively when his allowance came through and loved the hot climates. One summer a friend of mine was sitting in Dean's Bar in Tangier (an English bar in the heart of Tangier that welcomed all the British hags and saved them from the heat of the noonday sun) when a rustle of chains was heard by the customers as they were having their elevenses. It was assumed that a posse of prisoners from the nearby Moroccan jail were being given their morning exercise, but it was nothing of the sort. It was Pip out for his morning promenade, with his jewellery jingling.

I went to Pip's empire in Alexandria and Cairo several times for holidays and basked in the luxury and warmth. He was, and still is, a smashing host and a very kind man. His mother had jet black hair, a retroussé nose and a calm face which boasted it had lived several lifetimes while she told nothing. She was constantly on the lookout for spies and signs of espionage, for treason was rampant at that time. She referred to all taxicab drivers, errand boys, and tradesmen of all description as '007'. She spoke mostly in French, and was astounded that anyone could be allowed out of the dormitory until they could speak the language fluently. I always felt that deficiency went down in her little black book as very much a minus for me. She had been born to the good life, whereas her husband had come up the back way to become a leading figure in the world of finance, publishing and politics. Pip and his family were prominent under King Farouk until President Nassar and his followers took over. Both parents have been dead a long time and I speak to Pip in Alexandra often.

Pip was very popular with the customers of 'As You Like It', and many would have no one else to serve them. It was equivalent to asking the proprietor to see they were well attended to for Pip was always very much the tourist who was helping out for the moment until his allowance arrived. I always remember Joan Hickson, who at the time was appearing at the Comedy theatre in 'A Day In The Death of Joe Egg' and was always adamant that unless Pip served her and indeed prepared her supper for the theatre, she would fast. I wonder if she ever knew how rich and famous he was in his own country, and how delighted he would have been at her success in the television Agatha Christie series, playing Miss Marple.

Two friends who were with us for a long time at Monmouth Street were Diane and Denny Leroy. Denny was the grandson of the founder of Leroy Holidays Company. He had not followed his family into the business, he was a short, blond man, with high cheekbones, great style and glamour. He had a twin brother, Eric, who was similarly endowed and they were truly a very striking duo. Diane, who married Denny for her first excursion into the marriage business, was a psychiatrist, and a lovelier one was never seen giving counsel on a couch. She was a tall lass, with classical beauty, wide lips, beautiful bone structure, and a stunning impact. She looked as if she belonged to the days of Somerset Maugham and 'The Razor's Edge', and was one of the calibre that could give even Sophia Loren a rival. All three were a great help in the café, especially on Friday evenings when the traffic was at its most chaotic. When the pubs and cinemas turned out the queue to enter our establishment was long and vigorous. It was difficult to get in or out to attend to the customers from our counter and we ended up handing out the orders over a sea of heads, such was the commotion. All the seats had been taken by regulars much earlier, so everyone else had to stand to devout their sandwich and coffee. Diane was extremely adept as this sort of pandemonium and could control even the wildest of tempers.

Diane married Denny Leroy one spring and then divorced him after he had acquired a yacht, so he immediately set sail for the Greek islands, a new romance, and peace. He was not seen again for many years, but I hear he is now back selling antiques for an appreciative public. Diane rules Jersey with her second husband and all is well. Eric Leroy, after a very good few years as a strong, light comedy actor much in demand, got fed up with the whole ball game and now has joined his twin brother selling delights from his venue in the Portobello Road.

*****

About this time a group of movie enthusiasts, who met regularly in Endell Street, drifted into the 'As You Like it'. They were a strange mixture and could almost have passed for members of a Tory convention with their tweeds and pipes. Dedicated to the cinema, they called themselves 'The Grasshopper Group'. They hired a private cinema in a nearby street, opposite the pox hospital, and showed films of varied origins, mostly virgin production from their own group, or others of similar calibre. I hit on the sudden idea – most of my ideas are sudden – to start Sunday film shows. Way back in the sixties, there was precious little to do in the Sabbath except get over Saturday night and read *The News of the World*. After all, movies were always better than ever, and never more appreciated than by the gay population and the café society.

I consulted the leader of 'The Grasshopper Group' and a deal was struck, consisting of my hiring the cinema on most Sundays and running either one or two shows. The idea caught on like a pampas fire and we were regularly sold out. We attracted theatre people, choreographers, directors and would be ones, 'has-beens' and even 'never-was' types, but all in the business. Sometimes even stars attended. Greater fame even Graumans Chinese Theatre could not rival.

One Sunday we were due to screen Jessie Matthews and John Mills in a little trifle called 'The Midshipmaid', and Marlene Dietrich's 'The Blue Angel', a truly formidable double. Both stars had expressed interest in attending. Alas, at the last moment this was not to happen. Miss Matthews was rehearsing for her cabaret season at Helene Cordet's nightclub in Jermyn Street, (whatever happened to Helene Cordet?) and La Dietrich had a sudden cold. The idea of the two stars attending this double mass was so intoxicating, that both houses were sold in two shakes of a lamb's whatsit. I used to open for pre-cinema lunch or coffee on Sundays with cold sandwiches, cakes and pure julep wine in the intervals at the Grasshopper Theatre. Richard O'Brien could well have picked up an idea for his usherette in his 'Rocky Horror Show' from this riveting scene. I then opened again at the café for high tea and later on supper, while the cinema emptied and re-filled. It meant giving up my Sunday, but it boosted takings and showed that if you're prepared to work, the sky's the limit.

Other films screened at the cinema at this time included Garbo and Lew Ayres in 'The Kiss', when Garbo smoked 'De Reske' and made that brand immortal and a must for all debutantes from Mayfair to Mandalay. Then there was Norma Sheerer and all the girls in 'The Women' and Greta Garbo hiding under a tutu with her size eleven ballet pumps peeking out under the long body in 'Grand Hotel'. Double features were definitely in at the Grasshopper, and we staged two shows each Sunday at 2.30 and 6.30. Other favourites included Paulette Goddard in – 'Kitty' with Constance Collier acting herself and everyone else off the screen, even before she reached the whisky flask. Ida Lupino was seen drawing a little ditty called 'Again' in a Twentieth Century Fox romp entitled 'Roadhouse', and Marlene Dietrich's 'The Scarlet Empress'.

Betty Grable came and mostly went in 'The Dolly Sisters' and 'Diamond Horseshoe', 'Hot Spot' and 'Mother Wore Tights' were seen during this period. Alice Faye also went down very well with such items as 'Tin Pan Alley', 'That Night in Rio' and 'Weekend in Havana', with everyone swearing by their chastity belts that Carmen Miranda was a man. This speculation has never been confirmed or denied to this day, as she collapsed without warning and left us somewhere around the age of thirty-three. I think Grable and Faye were the two perennial favourites of the film club. Closely followed by Miss Garbo and Miss Dietrich.

Tommy Deane (Roscoe to his friends) was always in and out of the Coffee House. He came from the Kangaroo country soon after the blitz stopped and has been here on and off ever since. He was a comic when he arrived (and some still swear he is) and for a few years did every gig from here to eternity.

Then he retired to become a talent spotter and press agent. He bore a marked resemblance to Bob Hope, who has been his guru since Bob took to the paths of stardom. With his eagle eyes and sharp nose, he was not unlike a better looking Mr Punch. Latterly he gradually turned to journalism and other avenues of pure delight in the world of show business. He gave up the stage when Lenny Bruce would not marry him, and has dined out on Bruce's jokes for a very long time. Tommy was as sharp as an eagle and could sell an idea to newspapers faster than any man I know.

I joined forces with him for one season for a foray into scriptwriting. We wrote for Frank Berry, a six foot Canadian, the late Don Arrol and sever other semi-names, including some artistes on 'Sunday Night at the Palladium'. Tommy expired and died two years ago at a very ripe age and we miss him still.

An actor called John Trigger was also well known at the 'As You Like It'. A Cornish boy, he was the poor man's Michael York, and for a time looked like the boy most likely to. He appeared in a succession of West End plays. He was talented, and with his devastating good looks a very promising young man. Alas, he was something of a gypsy, and after a time in the factory which is show business, he decided to fly away to become a stilt walker in down-town Ankara. He is probably still entertaining in some distant pathway out East. When asked to explain his good fortune in appearing in nine plays in the West End in the short space of two years, he would shrug his shoulders non-commitally and go on to discuss politics or world affairs until everyone had gone home to their Horlicks or some other stimulant. On this travels he took as a companion, a very clever young mime artiste, Mark Ferneaux. Together they played all over the world, whether to amuse themselves or excite the natives I know not. The Arts Council came up with the cash, so that was that. Before the Romany instincts got the better of him, he married a charming girl, Christine, and had four remarkable little Triggers.

Unfortunately, she asked herself, "Is this enough?" and alas it wasn't. So one day while John was high on his stilts, she went and divorced him, and flew off to America with husband number two.

John had a rare and special talent and a most extraordinary personality. He is sadly missed. He resides at this very moment in New South Wales, Australia.

*****

When you have a business, people come and go like flies on a window pane. When one has a moment to take stock, it is a job to imagine where they have all gone and why they were there in the first place.

Not such a problem with Quentin Crisp. I first knew of Quentin's existence when I was a dictation typist at Catherine Billinghurst's. It was one of my duties to work for an actor, Gordon Richardson, who lived in Chelsea. I looked after Mr Richardson's correspondence and visited him once a month. In this very house dwelt a gentleman known as Quentin Crisp. At that time he had not cleaned his room for over twenty years, so the havoc was not quite as considerable as later on when he made the gravy train. Not that it made any difference. I remember Quentin being interviewed in the short programme 'Man Alive' on BBC television. He started the interview by looking out of his window to the heavens above and quoting, "On a clear day you can see normality."

I had told my mother and father to watch the programme, as I said it featured one of our regular patrons at the coffee house. Father said, "Jesus Christ!" and my mother exclaimed, "What a funny man!" Quentin Crisp progressed, unabated.

The world was not quite ready for him at this juncture, but it did not take long for it to catch up and accept his genius. Quentin and I were cautious of each other in the early days, like a field mouse watching a hare. (I was the field mouse). I was not ready for him and he, in turn, was not ready for me. Bur gradually we came to like each other, little knowing that in later years we would be working together all around the country when I presented him in his superb one man show, as he preached the wonders of his lifestyle to the masses. He was at that time still modelling in art colleges and his circle of friends was vast.

"My, my!" he used to say when colliding with his fans, and after being rammed by some middle aged housewife who had finally got the message. Having seen Quentin's show, she would rush up to him and exclaim, "Mr Crisp, you have changed my life, tomorrow I will start anew."

To which Quentin would coolly reply, "How cosy!"

When asked whether he wanted to eat, drink or merely be merry, he would reply with, "Whatever you want, I want!" One can scarcely quarrel with that. He never visited the cinema for an English film, and only an American one when he could get in for one shilling and ninepence. Some sage remarked that there is a book in everyone – and he could be right. Quentin's life produced enough material for a number.

Now Quentin (as Tennessee Williams put it of his character 'Sebastian' in 'Suddenly Last Summer') is not so much a man, as a vocation. He first arrived in Monmouth Street when French's in Old Compton Street closed forever, and Bohemian clientele were cast adrift on the Soho waters. In French's, Quentin would offer conversation and wit to anyone who would care to listen for a few hours a day. The only difference is that nowadays he plays to much larger audiences and they pay him for his genius. It is extraordinary how, for all those years, we could enjoy Quentin just for free.

Quentin chose for his entrance at the 'As You Like It' a cool pair of linen trousers, shirt tied in a bow at his naval, banana fashion, and high platform shoes that were straight out of 'The Teahouse of the August Moon'. His hair was electric with mauve tints and he appeared and gestured as if he was the prophet and we merely the followers. His rouge would have done Max Factor credit, and naturally his first appearance caused quite a stir. Even the trifles melted. The bistro was one of the few that were ready for such a star patron, being very ahead of its time. It was obvious that Quentin had recommended that Boy meets Boy long before his teens, and had the courage not to care a jot who it upset. After all, the Greeks had a word for it and they never looked back.

Quentin, however, I feel has more the calibre of an Oscar

Wilde. After all, who cares who had who except the prudes, and possibly John Junior in the *Sunday Express*.

Quentin, is a very kind, quiet and compassionate man. He understands and sympathises with life itself, and the only time I ever saw him lose his cool was at the New Theatre, Oxford, now the Apollo Theatre, when a woman stood up and ranted and raved that animals were more important that humans. She might have had shares in 'Winalot' or 'Kit-E-Kat' for all I know, but she would not tolerate the species known as humans. Quentin would have none of this and gave the woman as good as she delivered. The more they fenced, the greater the excitement in the audience. In the end the woman flew out to retire to her kennels or her own particular zoo.

Quentin would have parties of anything up to nine to hear and savour his particular message of the evening, and they would sit, for all the world like the onlookers at The Last Supper, savouring their coffee and each other. A few years back, Quentin journeyed to New York for good. He was a celebrity and he died a few years later silently and was gone.

On Saturday evenings the entire place would come to a standstill while our delivery service got off the ground. Either delivery boys (usually the Brad Pitt's of tomorrow) would appear, go to the theatres before the first show and collect the orders, and then came back and make up the avalanche of sandwiches, cakes, pies and soups. That is not to mention teas and coffee that would also be ultimately delivered in between shows for the ravenous clients. Each delivery boy made up his own order. I had to ensure there was enough to go round and that no one was disappointed. If any customers came in to the café during this time they were disdainfully served under protest and dismissed with hardly a smile. Regulars would either help themselves or keep away. The speed of the service, once we gathered momentum, was the force that had to be with you. To cause any sort of obstruction meant total liquidation!

We serviced at one point twelve theatres in the West End, a record never equalled since, though many have tried. Several more 'up-market' establishments have attempted a dressing room delivery with silver service to add more elegance, but in the end they fail, for theatricals rarely like to spend much on eats when working. A common old sandwich generously made, and a cuppa is much more up their street. And that, my friends, is show business.

Chapter 7

The Late Sixties at the 'As You Like It'

Life sailed on in Monmouth Street. The German assistant left and the natives took over the serving. The clientele stayed more or less the same, the crème de la crème by day, the other world by night.

With the constant growth of the delivery service, the enormous contracts for the Festival Ballet and the improvement in general trading, I could walk into the Midland Bank without a disguise, even flirting with the bank teller when I deposited my worldly wealth. No one could really ask for more from life than to enter the portals of the 'listening bank' with such camaraderie.

About this time I was getting more and more jobs for actors and actresses who came in for coffee and went out with an audition. I always knew what was casting and for whom, and the types required, and I gave clues out with abandon. How I remembered all that was going on amid the hubbub that was catering, I shall never know, but I seemed to get a kick out of it.

When I delivered the food to the theatres I gleaned quite a lot of information, and got to thinking I should be doing better than I was.

My mother remarked, "As you get so many actors engagements, why don't you charge commission?"

I couldn't, because I was not a bona fida agent.

So she said, "Become one!" And I did.

*****

The authorities in those days ask for references that back to the Ark, and even the sex of the animals. My godmother, Kathleen, who taught me many years previously at the council school in Christchurch all the few bits of common sense I possessed, now gave me the required reference and testimonials. She said I was honest, bright and a good citizen. I gained my licence soon afterwards in nineteen sixty-six, and was renowned as the only agent who served a salad with one hand, and a casting requirement with the other. We had a very busy telephone line in the kitchen, and clients of the agency were asked *never* to telephone in the lunch hour. Of course they always did, and caused havoc. I was always very short and quick tempered to the fools who did this, and often came unstuck as the tone of my voice started off icily, and when I realised it was a casting director or producer on the line, it changed to a voice of pure syrup and honey. Then I wrote the casting on a sugar bag, while I got down to serving the lunches and catching up with my orders. If you were around at that time and had an undue wait for your lunch, you now know what happened.

I started my life as a theatrical agent alongside my role as café proprietor, and a most knowing pair of actresses, Rosamunde Hartley and Patricia Samuels became my first agency assistants. They were most efficient and knew the ropes, and Rosamunde in particular stayed for quite a time to form a basis for what was to follow. Patricia Samuels was hardly ever out of work, so was not available for very long. I always remember Rosamunde alternately answering the telephone and discussing a casting and the next minute serving the bald old man on table four his chicken soup.

Tommy (Roscoe) Deane, who could find water in a parched desert, came across a small office in Henrietta Street. True, it was only a shoe box, but it was fine for a start, and for a lowly sum of three pounds a week, who could argue? We took the office and were in business.

I used to get up and prepare the food for lunch, then at eleven o'clock in the morning run through Covent Garden and open the office up for a little action. I would rush back to help out at lunchtime at the 'As You Like It' and return later to the office to mop up the afternoon enquiries.

Thus the world was a passing carnival, while life within

my own little tinsel empire proceeded and prospered. Quentin's book *The Naked Civil Servant* had been published with an astonishing cover. Half was Quentin at twenty and the other half Quentin on the day you read the book. Amazing!

Other items of the day were entertaining. Sir Francis Chichester had rounded the Cape of Good Hope and Lady Chichester had been seen in a dress. One wag of our acquaintance had the curtain brought down around his ears in an evening of variety at the Arts Theatre, with the line, "When Sir Frances Chichester round the Cape it was the only time he had a horn on in twenty years!" Lewd, by any standards. Cilla Black had developed laryngitis and thanksgiving services were held throughout the country. So what else was new?

In a down period at the café when Florentines and their counterparts were not in favour, I received a call from Bill Keating, a great friend, who said he was stage managing a little epic at the Theatre Royal, Stratford East, and would I like to be his assistant stage manager? Of course I would. My helpers could run the coffee house efficiently and Rosamunde could cope with the casting that came through the door at Henriette Street. The Christmas show on the stocks was the American trifle called 'Tom Sawyer', with music and a good cast. I found it delightful.

Anthony Linford, fresh from drama school, played the lead with authority, and Patricia Kerry was responsible for the choreography. We enjoyed many parties at her home in Gloucester Street; sadly she left us for gigs far away eight years ago. Anthony Linford is a good, respected actor who never stops working and has latterly become a director. Amanda Reiss, whose mother was the delightful Ambrosine Philpotts, was making her stage debut. Ambrosine was one of the core of the profession, not quite a star, but certainly more than a twinkle. The West End would know her, but probably not the provinces. Paul Mead arranged the dances for this saga of the American South.

I was a reasonable assistant stage manager as long as I did not have to go into the flies. Happily, this did not occur. Also, I had one big fault. I could neither iron, sew, or repair, and this saga boasted a large wardrobe, not to mention starched 'little Lord Fauntleroy' collars. As the wardrobe mistress expected the ASM (Assistant Stage Manager) to assist in every way, she was not the only one that needed help. However, after my feeble efforts with the smoothing iron, a singe or two was more than evident on Tom Sawyer's period shirt, not to mention the large, floppy tie.

The wardrobe mistress was around thirty-five, going on fifty, as tall as a reed, with hair bunched at the back framing a thin, angular face. Perhaps a trifle starched, which is as her shirts should have been. She was obviously longing to play Mrs Danvers in 'Rebecca', but, alas, Daphne du Maurier was not popular that season, so this frustrated woman was shacked up at Stratford East doing the drag for this Christmas cabaret.

She got herself into a fearful frenzy when I couldn't get the shirts right, and relished lashing me each and every day with an excitement that bordered on the macabre.

"What can I do?" I asked Bill. "The woman hates me and my incompetence in the costume department."

"Oh Jesus!" he replied. "Tell her to go and stuff herself!"

I wasn't quite up to that and I don't think she was either, but the affair died down when she attacked me one dark Wednesday in the middle of the theatre's coffee area.

"If there is anything I cannot stand," she said in a loud voice, "it is a coffee bar actor!" She looked at me with a stare that would have turned Peter Cushing into stone.

Suddenly one of the cast got up, fresh from playing a pirate in the play and faced 'safety-pin Alice' with a smile. "For my part," he said, putting his left hand in his pocket like a good gangster actor working for Republic Pictures, "I prefer coffee bar actors to bad ones."

I loved the man then, and I love him still.

'Safety-pin Alice' took to her heels and was not seen until the 'half' (half an hour before curtain up). Where she went I do not know, but she went, and I was never asked to iron her shirts again. The show continued thereafter to steam along with great speed.

Wages in that day and age were not decreed by British

Equity. I asked the company manager when I could expect to get paid. He was a lovely old ham, as big as a house, with half his breakfast permanently worn on his waistcoat. His large, red face lived only for the moment the bar opened.

"Lookee 'ere, lad," he began, "if you come to me on Friday, just before twelve, I'll give 'e what y'deserve. No man could be fairer, could 'e?"

I had to agree – what else could I do? And sure enough the following Friday, naturally it was the thirteenth, I arrived and collared him. He took out a few pounds from his pocket, gave me seven, and said, "There y'are, me boy, and don't spend it on any wild women you may find behind the theatre. They all have the pox, and I should know!"

With that he vanished to the saloon, or the pox doctor, whichever was the most urgent, and I hardly saw him again until the following Friday. That really was the gist of my four week stay at the Theatre Royal, Stratford East. It remains an outpost of the islands for the East End, and still puts on excellent fare for the theatre lovers in the area.

I enjoyed a close friendship with that true son of the shamrock, Bill Keating, and had many wonderful adventures. Bill was a slight, wiry little Irishman; dark, with almost a cheeky urchin face, he was the eternal leprechaun, and his sense of humour would worry Woody Allen. He had been around for ages, and had helped us at the 'As You Like It' Coffee House on many occasions when waiting for the next stage job. He had been producing for the theatre, and his talents were gradually being noticed. He had done a great job on 'The Hostage' for a fellow countryman at the Little Theatre, in Saint Martin's lane, and what he would have done for the hit play 'Once a Catholic' defies description, with all its copulating and 'Hail Mary's', Eventually he took to the land of his birth where he became the head of variety. Sadly, our paths have crossed very little in the ensuing years. His fervour for the bottle was constant and not far behind that of his countrymen, Peter O'Toole, and he is the only Irishman I know to get pissed outside a police station and lie down and await an invitation into the joint. Why he never got a part in

Carol Reed's 'Odd Man Out' I have no idea.

In addition to my work as a restaurateur and my stage duties, I found time to write regularly. I had that six weeks' experience behind me with *The London Weeks News* which employed my talents for a short period gossiping and commenting on the latest offerings in the world of stage, screen and cabaret. During that period I met and made friends with an actor, John Stuart Anderson, when he invaded the Arts Theatre in Newport Street with his one man show for a week or so.

Reid Anderson, one of my helpers in Monmouth Street, who also doubled as stage manager for John Stuart, brought us together one cold Wednesday when he brought John and his manager, Ricky Church up for coffee at the café. I was cleaning the windows at the time so looked more like a skivvy than was usual. John Stuart was strikingly handsome. Being tall and distinguished for one so young he had a superb wit which, with his manager Ricky, as an excellent foil, made them a very entertaining pair. Although strictly speaking, Ricky managed John Stuart, which sometimes was a job, off stage they were quite a double act and had toured widely for some years. At one time John Stuart was one of the Arts Council's top earners abroad, apart from the Beatles, who had a distinct advantage over my actor friend, as they could play the guitar. John Stuart excelled in his one man show, but he was as restless as a gypsy. He frequently bought a house, sold it and moved on, usually within the full moon.

He made a good living in America, where the matrons fêted him, and their husbands didn't quite know how to take him. Clifton Webb couldn't take to him at all, and even Orson Welles was quizzical. We have been firm friends for a long time, and later John did a play for me at the Georgian Theatre in Richmond, Yorkshire, which was a great success. It was a lovely Restoration piece called 'The Careless Husband'.

Ricky Church (real name John Church), had previously worked for J Arthur Rank, but after meeting John Stuart, he decided to join Mr Anderson's merry band, and from that moment on has managed the other John's career with aplomb and style. Sadly John died some years ago. Ricky Church emigrated to Greece and so did Reid Anderson and are there still.

At the 'As You Like It' everything was going well, and as we were keeping our head above water, I was beginning to relax a bit. Madame Torres was a new devotee to the cause, and came in every evening to eat a mammoth salad and drink endless cups of black coffee. She was always dressed in black, with a large sombre hat perched on her small head, and glasses balanced on her nose. Her small, pinched face was of a poor complexion, and her lips were tight, and exposed very uneven teeth. She was only five feet in height, and it was assumed that as a spinster of the parish she was not into men, and her family had probably given her up in despair. She lived for, and adored, books, books and then more books. She smoked Sobrani cigarettes of the very highest quality which she purchased in Piccadilly proper from a very old established tobacconist of her acquaintance. She dealt in second-hand books and her personal collection numbered over a thousand. The periodical *The Clique* was her Bible, and her livelihood depended largely on the Post Office regularly delivering this noble book.

We called Madame Torres 'Mother Medea', mostly because of her affection for black. She must have been seventy, but could well have been eighty as she seemed to have looked the same for eternity. She coughed as much as she smoked and it was always generally expected that she would depart for the heavenly choirs at any moment. In actual fact she lasted out most of the cronies of her period.

In the middle years of the 'As You Like It' she dwelt in an attic in Coptic Street just above St Giles' Circus, but after a contretemps with her landlord, who ungallantly called her a witch, she was thrown out without warning. On one of the coldest nights of the year she knocked on my door just as I was putting our cat out, a leftover from a horror film, with just one eye, in fact, the only one-eyed cat I ever did see. Madame Torres came in and proceeded to pour out the unfairness of her situation, and asked if she could spend the night in the café. I knew I had made a bum decision, for she slept on the wall seating in the café for over a month before she persuaded my landlord to let her have the basement.

It took a team of navvies to move all her books in. she had little else, except an old straw hat in blue, which she wore on Good Friday and Christmas Day. She received an allowance once a month, when she paid me for the food she 'ticked' up, and squared anyone else who might be due some money. She had a wonderful sense of humour, and nothing in this world would shock her. To practically every remark passed to her, she replied, "Thanks awfully!" She was one of the old school and belonged to the world of Jane Austin and possibly the Brontes.

Soon after she moved downstairs we had a disaster. One evening I was just going to bed and drew back the curtains (I never sleep with the curtains drawn) when I heard a rushing sound, like a river. I looked out and water was gushing down the road. What could have happened? I telephoned the Fire Brigade and the police, who, after waking from their slumbers, or their amours, arrived in droves.

Water still cascaded down the street and was beginning to flood the other side. It seeped into the basements and indeed the ground floors of businesses along the street. We seemed to have a slight rise in the ground on our side of the road so were escaping immediate danger with the flooding. However, that proved to be only a temporary lapse.

I tore downstairs with my trousers half on, half off, and saw the street was now awake and viewing the situation with growing alarm. What were the water board thinking of? It turned out that the man who had the key to turn off the water was missing. Everyone was powerless to stop the torrent, and flooding continued. I began to panic when the water was level with my steps and suddenly remembered Mother Medea in the basement. I ran downstairs and there she was, up to her chest in dirty water, trying desperately to reach rare editions of her books as they floated around like toy boats in the bath. It was then realised that Mother Medea, for that is what we called Madame Torres, always slept in her hat. I joined her quickly to assist in rescuing or attempting to save the only things she had left in the world. It did not help that the water was filthy and as cold as ice.

The police arrived and ordered us out. Mother Madea refused to leave until they helped rescue the books. So there were three policemen wading around in the water and reaching out in the murkiness for a rare edition of *East Lynne* or Bernard Shaw, in addition to us.

The flooding suddenly stopped as the water seeped through the restaurant floor. I thanked God on my knees that he had seen fit to pardon me this time. Across the road the restaurant known as the 'Mon Plaisir' was ruined. The basement which housed the kitchen was flooded and chaos reigned.

After a while a kind of tranquillity descended and Madame and I sat on table one at five thirty in the morning and reviewed the situation. Here was this tiny little woman with all her worldly possessions up the spout. She had managed to save the shabby old handbag, but sat as large as life telling me all was not lost. Certainly not her hat, which was where it should be, on her head. Such women are the backbone of England, and do not come sweeter anywhere in the world.

"Madame," I said, "whatever shall we do?"

"We shall do what we always do, you and I, and enjoy a pot of the strongest tea," she replied.

And that is exactly what we did.

"Thanks awfully."

*****

The years at the 'As You Like It' were marvellous, colourful and exciting ones, and I learned more from the characters that came and spent their daily bread with us than I would if I had sailed the seven seas. The area was at its best. That scene in the sixties was slowly drawing to a close, and it was, as with all sections of one's life, personal, touching, and never remotely like anything one would see again.

By now, all things being equal, it became increasingly

clear that I could not expect to run the 'As You Like It', as well as my own agency and the production company as well. As so often happens, fate forced my hand. We were offered a reasonable sum by the Shaftesbury Hotel to vacate our premises, as they had plans to build onto the café.

I accepted their offer, but with the agreement that we could stay on upstairs until alternative accommodation could be found. Poor 'Mother Medea' was also a problem. So we took a shop on the corner of Seven Dials, opposite the Cambridge Theatre, and we opened, selling rare books for 'Madame', as well as a selection of soft toys, several of which were made by friends and associates. There were some beautiful lampshades made by the lovely old actress, Chilli Bourchier and odds and ends of bric-a-brac. For the moment, this took care of 'Madame', and we did a reasonable trade which did not demand too much of my time. Obviously, it was time to take stock.

After a while we had problems with 'Mother Medea'. She had occupied the basement under the new shop in Seven Dials, for her books. It was also her own bedsit, and someone had obviously told the landlord she was sleeping there. We had a threatening communiqué from the landlord saying that 'Madame' had to stop using the basement as a residence, or else!

'Madame' took very little notice, except possibly to smoke more Sobranie cigarettes! The problem remained.

She started sleeping in the shop. The windows were wide, and one could easily spot her, as she was sleeping underneath the counter in her slip. The hat, of course, remained on her head throughout. When I found out, I said, "For God's sake get up early and quietly before the streets are aired."

What a hope. She started rising around twenty to nine in the morning, when the streets were filled with office workers. She became a curiosity struggling up from under the counter in her slip, smoking furiously.

I knew this could not continue, for sometimes a small cluster of people would gather, looking forward to this cabaret. So I did the next best thing, and went and saw the Covent

Garden Association to see if they could arrange something for my lodger. They refused abruptly, saying nothing could be done. I knew they could help if they wanted to, so a little push was required. I flatly told them that if they did not find anywhere for 'Madame' by Monday morning the following week, I would be forced to put her out in the bitter winter cold.

"You wouldn't dare!" they said.

"Don't you count on it," I replied.

By Friday, they had found her a new flat in Macklin Street, which was just the style for this lady. For a time this worked, until 'Madame' set fire to the place with an unusually ferocious Sobranie, and was once again on the road. They shifted her soon afterwards but, sad to say, her cough turned into something more sinister, and she died on Christmas Day. Another link with my past faded into obscurity.

*****

I chanced one evening to invite Stuart Hopps to supper. Stuart was an old friend who had studied dancing with the legendary Martha Graham in America, and was now doing classes with a dancing school around the corner. I was impressed with Stuart and his ideas, and felt that with a little help from fortune, he could reach fame.

Stuart was tiny, five feet two inches in height, with a small, round face and bunny teeth. He was little like a miniature Mr Bennett from 'Pride and Prejudice', but in his twenties. Stuart possessed a raucous sense of humour, which suited me, as I laughed like a drain. We got completely sloshed upstairs on this particular evening, and in a moment of pure madness, decided we would stage a show. After all, Judy Garland and Mickey Rooney had done it in countless metro-Goldwyn-Mayer musicals, so what had we to lose? Plenty. But when one is young and carefree, who cares?

A friend of ours lived opposite Monmouth Street, a young actor of twenty-three, and who had recently been appointed administrator to the Gulbenkian Theatre in Canterbury. We phoned him, and as luck would have it, he was in, and came over. After a few glasses of my punch, which, as all my friends will testify, is lethal, he was as drunk as we were, and clamoured to stage our show. It was to be 'In Circles' by Gertrude Stein and Al Carmines. Stuart had done it in America and could get the rights. So the dye was cast for the pattern for the subsequent ten years, ten wild and wonderful years of producing shows. However, after this period most of the jewellery had gone, the little pad in the country was no more, and I was left with little more than a dozen pairs of knickers. But in this business you have to hang in, and the Gods will eventually smile on you.

Stuart worked and worked, became the choreographer, most likely and directs musicals from Istanbul to Peru. He recently bought a house in Deal which is his little home when in the UK.

Chapter 8

We Take a Show on the Road

At the time I started my career as an impresario, the Beatles had set up a company known as 'Apple', so not to be outdone, Stuart and I decided to call out production company 'Grapefruit Productions'. Its first venue, the Gulbenkian Theatre is a small, but very pleasant college theatre on the campus at Canterbury.

Stuart was pleased as a cat with cream, and I was not far behind. We could but wait, and see how students of the Gulbenkian Theatre would react to our premiere production. On reflection, it did not seem a bad thing to stage the play there, as students were surely on Gertrude Stein's wavelength.

My mother wasn't, and said Miss Stein was surely a screw loose. However, I do not think that screwing was in the lady's curriculum. Miss Stein was, however, unknown territory to me. A Messiah for some, a puzzlement for others. She was 'in' when 'in' was 'out' and vice versa. I always mixed her up in the same teapot as Dame Edith Sitwell, who used to dwell in Carlyle Square, Chelsea for a time.

Freddie Lees had a bed sitting room in that very area, and we used to sit drinking Mazawattee tea on early closing days, and occasionally got to hear of this noble lady's witty remarks. My favourite was when she rang the police station and shouted at an unsuspecting police sergeant, "Noise at night I can tolerate! But noise in the day I *will* not stand!"

The show was called 'In Circles'. Gertrude Stein had a style all of her own and 'A Rose is a Rose is a Rose' was one of the compositions which meant little to me, but seemed to spell a world of meaning to her followers. The music was zany and bright. One song was supposed to be Marlene Dietrich singing a ditty entitled 'Cut Bread'. The whole thing looked fun, and perhaps I could learn to love Miss Stein a little later on. Stuart Hopps did have the performing rights. How he had them I did not know, they were either won in a poker game or first prize at the rag ball. But have them he did, which meant we could stage this riotous affair at Canterbury for a week's run.

We set about casting. Shirley Hafey was perfect for one of the parts, and two girls I have always liked, Myra Sands and Rosemary Faith, were the other femmes together with Felicity Harrison, a lovely singer. Mike Fields, a pocket marvel, was the compere, and also played the pianola which accompanied the production. Several other good artistes were hired to re-enact this 'way-out' carnival.

The first night went well. Stuart had directed and choreographed with panache, and the cast seemed happy and vibrant. Business was reasonable, though whether the local students knew they had a theatre in their midst, it was difficult to tell.

Canterbury is an enchanting old city, and I did, when later I developed as an agent, get a lot of clients into the Marlowe Theatre. There they did superb musicals which were usually directed by the very talented David Kelsey, a man with vast knowledge and technique for this particular medium. The *Daily Telegraph* came down and gave us an excellent review. I have a sneaky suspicion that the critic, Eric Shorter, was a great fan of Miss Stein. All in all, it was a good production and one that filled me with hope for at least a day. The audiences dwindled as the week progressed. Saturday was good, but we still finished up five hundred pounds in the red. However, it was worth the effort, and the production, I felt, did us credit. I could not have done it without Stuart Hopps.

This primary adventure whetted my appetite and I carried on 'Grapefruit Productions' with a short tour of Dylan Thomas's 'Under Milk Wood'. This, I fancied, would beguile the whole of Cambridge, long one of my favourite cities, and indeed, Cambridge was first to give me a booking. So then I needed a try-out week to run the show in. We opened the tour at the Adeline Genée Theatre in East Grinstead. Originally it was built as a ballet and festival theatre, and named after

Madame Genée, who knew a pirouette or two. But it was badly planned, for it is situated in a forest. It had no restaurant to speak of, but that said, the theatre is bliss. The next thing it didn't have was money. So the poor theatre was a goner from the start. And if you braved the elements to get to the damned place, there was every chance you would go astray on the way home, as the path was dark and very murky. What was a poor theatregoer to do? The late Myles Byrne, the Brighton impresario, who was really into the movies, owning several cinemas all in the Brighton area, had bought the lease and was aiming to satisfy his ego in opening and running the place. It was a far cry from his offerings at his cinemas, with such jewels as 'Emmanuelle' and 'Who Pinched Rosie's Knickers?' which paid for his French maid and caviar at least. At the Adeline Genée, Myles booked in tours, an occasional repertory season, which usually was directed by the lovely Sorrel Carson, and a pantomime which invariably did quite good business. The only danger at the Genée was, if you had a matinee and the curtain was not down by four o'clock, all the electricity was turned off and the audience and artistes were literally in the dark.

Myles had an arrangement with the electricity board and this was the winter regime. All very difficult if the play went on too long. Myles did his best, however, to keep the theatre from sinking for a few years. It finally kicked the bucket around nineteen seventy-eight and now belongs to the Bush Davis Dancing School next door. Sue Bishop, who occasionally present first class productions at the Genée, also supervises the dance academy next door, and turns out a superb array of talented girls, dancing and singing along with the best. The Adeline Genée is now a real shanty theatre, more's the pity.

We opened 'Under Milk wood' there, and much to our astonishment came out with fifty pounds profit. A miracle, indeed. However, it did get the play off the ground. A week's rehearsal nowadays, even with actors pampered and spoiled by grants, is scoffed at. But really if actors cannot learn a script in a week, and give a reasonable rendering, and there are many that cannot, I maintain they should not be in the business. Some of our actresses can get a script at ten o'clock in the morning, and by four o'clock the same day have learned a whole act! A fortnight's rehearsal is bliss if you have enough money. Three weeks rehearsal for a musical is very admissible, but not for a straight play. Come on! If you cannot get it together in a week, go and be an insurance clerk or perhaps work on the desk at the local dole office.

Many of today's stars played in weekly repertory for years, and it did them no harm at all. None of them will ever have any trouble learning lines. That I promise on my rosary.

We did our first major week with 'Under Milk Wood' at The Arts Theatre Cambridge. It was commanded in military fashion by a gentleman by the name of Colonel Blackwood. The venue was a joy, well run, and packed it from top to bottom with our Welsh extravaganza. James Jordan, who had become my resident producer, I had found him through a colleague at the Grand Theatre, Swansea. James always wanted to produce, and I was glad he did. I always got on with him famously, for not only was he a good director, he spoke my language, be it blue or grey.

We assembled a very good cast including Gareth Armstrong, Jill Mears, Jonathan Prince and Ann Emery, Dick's sister. Ann was a major talent, with a voice like Streisand and a talent to match Danny Kaye. She was a lady to be reckoned with. She had not done a straight play before, but with this Dylan Thomas tale everyone had to play at least three parts, as we only had ten in the cast.

Ann managed to excel with every portrayal. Just the sight of her as 'Mrs Organ Morgan', eating fish and chips was something extraordinarily amusing. It was a joyous week. And believe it or not, I could not get a seat morning, noon or night to see my own production. Ann Emery is currently in Billy Elliot at the Victoria Palace.

James was very pleased with it, as were the theatre, for they made a nice little profit to store for a rainy day, and let's face it, rainy days in the theatre are numerous. The following week we were at Folkestone. We shouldn't have been, but we had been offered a week at Swansea and therefore had a week in between to fill. This is where luck figures so much in the theatrical life. If we had got the week in Swansea to follow Cambridge, I would have been home and dry, but I *had* to have a week in between.

Folkestone's Leas Pavilion was run at that time in the summer by Richard and Peggy Burnett, true thespians of the highest order, who did so much to help and mould many stars of today with their high standard repertories. The theatre on the front at Folkestone, is small and intimate, really a music hall theatre.

We went there in the winter, and the only living soul along the sea front were the gulls. It was cold and bleak, and only on Saturday night did we attract anything like a full house. I lost all I had made at Cambridge, (which was nothing to get you in a lather, anyway) and at Swansea we did reasonable business, but did not end up with anything worth celebrating.

Meanwhile, back at the café – in the last few months of our reign at the 'As You Like It' we were doing excellent business, as if all our friends knew the joint would shortly be no more, and were trying to make sure the place went out with a bang. So the business was able to sustain the losses incurred by 'Grapefruit Productions' with the little Gertrude Stein exercise, I joined the Association of Producers and Theatre Managers, a most noble organisation, and as I spoke out strongly at things I disapproved of, I was elected onto the council in no time at all. The Association was a fine one and did much good work for its members, especially the young actor manager, before being merged with a senior group, the Theatrical Managers' Association, to carry on the tradition.

A year later I received a telephone call from the manager of the new Brunton Theatre in Musselburgh, a little town on the outskirts of Edinburgh. We were asked to tender for the theatre's annual pantomime. The burgomaster there at the time was Kenneth Lowe, who was not everybody's cup of tea, but nevertheless, packed the place for the Christmas show with school parties, so he was worth his salt, whatever the opinion.

The banqueting and cocktail lounges at the Brunton theatre were superb, and the theatre although in the round and a trifle small, was a dream. We got our tender accepted and produced the pantomime there for four years until Kenneth Lowe got himself a new job in Glasgow, and his successor preferred a Scottish management. We were literally told to push off. We did – just as far as Dunfermline, and at the fine Carnegie Hall set up shop there with pantomime for the next five years. Wherever I present pantomime, I always give a pantomime party which destroys most marriages, and creates many an illicit coupling. But on the whole it is an enjoyable shindig, relished by all. The punch is powerful and if you live through it, tomorrow has to be better. On some occasions the soirées, it was whispered, were even better than the show. But this report is anonymous.

The banqueting table at the Brunton Cocktail Lounge was laden with all kinds of exotic foods, especially prepared for the pantomime party, and was an impressive scene. All the local dignitaries came, and we said our thanks to each other in speeches, in between rounds of the demon brew.

Mr Taylor, the Town Clerk at Musselburgh at that time, with his lady wife who was also called Taylor, were present that first year for the 'do', which started on the Friday evening and went on through to the early hours. It was agreed that my punch was more successful than usual because James Jordan, the next day, shortly before noon, was found on the seashore of this Scottish resort, ordering the waves to go back, obviously convinced he was King Canute.

Poor Mrs Taylor was taken home in a near coma and only after four glasses of punch. At four a.m. on the Saturday morning or what she thought was Saturday morning she took the shopping bag out to go for the weekend groceries, only to find that time had flown and she had lost twenty-four hours somewhere, as well as missing Family Favourites. It was, indeed, Sunday morning and she had slept all the time.

The years at Musselburgh were extremely happy, and we found the town generous and warm in support. Many artistes who have done very well since were with us at that time. Keith Hopkins, always a great favourite, was starring. Neil Martin, the all-time winner of the television competition 'Opportunity Knocks' played Buttons the following year. Neil hit the jackpot too early and consequently could not handle the success that came like a thunderbolt. This was a shame as he had a lot of talent to give, Tricia George, who starred in 'Tomfoolery' at the Criterion Theatre in London, and in several 'American Express' commercials, was there with Tony Taff, a very popular pantomime dame. Thereza Bazaar, now half of the famous duo 'Dollar' was also a chorine with us.

Meston Reid, the D'Oyly Carte tenor, joined us one Christmas to play Principal Boy in 'The Sleeping Beauty', while an old friend, Wendy Pollock, played the title role.

I should add that the children at Musselburgh seemed to be very adult for their age. In the scene where Princess Aurora has slept for so long her only hope was to be awakened with a kiss from the prince, Meston leaned forward to plant a kiss on her lips, when a nine year old, with ambition, shouted from the front row of the stalls, "Give her one for me, mister!"

Wendy Pollock opened on eye form her royal bed and declared, "With what he's got, you must be joking." This was a line which wasn't in my script and did Meston untold harm when later he was attempting to interest the local damsels. In any event, Mistress Pollock was a little wide of the mark. Our Wendy, renamed 'Bollock' by her enemies, had much to answer for on this occasion. At somewhere between forty and death, she makes middle age a joke. She was always ravishing and her top note could worry Sarah Brightman if not Katherine Jenkins.

James Jordan was always a source of comfort, as he stayed with each and every show he directed for me, ensuring that the quality and standard never slipped. Brian Cooper, our good friend and associate, a large friendly man who looks a little like Russell Harty, used to drive me up to Musselburgh every weekend, and as we made the trip from London in seven hours flat, you can tell that Brian was not a man to mess about.

James Jordan was adored by his cats of which he had many, but was never a happy man. He had not come to terms with what he wanted out of life, and was constantly searching for the unobtainable. There is no doubt he was a smashing chap, and an excellent actor and director. Whether working and directing for me for seven years did him a mischief I shall never know, but the poor man dropped dead at thirty-five, and we lost a good friend and the theatre a fine artiste.

Lindsay Kemp had been at Musselburgh a little before us. In his company was a newcomer by the name of David Bowie, and he offered David to us for pantomime at Musselburgh for thirteen pounds a week. I turned him down, and said he could not sing! Lindsay, as part of the vast Edinburgh Festival, later moved to the Town Hall at Portobello, a little town on the way to Edinburgh, which boasted a tiny seashore and reminded me of Northam, near Bideford, Devon. Princess Margaret, who always knew a good thing when she saw it a week before anyone else, visited Lindsay and his wandering band and saw nude bottoms on stage for the first time in Scotland. Incidentally, the Scots were quite taken with this revue, so unlike the ones normally unveiled for the Festival in Princess Street.

For a while Lindsay was not allowed back in the capital for one reason or another. Ironically, if they could have foreseen what Lindsay's production of 'Flowers' would do to London and the rest of the world, they would have had a seizure there and then. It must be said that apart from a lot of nudity, 'Flowers' had some superb artistry in it, and, in time, was received with acclaim in many countries, apart from the court of Bohemia in London.

We later shared a double bill with Lindsay at the Little Mercury Theatre in Notting Hill, when I presented a late night revue which was preceded by Lindsay's company performing 'Harlequinade'. This was as you have never seen it before – not even in your wildest dreams. We both had a good season. I was presenting an outrageous adult revue starring a camp duo, 'The Funny Affair' and both casts loved each other with passion, which always helps to create a fine team spirit. This almost excited some journalists, but perhaps not Marjorie Proops. She possibly had to read up on the situation at that time.

*****

A London booking agent, and impresario Keith Salberg, rang me with offers of work. Keith is a short, squat, Jewish gentleman of middle age, who for all the world, looks like a tailor or jeweller. Jewellery would be much more apt, as he is, without doubt, worth quite a few bob. That said, he has seen the ups and downs of the business as vividly as most, and like the rest of us, has often had to walk home from a theatre not having the required fare. He had almost no neck, and wears a little trilby hat perched on the top of his head. Keith has a sharp wit, and a capacity for work that would make the Japanese delirious. He smells out news like a vacuum cleaner on a dirty carpet and can tell you the takings of any show from here to the Orkneys within a hundred pounds. Keith has seen all of the parade which is show business pass by, and I would give much to glean half of his knowledge. He is outspoken, often to the point of rudeness, but as he always pays for his seat in the stalls, he is entitled to say what he thinks, regardless of who it offends. He has a small stable of well-known personalities, though, alas, as a few have withered and died during the past five years, so his ranks are more depleted than they were. A few stars who were under the Salberg banner that I have worked with and now sadly departed are Walter Landeur, Sandy Powell and Leslie Welch (the Memory Man).

I always had kind thought for Joyce, Keith's wife, who was on the boards with the rest of us in many a comedy farce. At that time she enjoyed the comedy which is the house of Salberg, along with her regiment of pussy cats, never more than twenty, never less than fifteen, which form the core of the family. There are also around four hundred and eighty-five teddy bears, but they are less demanding, although it has been said that Joyce and Keith have a name for them all. Joyce was always chatty, and optimistic, a quality rare in the land of sawdust and mascara. Keith goes to sleep with the telephone clutched to his ear, and only leaves it to relieve himself or go to the bank, two functions he defends with utmost ferocity. In the evenings Joyce manned the telephone as well as Judy Holiday did in 'The Bells Are Ringing' while Keith attended the theatre. He went every night, and matinees twice a week, but on Sundays he did his accounts. The last time I sat with Keith in the theatre was for a revue at Wimbledon entitled, 'The Jolson Revue'. Kevin Devane, a very talented young light comedian who practically started his career touring in my one nighters, came dancing out to a thin house and quickly started to warm us up. He asked if there were any married couple in that early evening. Keith shouted from his seat in a very clear voice, "Yes, two sailors in the front row…" A very remarkable chap.

However, Keith had on this particular night rung and asked me if I would like to present pantomime at the Carnegie Hall in Dunfermline. As I was no longer at Musselburgh this was a good idea, but at that time I was still so besotted with being an impresario, I would have presented it anywhere in the world. To illustrate how times have changed, I received a guarantee of six hundred pounds a week for presenting pantomime at Musselburgh, and after paying adequate wages and dues, there was always something left over for myself, as manager. This will give you a little indication of how much wages and production costs have risen as the year was 1974. Now I cannot do a reasonable standard of pantomime on a small scale for anything under ten thousand pounds a week.

We had only worked for Keith Salberg once before, when we presented a version of 'The Wizard of Oz' (long before I had penned my own version of this well-loved classic) at the Little Library Theatre in Grays, where our good friend Brian Pridmore was the manager. This had obviously not deterred Keith from coming to us again and here he was, asking if we could do a pantomime for him at Dunfermline. We would and we did.

The administrator at the Carnegie Hall, a Mr Colin Reed, was so bowled over with the show, and especially the performance of Malcolm Terrey as the Dame, that he booked us immediately for the following year, almost before the paint was dry on the current year's set.

Our stay at Dunfermline lasted five years and included pantomime each year, children's musicals and the occasional variety show. We sadly relinquished the venue when rising costs made us realise that we could not keep up the quality without sustaining a loss.

Keith booked many shows and concerts for me and we worked with many names; one, in particular, Leslie Welch, billed as 'The Memory Man', talked like an express train and it was extremely difficult to get a word in edgeways once he had started. His wife only came to see the act once when they were first married, and was never lured to see it again. Nevertheless, she loved him all his years, looking after him like a faithful watchdog. For the uninitiated, Leslie was a star for a very long time, answering any question you would like to name on sport. He was very busy on radio and was top of the bill for ages. I can always remember him on bills with such stars at Cavan O'Connor, Beryl Orde, Turner Layton, Donald Peers, Larry Macari etc.

I remember Leslie on the last show he was to do for me, which was headlined by Jessie Matthews at the De La Warr Pavilion, Bexhill, one hot Sunday in nineteen seventy-seven. He asked the audience, as usual, for their questions. During the evening he got one question wrong when quizzed about Britain's amateur featherweight boxers in the nineteen thirties. Jessie Matthews came bounding out of her dressing room at the rate of knots and ran into the wings, thrusting a note into the fist of the amazed stagehand. It was to tell Mr Welch of his error and inform him that Miss Matthews' brother was the featherweight amateur boxing champion of that particular year. Leslie's memory and patter was in great demand until the day he died and no 'pro' could ask for more. A careful and humble man, Leslie was the epitome of professionalism. Joyce Salberg died very early but Keith Salberg, currently in Brinsworth House in Twickenham is sadly no longer an agent but still gives to the theatre twice a week (usually Windsor and Richmond) and still gives us his opinion as to what he has seen is super or crap! No one knows what became of his many cats.

Many creatures of this world have wanted to become impresarios or mere presenters of entertainment, be it plays, musicals, revue, concert or burlesque, but only a tiny percentage have succeeded. One has to expect to go bankrupt at least twice to qualify for the title, shared by the likes of Andre Charlot to Phyliss Dixey. Every time I leave the pawnshop or a far from understanding bank manager I remember this.

Casualties in this most precarious of professions, are

endless. To want to back or invest in a theatre show in the first place is pure madness of the heart. To actually hand over your gold or cheque is lunacy of the highest order. The pessimists always decree that the moment the money leaves your hands you can say 'bye bye' to it forever. This sadly, in many cases, is only too true. But once the wine has been tasted... many are hooked for life.

The thing to do is to go into the matter thoroughly. Firstly, look at the track record of the producing management inviting the investment. Have they a pedigree? Have they experience? Do they have the expertise, stamina and resources to mount a first rate successful show? What of their office? Or do they conduct business from a crap table or a telephone booth? I know one management which does just that. What of their accounts, and their accountants? There are more crooked accountants around than traffic wardens. Are references, credentials and books open for inspection? If the answer is yes, one then looks further into the proposed vehicle for production. Who will star? Who will direct? In this day and age of television, the names on the box command more consideration than the stars of theatre's yesteryear, but are they as durable, and can they act, and are they really names that people will pay to see? Common sense is always the best influence, and if you would pay money to see the proposed names, other people would; so go along with that.

Finally, small casts are less of a risk, and so is one set. It is essential if the show is a musical, that you realise you will have to drum up more money, as there are so many more expenses. Just think of the dancing shoes one would have to supply for '42nd Street'! But musicals are more popular with the theatre-going public, which is, again, something to think about.

If it is a straight play, make sure the subject is an acceptable one, and, if possible, penned by a known author. In many cases the author is the real star of the show. Look at the proposed dates for the tour. Are they 'number one' theatres, which will mean you are playing a well-run, efficient theatre, in a major town. A 'number two' theatre is a smaller one and not such a good proposition, not having the seating capacity. 'Number three' theatres are those where everything and anything can happen, and usually does. Often the so-called manager comes in only once a week, and then only to collect his laundry.

So for the uninitiated or merely stage-struck, to enter the world of show business as a backer or an 'angel' is as dicey as backing a horse on the race track, and just as much fun. I can scarcely say more except be prepared to flog the family silver and heirlooms twice every winter.

Let me move on and relate how it all started for me as an impresario and promoter, and how I came to move into the world of children's musicals, then variety, with ease, a little pain... and much success.

Chapter 9

A Little Further into the Jungle of Theatre Presentation

A great friend of mine, Peter Tod, who is now the most sort-after gentleman in the field of theatre management, was under-manager at the New Theatre, Hull, when Alexander Bridge presented a revival of 'Flare Path' for a week. I had worked for years as a casting advisor to Alexander Bridge. His real name was Peter, but as there was already a famous West End producer of that name, Peter changed his professional name to Alexander. I cast 'Flare Path' for him and it turned out to be an excellent production. This was not unexpected, as I rate Alexander Bridge to be one of the cleverest directors it has been my privilege to work with. The week was a good one and enjoyed by all.

In due course, it was Peter Tod who beat a mass of applicants for the job of administrator at the Civic Theatre, Darlington, and he proceeded to transfer this outpost from an audience percentage of twenty-two per cent to ninety-four per cent in the space of two years. A major feat, and if you know Darlington, you will understand what I mean. Peter has imagination, application, and knows his stuff. He has now enjoyed a remarkable career, and retired after managing the Hippodrome in Birmingham. He offered me pantomime at this particular theatre, and we presented 'The Sleeping Beauty' once again. How that woman of slumber gets around! Unfortunately, the script was by an old established writer at whose altar I did not worship, but that said, we assembled a good cast and proceeded.

Tom Mennard was approached through an associate of mine, the fine agent Jean Charles, and over lunch the three of us did the deal. We took lunch at the Piccadilly and Little Cottage Restaurant in Windmill Street. There, the variety of food, quality and cost cannot be rivalled anywhere, and the warmth and cheek of the waiters is unique. Tom liked me, and the food, and all was well. He is a great practical joker, and has a dry wit. He was previously a bus driver and he identified beautifully with the warm Northern audiences.

Marienne Parnell was 'Beauty'; she had previously played 'Gretel' for me in 'Hansel and Gretel', and was a smashing singer who could also act, a very rare combination. She has since retired from the business and is married to a wealthy industrialist. Another friend who was in the cast as a dancer was Michael Blaise (known as 'Modesty' to most people), who had been spotted and cast in Franco Zeffireli's 'Jesus of Nazareth' as a pretty disciple. He was probably one of the most handsome youths I had seen, which Mr Zeffirelli wasted no time in noticing. Michael was last heard of at Sun City in South Africa, compering a bum and tit show. It is a shame he did not pursue his career over here, as he did some good work watering the camel in 'The Desert Song' and was excellent in 'Let My People Come' at the Regent Poly in London, which enjoyed a very long run.

For this production, and in fact many other shows, I used the 'Jackie Palmer Babes'. This admirable school still operates in High Wycombe, and was then run by Dick Hughes and his wife, Jackie Palmer. The girls were schooled like 'The Tiller Girls', and to my knowledge they still are. All the perfect young ladies. Jackie Palmer always spoke my kind of language. There was no messing about. She had immense common sense, as she had danced in the business from here to Hong Kong and knew every back-flip there was to know. Furthermore, she possessed that wonderful sense of humour you gain in the chorus. There are a few exceptions, Elaine Page is one, but Jackie could also be as hard as nails when any of the spoilt kids threw a tantrum. She is a rare and exotic bird, a breed that is becoming extinct, more is the pity. She has been succeeded at High Wycombe by her daughter, Marilyn, and if your daughter or son want to go on the stage and become a professional dancer, there is no better place to start than here.

When the Darlington pantomime was running, Tom

Mennard would stroll around the town with 'the Jackie Palmer Babes', six little misses in red cloaks, all looking like applicants for the lead in 'Red Riding Hood'. Tom could be very wicked, and his practical jokes did not amuse everyone. In this particular pantomime prior to rehearsals the principal boy had not booked her digs early and at the theatre they recommended a Mrs Anderson, who said she was descended from the incomparable Hans Christian. She certainly did hear fairy tales from her guests.

Tom arrived one Tuesday and rang the bell at the Anderson residence. Had Mrs Anderson a certain 'Miss' coming to stay? She had, indeed.

"Well," said Tom, "I wouldn't like to worry you unduly, but she has... er... a small problem."

"Oh," replied this astute lady, "but almost *all* pros have."

"This is true," said Tom, "but her problem is the needle... and I don't mean those you sew with."

Mrs Anderson was not amused, especially when Tom rolled his sleeve and mimed the needle being injected into the skin.

"Only trying to be helpful, Mrs Anderson," quipped Tom, as he skipped down the steps with his giant Alsatian.

The poor victim arrived the following day. A demure 'Miss', obviously only a few steps away from the convent.

Mrs Anderson pounced on her before the poor girl could catch her breath.

"Now, I know all about *you*! I am not having any of that carrying on in this house."

It took four pots of tea and a good ear before the mess was straightened out. If you played with Tom Mennard at this time I don't mean roulette, you had to watch your step. Tom Mennard left us, I'm afraid, many moons ago. That said, he was a great guy, and it was through Tom that I started doing business with Russell Hills, the administrator of the Empire Theatre, Sunderland. He shortly afterwards ran the New Theatre, Hull, which was his last appointment before retiring. A most astute and clever gentleman in the turbulent world of the theatre administrator. His knowledge and help has always been a great bonus to me during my years as an agent and impresario. Many have been the shows I have cast for him at the Empire, Sunderland, not to mention other houses he has managed, such as the Connaught Theatre, Worthing and the Theatre Royal, Lincoln. We have played over fifteen major scale musicals for him at the Empire Theatre, Sunderland, thereby cementing my many ties with the Tyneside area.

Peter Tod also introduced me to Mr and Mrs Fairbrother, who ran the charming old Georgian theatre in Richmond, Yorkshire. I did five plays for them over a period. The Fairbrothers were the 'Mr and Mrs Miniver' of the county. They loved the theatre and ran it as a trust, with many old dears coming in voluntarily to sell programmes, coffee and whatever. This is very Conservative country. The Fairbrothers have since retired, and when I took a production there with John Hanson, it was not at all the same. Anything revisited I fear, is totally disappointing; one seems to have lost the continuity.

We were to present the Neil Simon play 'Barefoot in the Park', and fancied Imogen Hassell to play the lead, for many reasons. I arranged to have tea with Miss Hassell one sultry afternoon in town. She was well known for her first night film appearances rather than for the films which she had adorned. Generally, the profession knew her considerably better than the public.

Imogen came to tea in a large picture hat, the thinnest chiffon dress, and looked absolutely beautiful. She was fluffy, sexy and infuriating, therefore utterly feminine. We got on like a house on fire. She was obviously not going to give Dorothy Tutin a hard time. Nevertheless, she looked ravishing and full of promise. Her outfit was straight out of 'A Yank at Oxford'. After two cups of tea we were inseparable, and swore on an oath to do the play – or die.

Her co-star was to be an up and coming actor, Lawrence Davidson, who had attracted much attention in a lead part in an art movie called 'Blanche', which had hit the bull's eye at the Curzon Cinema in Mayfair, and other art palaces. The film 'Blanche' was extremely stylish and pictorially stunning. It also went on to entrance the clientele of the little Paris-Pullman cinema off the Fulham Road, which catered for the intellectual and carriage trade.

The opening of 'Barefoot in the Park' at Richmond was to a packed house and a most appreciative audience, although Imogen was not going to worry Jane Fonda either, in the acting department.

Imogen occasionally forgot a few lines, but Lawrence Davidson spoke them for her superbly, and with her sex appeal the audience were not following the same line of thought anyway. The other members of the cast, Mavis Rogerson and Derek Wright, gamely kept everyone's end up, good pros that they were.

We hired the set from a firm in Bradford, as we had not reached the grandeur of our own store, and I felt it must have been left over from 'Gaslight'. Thankfully, no one complained, and we sailed along to the next port of call, the Rosehill Theatre in Whitehaven.

'Barefoot in the Park' finally completed its run at the King's Theatre, Southsea. This theatre was masterminded by Commander Cooper and his wife, Joan. When the Navy got wind of Imogen, no boats were put to sea. So when we had the press reception for the play, the Navy turned up in such force to meet Imogen that if invasion had taken place that morning, we would all have been gonners. During her stay at Southsea, Imogen was loaned a flat by the Commander, and we had quite a week.

After Southsea, we were to work with Imogen again in pantomime at the Civic Theatre, Whitehaven, when she played in 'The Sleeping Beauty'. (How that piece follows me around.) She was very nervous, a little temperamental, and prone to several horrendous outbursts. I remember one evening when she threw a bottle of whisky at our choreographer, Toni Harris. Toni had been with me for several years, and was a smashing lady and a tremendous worker. She had great style and attack, and was able to fend for herself. Whether Imogen threw the whisky more in anger than spite, one will never know, but Toni caught the bottle and threw it straight back. Imogen went on with a whisky rinse hairdo. This is probably preferable to a beer treatment, which we are all told can be stimulating. Toni later became part of a singing group called 'Valentine', and retired to have babies, producing two. I cannot wait for her to come back and create some interesting dance routines again, but it has been a long wait.

Malcolm Terry, as I have said, played the dame at Whitehaven, and our favourite joke of his, every time Imogen 'died', was, "Oh, daughter, you haven't got lost in the woods again? You must stop picking daisies." I wish I had spent more time with Imogen. She needed love and attention, and had much more potential than she was credited for. She needed to re-think her image, as it is always later than one thinks. The train of life never slows, not even for a passenger as beautiful as Imogen Hassell. Her early death was a sad blow and ended what could have been an interesting career. She used to ring me at four a.m. just to chat and invite me over. After an hour, even the mightiest weaken. She used to threaten that she was going to commit suicide, and I would often jest to friends, "I think I'll send the razor blades over." How very sad that she really meant it. It also teaches one to be a little guarded in such cases.

*****

Amongst other places we presented pantomime were the Civic, North Peckham, the Town Hall Theatre, Ealing, and the Lloyd's Park Pavilion, Walthamstow. Not the London Palladium, but they were nice little runs which gave everyone work, and kept them off the streets. At most of these places we returned annually for four years, but as we progressed, it became increasingly clear that with rising rates and prices, if I was to continue the same standard of shows, we were going to lose a fortune. And this had already started.

So, in 1978, I reluctantly called a halt to the schedule. We were then mounting at least five productions each Christmas. Gradually, I withdrew from the Yuletide scene. Tis also meant an end to the pantomime parties which had been a feature of the circuit. Our main star at these parties was J J King. He was a vocalist of great power, and a great entertainer. He would quickly melt his audience into a sensuous trance. The more he rotated his body to the music of the song he was singing, the more the excitement grew. The ladies in the audience would get highly feverish and forget any man they had with them, while they savoured the sexuality and vocal talents of Mr J J King.

At the last pantomime party we gave the Civic Theatre, Camberley, the mayoress forgot herself during JJ's act. It was where he took off his tie, swaying the lower half of his body like a snake charmer when... wham! This noble lady, with breasts a-heaving, threw her chair of office onto the stage and shouted, "I want him!"

Mr King, never at a loss for an answer, replied sensually, "Take your place in the queue, ma'am, like everyone else"

The funniest act I ever booked for a pantomime party, was a Scots magician from Dunfermline. He turned up for the main spot, not the supporting one, and is the only man I have ever seen to put the lady in the box, secure it, then turn to the audience and say, "Fuck it, I've forgotten the knives' – and walk off. Happy days!

Looking back, our favourite place was the Floral Pavilion, New Brighton. It is a large theatre, masked by an outside which looks like a warehouse. Not to be deceived by appearances. It is one of the warmest and most exciting venues to stage a pantomime – or a variety show. We were resident for six years and they were the most enjoyable anywhere. Unfortunately, when we started to make real money after a period of just breaking even, the Council went 'up market' and demanded stars and a new set-up, and have recently spent two million tarting the place up.

*****

In 1977, I had the idea of writing a musical comedy spoof, based on the Garbo movie version of the French classic 'Camille'. Everyone has tried to play Miss Marguerite Gautier,

179

from Arletty to Joan Sims, and I felt with good music and a funny script, it could be a lot of laughs, especially between coughs. More of this later.

A repertory actor Terry O'Sullivan tried to get the piece together, but was not strong enough for such a production as Oh Camille! Which needed a director with panache. To be fair anyone would have had quite a job as we hardly ever had the cast together, much before dress rehearsal. However, I had chosen the cast carefully and well, kids who knew their stuff, it followed beautifully. The choreographer was one Henry Metcalfe, who I later got a job choreographing 'Joseph and His Technicoloured Dreamcoat' for Bill Kenwright. To my knowledge he is still with La Kenwright and the show some thirty years later.

Ruth Madoc was something else again. She played Marguerite with or without camellias and scored with her many one liners, her comedy artistry coming to the fore majestically. A leading lady par excellence, she learnt her trade in the hills and dales of repertory and was a strong lesson to all those fillies tipping out of drama school each year on how to learn your trade before screaming for television exposure.

Ruth took the script by its ears and made marguerite a leading lady of quality. Her three and a half octave voice was used to great advantage. Russell Grant also displayed his considerable talent (often overlooked when he is dicing with the moon and the stars), currently achieving much attention – 'Strictly Come Dancing' on BBC. He caught the sweep and humour of Max, courtier to Camille, splendidly and was assisted by his onstage partner-in-crime. Madame Prudence, played with style by Mary Dee. She was just right for this old character lady with her curly grey hair, mischievous face and odd ad lib at the right time. She recognised a good line when she saw one and delivered it with gusto.

The show opened to half a house. Some were stunned, some were pleased, and some ecstatic. We did two shows on the first Sunday, which was just as well, for with such bare rehearsals, one was never really sure what was coming next. In the final scene the bed chose to collapse with Miss Madoc on it, singing 'That When The Coughing Has To Stop', and as there was much coughing in the auditorium, it was received hysterically by the audience. Audrey Leybourne, as the 'Maid' did calm this proceedings down a little by fanning Ruth Madoc on every available moment, but it was at least half an hour after the performance that I dared to set foot backstage.

The scenes were linked by an excellent Gallic trio, led by my stalwart musical director, David Carter, who dispensed the musical tapestry. It was admitted by all and sundry that the whole show was as 'camp' as a row of tents, if not a marquee, and might not be understood by everyone.

The period costumes on hire from the Queens Theatre, Hornchurch, were delightful, while the quaint furniture hired from the Old Times Furnishing Company added to the illusion.

The billboards described the piece as a camp spoof, and I think the dialogue bears this out:

Madame Prudence:	Marguerite, I have arranged an introduction for you at the opera on Tuesday night, 'Box B'.
Marguerite:	Indeed! What is his name, pray?
Madame Prudence:	Count Bonaparte!
Marguerite:	Tell me, which part of Count is Bona?

Which leads on to Marguerite, taking stock of herself in preparation for this momentous meeting:

Marguerite:	Make way, and let me give the mirror a bad time!

The press were puzzled, and the radio station bemused. On the second Sunday the queue was long and lusty, and by the second house they were standing. It was, all in all, a fun show, and by the time everyone knew their lines it had quite a sparkle to it. The music, in particular, was catchy, unlike so many of today's musicals, and the audience laughed long and loud.

Whether it was in hysteria or madness I do not know, but the guffaws came thick and fast. I went home relieved and fairly happy, and of the opinion that with three weeks rehearsal and a few thousand pounds to back us, we had a show that could take off.

Next time around, Miss Madoc (Gladys Pugh) would not, I fear, consent to play the lead. The coughing and the collapsing bed were all *too* much.

Many memories come flooding back of that production at the old Arts Theatre. Ruth Madoc, coupled with Russell Grant, and old favourites like Audrey Leybourne with names like Simon Clarke and Margo Waine, and Keith Hopkins.

'Oh Camille' was revived at the Shaw Theatre, London, just three years ago to great attention, which I will tell you about later.

Chapter 10

I Become a Mister 'Ten Per Cent'

To become a theatrical agent appears, on the surface, to be relatively simple, but in fact it entails more red tape than one would imagine, and rightly so. The difficulty in obtaining a licence is not a bad thing, as we have all heard of agents or managers who have flown to Monte Carlo, with monies earned by clients in soap operas or television commercials. Rogues there are in plenty, but that is true of every profession from politics to barristers.

Most agents are, in some ways, frustrated actors, and scenes played out in their offices in one way or another can range from melodrama to farce. Agents are renowned for usually talking fast and promoting slowly. But the work is hard and the hours long. At the end of some days it is difficult to know who needs the psychiatrist more, agent or client. Many hours are spent travelling, which I consider a must if you are a caring agent. One should go to the provinces at least twice a week, looking at the work of clients, and sometimes discovering new and promising talent. This also means you get to know the theatre managers and producers who could, on another day, perhaps give you a casting and opportunities for your 'stable'. Socialising is a duty – or a pleasure – of the job, and it's a profession where bed is a paramount topic. The only other job offering a similar pre-occupation is as a mattress salesman.

The casting couch must be obviously touched upon. Today's students, I fear, are more likely to seduce the agent or impresario than vice versa. One young would-be actor of my acquaintance actually came out with, "I suppose a fuck is out of the question?" (Shades of 'Who've I got to fuck in this place to get a drink?' – by courtesy of 'The Boys in the Band'). Whether this remark was directed to Angela Graham-

Jones, my blonde and lovely assistant, or myself, would be the jackpot enquiry.

There are stories and fables about 'Mr Ten Per Cent', from here to the salt mines of Siberia, but it is true that ten per cent certainly does not take you to the ball in most cases.

The moment the word got around I was applying for an agent's licence, I was inundated with photographs and telephone calls. Hordes of people called in for lunch at my café that had not been in before.

As an actor, I have many memories of climbing a million stairs to see agents who always seemed to dwell on the top floor (probably nearer to heaven). One started with the carpets on the ground floor, which gradually gave way to bare boards at the top, to be told, "You seem like a nice boy!" This should have been enough to send you to the monastery at once, if you possessed any sense. Then they added, "We'll let you know!"

One very helpful man was Eric Blythe who ran the 'walk on' and 'extras' battalion in nearby Great Newport Street. Here, the newcomers, the old hands and the people in the middle, came every day to sit around the waiting room, which had shades of every Hollywood musical from 'Shine on, Harvest Moon', to the 'Dolly Sisters'. Around three o'clock, Blythe would come out of his slipper box of an office, with a cigarette trailing from his mouth, leaving a line of ash to decorate his already out-of-fashion suit from Burtons. He looked at everyone incredulously, as if we should all be in HM forces or the Salvation Army, point to one or two and say, "You – you – and you!" then sigh and tell the remainder there was nothing else for them that day.

We would file out like rejected waiters at a Jewish wedding and go to the Arts Theatre Club for a cup of tea to drown each other's sorrow. Often Eric Blythe would say when giving you a day's work, "Wrap up in a warm coat, flowers are expensive at this time of year," if the wind was cold, or enquire if you had enough money for the fare. 'Walk on' and 'extra' works is usually frowned upon by many, because it is assumed that if you did this sort of work regularly you would never become a star. I have never quite gone along with this theory, as many have made the big time from 'bit player' to movie star, but the belief is there forever. There are a few who love 'extra' work, live well on it (you can make two hundred pounds a week quite easily in a good period), and want nothing more out of life and the profession than waiting on a set, chatting about everyone else to pass the time of day.

Eric Blythe was a kind, warm old professional if ever there was one. Most agents would not bother with those starting their career, as there is no great profit to be made from a struggling client on 'extra' work.

For me, the excitement of the job is finding new talent, and this country has a wealth of it second to none. Our downfall is that we scarcely know what to do with talent, even if we can discern it. Nowadays, there is a fight to get an Equity Card, which can take as long in coming as labour getting back into power. We have been offered cash up to five thousand pounds, sex, total adoration and a trip to Valhalla in exchange for an Equity Card. These offers, were to no avail, of course. You fight for the chosen ones on your list, and they move up as you exercise your allocation of Equity Cards. Here I should explain that when you are a manager and present shows, under the current system you are allowed four Equity Cards a year. These are for newcomers, and given by the high priestesses at the Equity stronghold.

Pat Samuels was still a great help running the agency. She answered the telephone with great decorum, and a speaking voice straight out of 'Debrett'. Of course, acting requirements were few in those early days. Either casting directors had not heard I had set up shop, or they just couldn't believe it.

Incidentally, Pat was later offered the part of 'Miss Casewell' in 'The Mousetrap', a saga that has run longer than 'Coronation Street' and has, I fear, never caught a mouse. The tourists include the play on their list of monumental sights, and pack the theatre year after year. In truth, the play is not all bad.

Gradually we received calls, and I gently tried to push the right numbers into the right slots. Clients were no problem at all at this time. Later on, it was another story. They came by clipper, tandem, magic carpet and on foot. From Wigan,

Wimbledon and Weymouth. In one week we have over three hundred enquiries from the stage-struck, the idiots and the true professionals.

When interviewing a prospective client, I would have a test situation. I would be wearing a pair of glasses, without any lenses. If the person sitting opposite was too timid or unobservant to mention it, I tended to be somewhat unimpressed with his or her potential. I would therefore not jump to represent that individual. If, however, they remarked, "I don't think there is any glass in your spectacles,' I would shout with enthusiasm, almost splitting a gut. That person would then go to the top of the class.

Drama students are known to gossip like tarts in a brothel, and very soon all the Webber Douglas Academy knew my little tricks. By the way, Webber Douglas and Mountview Theatre School are my favourite nunneries, where the novices are knowing, and the tutors skilled enough to wield the whips. No wonder so many of them do so well. After that, I found a new ploy. I would ask the aspiring Bette Davis, the following question. If she were given one hundred thousand pounds to stage a play of her choice, which play and which part would she choose to show off her individual talents? If she answered within one minute, this truly was knowing and she could, with luck, make it to the summit of the profession.

Some actors when asked this became as mute as 'Johnny Belinda', and some had a stroke, while others told you without hesitation the play and part they would choose. The latter were the babies that I would sign straight away. If only as many of our flock would be as quick and as astute.

I remember interviewing a charming young woman, Maggie Ryder, hot off the baking tray from Webber Douglas. She had looks, intelligence and a delightful personality. Her sense of humour would make Buster Keaton laugh, and we got on like a house on fire from the beginning. She knew what part she wanted to play. 'Mary Queen of Scots'. When I ventured to say that she was beheaded, Maggie came back with, I should make sure the executioner was missing!"

*****

Drama schools are a funny lot. Reminiscent of Gertrude

187

Stein's observations, there are drama schools and drama schools and drama schools. Some build character and some want to change them. Some leave them alone to mature and come of age. The Royal Academy of Dramatic Art will always be the magnet for the carriage trade, but they too, can take and make someone from the wrong side of the tracks. Their record is excellent. The Guildhall, the Arts Educational, and the Guildford School of Acting are not to be sneezed at, and the Academy of Live and Recording Arts are on the up and up.

I must tell you a lovely story that went around back in the sixties. It concerned the Central School of Speech and Drama, based as they were at the Embassy Theatre, Swiss Cottage, and the late Dame Edith Evans. It seems Dame Edith was asked to go along to the school to speak at a fund-raising seminar.

Dame Edith arrived as large as life, or possibly larger, and when motioned to rise, stood up and said, in that wonderfully booming tone, "I have been asked to come here today, by your Principle, Miss Elsie Foggarty. I knowest not why, as the only time that I met the lady, we disliked each other on sight!" She then looked around, drew breath, and continued, "Be that as it may, it appears the school needs three thousand pounds without delay. So will three gentlemen kindly raise their right hands and promise a thousand pounds each, and we can get this measly business over."

So ended the prayer meeting.

To be a good agent is not easy, to be a fine one is miraculous. No one is more vulnerable. Some think they are God, but that is a malady so common to many of us. Artistes hover like dragonflies, moving from one agent to another, whatever the reason. A few loyal ones stay forever. The agent has to be patient, have stamina for the long, and sometimes frustrating hours, and be ever aware to today's castings and tomorrow's requirements.

There are always disappointments. As, for example, when a favourite of the agency decides, after you have guided him or her through the rapids, that they really need another agent to get them that starring part on television. For that, perhaps, I am not that well connected, or so they think. So the lady picks up her handbag, the man his portfolio, or vice versa, and probably wearing rose tinted spectacles, skip away to the well-heeled personal manager, who dines at the 'Ivy'. That's where the carousel element of our business comes in.

There is, thankfully, the other side of the coin, when an artiste comes in with a bottle of wine and a kiss, and makes the whole day Mother's Day, and you forget about all the others. Some big talents, when they reach the stairway to paradise, turn and smile their thanks, while others dismiss you with a frown, and go back to their caviar.

Such is life in the show business jungle.

*****

After ten full moons and a couple of Halloween parties, I moved to Number Five, Egmont House, Shaftesbury Avenue, which sounded much more plush and imposing. It wasn't, though it was slightly larger. The way I came to move was by an invitation from a lady called Pearl, who was well known in nightclub circles, and various others. Pearl ruled the large middle office, while I had the smaller one. This could accommodate at least four people, in comparison to my old offices, which could just manage three. Pearl sub-let the office to me for seven pounds a week, which was still inexpensive, bearing in mind we were actually on the famed Shaftesbury Avenue. Pearl ruled the world of the floor show, and I do not mean demonstrations from carpet salesmen. She dealt with dancers, tall, leggy, short and stubby, male and female, and those that hadn't made up their minds. She arrived and left by hire car, whether it was dawn or duck. She was an entirely new breed to me.

She seemed to be straight and honest, until she disappeared on a lost weekend, and was last seen in Canada, making Maple Leaf necklaces in the local gaol. One can't always be right, Alas, the rent had not been paid since Firework Day, two years back, and one day the landlord got tough, so the till was emptied again, and I returned to bread and cheese once more.

Working for youngsters just starting is not a popular

pastime with many agents. For an agent who wants to travel on the streetcar of success and good living, the new blood from drama school does not offer the right fare. I do, however, favour establishing new talent, probably stemming from my short look at the world of tinsel in my Carroll Levis days.

In this year of grace when I had put up my agency licence, everyone would go down to 'Le Gran' in Old Compton Street or the Arts club for coffee and a little gossip. Since no agent can possibly know everything, a little listening with one's good ear to all the badinage is often a most useful thing. It also helps to know your artiste well, as work more often than not, involves going away from home. Has the wench on your books got a husband, or a lover who is possessive? Possibly they may be a jealous type, adept with the kitchen knife! You have to allow for all this before putting her on the train to Kirkcaldy to say a few lines as the 'maid' in 'Gaslight'. (Thinking back, the part did Angela Lansbury the world of good).

Slowly but surely, the managers rang and asked me to help them with their casting. Charles Vance was a manager I met and worked for. A tall, imposing man, with a wealth of experience and a reputation to boot. He was one of the real actor-managers. He has a memory to out-do the late Leslie Welch. If you played Ashby-De-La-Zouch in the monsoon season, he knew who was producing, and what plays were presented and when. He could probably predict which day the rains came. Many storytellers have fallen down mid-interview with the wily Mr Vance. Around this time, he had tripped over one dark weekend, whilst staying in the country, presumably chasing an idea or possibly trying to retrieve the takings which had fallen down a fox's hole. He appeared next with a twisted ankle, dragging his foot along as if he were a candidate for the lead in 'Of Human Bondage'.

He still takes to the boards occasionally to keep his hand in. he adopted a walking stick with a silver eagle on the top from that day on, and has used it ever since at all meetings, rallies and performances. Indeed, he should have been a solicitor, such is his prowess in the courtroom, and he could have no doubt saved Ruth Ellis from the hangman, had he been defending the poor woman. Charles is now in a care home, and one is hopeful this is just a temporary measure. He is a true gentleman of the theatre.

Another real man of the theatre was John Farrow. A shortish man, he had the ruddy complexion of a farmer, and a genius of marketing, casting and promotion equal to the finest circus proprietor. He has been through the hazards of the business a thousand times, sometimes falling, sometimes scoring, and could sell a show quicker than lightning. I first met John when Alexander Bridge was presenting pantomime at the Intimate Theatre, Palmers Green. Not well named, for it was anything but intimate, and needed help in every way. The woodwork was tatty, the equipment prehistoric and the stage settings were poor. However, the three of us set to and did wonders in four weeks, and the pantomime opened and was a great success. I have known and worked with John ever since, and he was a loyal and trusted friend. I like to feel we have learned much of this turbulent trade together. Alas, he died a few years back.

Nowadays, a splendid trade paper which helps all, artiste and manager alike, is the Professional Casting Report. This was masterminded and introduced by Paul Craig-Raymond, who started in the business when he was knee high. A very stout gentleman, he is really to be described as a better looking Sydney Greenstreet, with huge shoulders on a short but stoutish body. He had a wide forehead, smoked and handled a cigar as well as George Burns and his dialogue was not far behind. His empire stretched from London to Rome, New York and Istanbul, and his knowledge was a wonderment. He has two lovely daughters, Lee and Vaughan, both pro's in the business, who have done fine work and were often seen on their father's arm at openings and parties. Paul was a kind and considerate man, and always there to help one in moments of disillusionment and doubt. Actors have much to thank the Professional Casting Report for, both in information and employment and as something to cheer them up when things look dismal and suicidal. There is always something going on somewhere in the world of PCR.

In the world of judgement and gambles, no one makes more mistakes than managements, and in a lesser sense – agents. To mention gems that have been allowed to go to another jeweller one only has to remember Deanna Durbin, when she was thrown out by Metro-Goldwyn-Mayer and allowed to join Universal. It was a good job she did, as they were on their uppers at the time and she saved the whole studio from total bankruptcy.

I did much the same with Mike Reid of 'The Comedians' fame. I also had a row with Lewis Collins, so he joined 'The Professionals', and never looked back. The Cuckoo Waltz indeed!

You can easily see why I haven't got to the ball. But I have had the pleasure of starting off many artistes who have made it, and whom I can still number as close friends. Michael Cochrane is one, Patrick Ryecart, Marc Sinden, David Easter (Pat in 'Brookside'), Chris Hamill of Kajagoogoo fame. Then there are Neil France, Maggie Ryder, Tricia George and many others. If asked who were the three best light comedy actors of the younger variety I would not hesitate to say, Freddie Lees, Neil France and Michael Cochrane.

Other agents can also be friends, and harbour neither jealousy or bitterness. Such a woman was Mildred Challenger, known to most natives as 'Bonzo', she had been in the business since Pearl White stopped a train, and what she has seen could run longer than 'Emmerdale'. I remember first seeing her name when she was producing touring shows for the music halls, shows that I skipped bedtime for, and such fruity shows they were.

'Hylda Baker' in 'Bearskins and Blushes' was one, and the wicked contents were bordered with chorus girls and risqué comedians, but were jolly good fun, twice nightly. 'Bonzo' was a tall, striking lady, with a straight back from her years as a dancer. Her tongue could be lethal, and used to threaten all sorts of things, like calling in the 'heavies' if you had not paid your commission on time.

The payment of commission is one of the problems for an agent, for when a client does either a film or commercial, the fee is paid by cheque to the agent. The agent then deducts his commission and sends the remainder to his client. In the theatre, however, the salary is paid direct to the client, and if the agent does not invoice on time on the first of each month, or immediately he sees the new moon, the client often does not pay up. The saloon bar takes most of the pro's wages, and indeed without the theatrical profession, it is doubtful if many breweries would survive, such is the thirst of the thespian. On the other side of the coin, of course, is the fact that often pros have to maintain two homes, not easy at the best of times, and those with responsibilities have quite a time managing on occasion. For the few of the world is their oyster, but for the vast majority, due to the irregularity of employment in the business, life can be a struggle. Always the possibility of making 'the big time' keeps one hanging in, and indeed everything is possible – always.

The ratio for the black book (meaning those who have not paid up), is probably twenty per cent, which, for the junior agent, is something of a hazard, for the rent has to be paid… or its back to the streets time.

For a long time Mildred Challenger occupied an office in the same building as myself in Denmark Street. One Christmas, two lovers who swore to love until the end of time, forgot their oaths and attacked each other with venom, as well as axes. The smaller one of the two had been hit on the head with the axe by his butch counterpart, and ran screaming into Mildred, with blood oozing…

"Look what he's done," he wailed to this doyen of ladies.

Mildred, without batting an eyelid, replied, "Get out! I'm casting!"

She would never have made a nurse.

Agents come and go as quickly as restaurateurs. Some think it is a good way to get rich quick! Others start in the business because they are stage-struck, while some retire from acting to go into the even tougher world of representation. The skill one requires is based on psychology, intermingled with weekend courses in head shrinking: (whether for the actor or agent I cannot say) and a capacity for being able to work twenty-four hours a day. Some artistes call you at breakfast time, tea time, the 'happy hour' time, or just before midnight, and ask in their best dulcet tones, "Is there any work for me?" You can be criticised if you fail to get the work, ridiculed if you obtain something that is thought 'beneath dignity', and classed as a good time girl or boy, if you are out more than twice a week for lunch. Finally, you are abused if you fail to go to less than four parties or orgies in a week.

I gave up most parties, except with close friends years ago. If I do burn the midnight oil and arrive at the party looking younger than springtime, I am immediately assailed by thespians who bombard me with every question you've ever heard about work. And if you arrive looking older than God, they fail to recognise you, so you are off the hook. It is not easy. In spite of all the minuses, I would not give it up for the world.

I have always found it amazing how many artistes still want to be principal boys at fifty. There are others who still use pictures of themselves when they were hostesses in Leicester Square, when Jessie Matthews was a girl. 'Touching up' does not always mean a finger on the derrière, that's for certain!

My favourite 'bon mot' from one of our leading actors, is, that if, when he wakes up in bed and reads the *Times* and finds he isn't mentioned in the obituary column, he gets up.

One of my most faithful and dedicated artistes was Peter Carlisle. Peter used to partake of afternoon tea at my café, and I would sit by the window and watch intently all the comings and goings. I would clear lunch, then start some casting on table one, early in the afternoon. Peter, a large man, at least six foot in his stockings, had played with many great names during his years in the business. He was born in America; Virginia, to be precise. His mother, Kitty Carlisle, was a well-known leading lady, while his father was one of London's matinee idols. Peter looked a little like a high court judge at one moment, and with his natural vivacity and wit, and something like a George Sanders the next. He had appeared in every play from 'Tobacco Road' to 'Dorian Gray' and was busy until this very day on television and film. He took julep cups with Greta

Garbo at least once a year in Antibes, and vacations at Arletty's old house, during his many visits to his beloved France. What Peter did not know was not worth knowing, and his sense of humour was boundless. He could be a tartar if I do not come up with the goods in the job department.

There were occasion when we would have a shooting match, something like Bette Davis and Tallulalah Bankhead finding out they were both auditioning for the lead in Somerset Maugham's 'Rain'. Then – after the storm – we would forget all about it, having got it out of our system, and resume the relationship of client and agent over a bottle of champagne at the nearest hostelry.

Jean Charles is another agent I have worked with through the years. What a smashing lady she was. She looked rather like a riding instructress, wearing jodhpurs regularly. She totally loved the profession and travelled far and wide, looking at acts and checking up on the ones she had booked. Jean was one hundred per cent a club agent and knows more about this field than most. She must have shares in British Rail – or else she is a millionaires on the side, for she trains up and down the country like a jet-propelled cat.

In those days provincial repertories would decide to do a musical comedy, and audition specifically for this in town. Only the best voices and the most experienced artistes would be engaged say, to perform in 'The Count of Luxembourg' or 'White Horse Inn' I would cast regularly for places like the old Marlowe Theatre, Canterbury, and occasionally was successful in getting clients into theatres in Coventry and Leicester.

Roger Redfarn was beginning to make his mark in the world of theatre at the Belgrade, Coventry. This emporium was one of the first to build flatlets for visiting actors so they could live almost at the theatre, which is a good idea for some, and not for others, who would flee and behave like Greta Garbo when not performing. The theatre, though unpretentious, was a splendid one; warm, and caring – and a great –place to work in. Other artistes at the time working continuously in musicals were Janice Bean, Michael Boothe, Valerie Griffiths, Alan Rebbeck, the late Doreen Carminay, Audrey Leybourne, Kay

Barwick, Jean Hampson, Rosemary Butler, Fernand Monast, Roger Neil and many others from my agency who fled to Canterbury and Coventry and other lovely English towns to sing their heads off for two or three weeks. This truly was the age of repertory. Nowadays, theatres cannot afford to engage actors especially for a single show, because of the rehearsal rates. In repertory, one would rehearse 'The Merry Widow' by day and probably perform 'Murder at the Vicarage' by night – for no extra cost. Thus often when a musical comedy is performed at a repertory, you may get stunning vocal leads, but the rest of the cast is made up of whoever is in the company at the time, regardless of whether they can sing, warble or just croak. A sad omen in these precarious times.

I co-produced the first Sunday variety shows in the West End when licence was given in conjunction with Alistair Aitchison, and these were presented at the Mayfair Theatre. Alistair had a weakness for champagne and smoked salmon sandwiches; when enquiring about the state of the handbag he would ask, "How's the boodle?" A warm, passionate and talented man, he was a loyal and supportive friend, and I miss him very much.

John Dane was another good leading man, he had a passion for Devonshire cream and made off to Plymouth years ago, where he has run a theatre that specialises in musical comedy and has created quite a nice niche for himself in the stirring sea air. Others of the period that come to mind are Blayne Barrington, Marc Urquhart and Robert Meadmore, and a little later on Jonathan Kiley. They played all sorts of theatres in all sorts of shows, shades of leads and Bradford. Latterly Keith Hopkins, Barry Hopkins, J J King, Eric Flynn, Steve Devereaux, Jacquie Reddin, Charne Oliver, Michelle Somers and Julian Ochyra are others that come to mind, with a special mention for the very talented Paul Burton.

In passing, I would like to mention that someone should set up a school for would-be stars to learn how to dress and present themselves to the best advantage at auditions and elsewhere. Some of the artistes attending auditions look as if the cat has just dragged them in, 'Style' may be a forgotten word in so many theatrical dictionaries, but it is so important when meeting a manager for the first time. Ask Joan Collins.

Think about what Cochran, André Charlot and Ziegfeld would have thought of many of the ragamuffins posing as professionals today. It's enough to put Binnie Hale off having a nice cup of tea in the morning.

Equally, some promoters taking auditions, should also be sent to a college to learn the finer points of how to treat an artiste and get the best out of them.

"We'll let you know," can be said with great sincerity and kindness, and means a hell of a lot when you might have come all the way from Widnes on a slow train.

One promoter I have worked for was a problem occasionally at auditions. Heavily into the male species, he would welcome boy singers with a passion that would have excited a choir master, but when the girls appeared, and they seem to come to auditions in packs of twenty, (shades of 'Du Maurier') he would give them four lines of a song to sing and then scream, "Next! Next! Next!"

One day when I was present, a girl with a large bosom and an even larger voice sang, 'Boys were made to love and kiss...' with which the promoter wholeheartedly agreed. But when she heard, "Next!" she shouted, "I'm fucked if it is! I've come from Brighton to audition for you and that is what I am sodding well going to do!"

With that, she heaved her bosom to the skies, and the piano player hit the notes like a thing possessed. She sang the whole song superbly, She never stops working, the lass from Brighton. And that's a fact.

It is assumed that if you took all the gay boys out of the theatre, venues would be closed from Rotherham to Reading. But it really isn't as crowded a province of queens as one would believe. True, queens are there in plenty, that I will not deny. But there are also a lot of butch fellows to even the score and paint the picture as it should be seen.

After a few years in Shaftesbury Avenue my office was to change again. On some rainy days I could be seen in my flat in Charing Cross Road, arguing the pros and cons of some deal I was trying to clinch. One helpful thing about British Telecom is that I can have the same telephone number at the office (which is just around the corner) and my flat, so I can receive a call at any time just by pressing a button. It does have distinct disadvantages also, as you could be in the middle of watching 'Sunset Boulevard' for the umpteenth time, when the telephone rings and some droll extra from Milton Keynes asks, in her Veda Ann Borg voice, about her audition. When questioned, if by any chance I knew her, she would reply, "Oh no! I've just picked your number out of the telephone directory!"

After smashing my mother's fruit bowl on the floor, I would return to the wonders of Miss Swanson, not to mention William Holden, completely dented.

I had just completed a super tour of 'An Evening With Quentin Crisp' and I thought I could afford to move to a spacious third floor office which was 'to let' just around the corner from my flat. In fact, all six offices were going at number four. With my wallet full, if did wondrous things to my ego, and I arranged to see the place straight away.

It was big and airy and on the third floor. I made one of my instant decisions. Most of my decisions are instant. I called the agent immediately and agreed to move in that same month.

The space needed more care than a deranged Barnado Boy. We soon took it in hand. Although, to be truthful, an office of mine is never remotely like anyone else's and tidiness is not my strong point. The office always has a little bedlam spread here, there and everywhere. This delights some clients, and drives others into a nursing home, or immediate departure to a more rational agent. The other good thing is that there is no lift, so heavy lovelies with little or no energy, scale the summit to the top with the utmost difficulty. This way we get fewer people calling and getting into our hair than if we were on the ground floor.

So with the move we became members of the celebrated 'Tin Pan Alley' though our tune was very different from say, Noel Gay, opposite, although it must be said that some days the melody and music of the street reaches our ears and provokes thoughts of the good old days of the barrel organ and rehearsal piano.

The only disadvantage with Denmark Street is that you are burgled every month, with regularity, as if it were due. If they cannot get in the front way, they climb over the roof top like monkeys! So if you decide to become an agent, make sure you know a good carpenter. The office had moved once again and a new reign was about to begin!

Chapter 11

Life is Just a Bowl of Cherries – If you Throw the Pips Away

When you start travelling with shows your life is one of perpetual motion. Each day becomes a trolley car to the next stop. Towns and places glide by, and your knowledge of the country is suddenly quite remarkable.

But the time I had started presenting shows and pantomimes, not to mention routs, the theatrical landlady was almost a thing of the past. You either looked for a low cost hotel, or very often a pub with a room – hopefully just above the bar, so you could have a nip or two after hours. When touring, it is prudent to give the lady a ring several weeks before to book a room or a bed. Making sure that when you get to your destination, tired and exhausted, and looking quite unlike a star, that there is something available.

There are many addresses that one is given. Some are clean and wholesome. Some are run by widows or spinsters, quite misunderstood by the world. They tend to talk the hind legs off a rabbit till way past midnight, and you might even find them escorting you to your bedroom, not to mention gliding in between inviting warm covers or cool sheets. There are others that have a son or daughter on offer to make your stay comfortable, and on a cold winter's night they help economise on the heating. So many avenues are open to be explored before you stun the town with your considerable talents.

Some impresario, renowned for his paucity of sets and costumes, who was presenting 'Dick Whittington' in a market town, instructed his assistant stage manager, a well-endowed wench, to go into town and purchase four lengths of long green crêpe paper. She was gone through lunch and then some, and then returned carrying four packets of crêpe paper. The enraged promoter yelled, "Where the bloody hell have you been?"

The poor girl blushed as red as an impresario discovering he has no advance at this next theatre, and stuttered, "I am sorry. I went everywhere for the green crêpe, but could not find any. So I brought red…"

"Excellent!" replied the promoter. "We'll do Red Riding Hood instead. It's about time the poor bitch was done, anyway!"

The other equally amusing tale, concerns one Christmas Eve, when most pantomimes have either opened or are running dress rehearsals. A stage manager at a number three theatre, who was still wet behind the ears, and everywhere else, was told to go to each dressing room at six p.m. and collect every costume which was not hung up. This he did, and returned to the stage area, asking his boss what he should do next. "Put them in a skip and call a cab," said the touring manager, "then take them over to the 'Sleeping Beauty' company at Dunstable, and tell them these are the costumes for the show."

About this time, a young light comedian I represented suggested I did a large variety spectacular at the Gaumont State Theatre, Kilburn. This was a Rank house which often staged large scale live shows, and, of course, it was just around the corner from where I started my London life when I lodged with Mabel.

"Put two Irish names on the bill, you can't go wrong," the comic said. "Mother of God, the place is reeking with shamrock."

I fell for it, hook, line and sinker, and went to Rank and arranged to meet the manager of the place to discuss the project. His name was Mr Weir and he was great. Over numerous gin and tonics I agreed to hire the venue for a Sunday evening in October, nineteen seventy-six. The stars were to be Cavan O'Connor and Ruby Murray. And a supporting cast of thousands. Who did I think I was?

The evening arrangements were complete, and tickets were put on sale without delay. We had been advised to start at eight fifteen, so that everyone could get to Mass and back before the curtain went up. Perhaps we should have gone too.

Alas, alack, business was not booming. My own followers were buying well, and coming from all over town, but the locals must have buried their shillelaghs and their cash in a deep trench and forgotten where they were.

We toured the whole of Kilburn, putting handbills in every pub, shop, store, church, off-licence and loo on the Sunday before the show with the Lancashire comic, Tommy Trafford, who was on the bill with singers Keith Hopkins and Margo Wain. The latter was a very butch lady, with a superb operatic voice which went into upper register the moment her car started.

We all climbed into Margo's car. It was decided to whizz around to all churches and tabernacles in the area, so when the paddies trooped out after confessing, we could tell them about the event. I had said my prayers long before.

Margo drove through every red light at a speed that would have excited Barry Sheene, and poor Tommy Trafford who had a heart that was not very strong, nearly had an attack as Margo swung the vehicle round at hair raising speed, singing full blast as she went. We did, however, handbill the entire area without getting arrested or converted – which was quite a victory.

A lovely old comic I had on the bill at Kilburn was George Williams. He was a droll-faced comedian with white make-up who had come to fame on 'Variety Bandbox'. This was a radio show which also did the world of good for Frankie Howerd and Derek Roy. George's stage character always looked as if he was on his way to a cremation, hopefully not his. He possessed a dry, slow style, but produced a laugh a second, and was a brilliant artiste. I had known him for many years, and can even recall him when I was a child (well, almost) at the Boscome Hippodrome with Felix Mendelsohn and his 'Hawaiian Serenaders'. George must have been sixty, if he was a day, but as good as ever, and always working. He brought the house down that night. The show went well with the Jackie Palmer Dancers opening. They were thirty perfect young ladies in red costumes with headdresses to match and would have made Miss Bluebell proud had they been her girls. The only snag was the bill was too long. When Cavan O'Connor, who was closing the second half, came on and said, "Would you like me to take the lovely Kathleen home again?" which was one of his big hits, a raucous woman in the stalls shouted, "It's too late, love the last bus has gone!" This was very popular with the patrons.

Cavan and I had worked together many times, and he was a grand old trouper who has seen it all.

Ruby Murray closed the first half, and she was a delight, as always. The show was a noble failure, for we filled the stalls, but not the vast dress circle. It was, however, to be the first of many variety spectaculars I was to present in London. A lot of managers came to see it, and I like to think that a few more knew of me afterwards.

Incidentally, while we toiled in the street settling our show, an Irish character by the name of 'Big Tom' came and sold out his performance completely at the Gaumont State in less than two hours. The mere fact that none of my party had ever heard of this lad from the Mountains of Mourne speaks volumes. It taught me to keep abreast with who was selling, and who sold in what areas.

A little later on, Cavan and I did a show at the Kenneth More Theatre, Ilford, where we played for four days to packed enthusiastic audiences. George Williams was again with us. The theatre had not been open very long and was run by a friend of mine, Vyvian Ellacott. Vyvian looks for all the *world* like a young Jolson's papa in 'The Jolson story', or perhaps a shade younger! He learned his trade at the Grand Theatre, Swansea and won the administration appointment at the Kenneth More. There he staged many shows from operas to comedies. He kept the theatre active and bubbling when so many all-around have fallen by the wayside, and are now bingo halls or mausoleums. Vyvian should have been a lawyer, such is his prowess with the rule books. A court wig would have looked splendid on him. But if he had taken the law the theatre would have lost a young and devoted slave.

Vyvian Ellacott had to retire in 2009 being 66 and was last

reported to be teaching drama in Romania.

It was in nineteen seventy-four that George Williams and I were lingering over a hot toddy, when George said, "Why don't you do something like 'Hansel and Gretel'?" I vaguely knew it was a fable about a wicked witch who wined and dined on young children, so I read the story, devised a script, added some songs and a huge bear named Joey and we had a show. The production opened at the little Library Theatre in Grays, where it played to great success. The manager was a tall fellow, with thinning hair, bunny teeth, and a great sense of humour. He also had a weak spot for bears. Whenever Joey came on, he bounded into the theatre and sat entranced. Brian Pridmore was definitely partial to this type of entertainment.

Brian had ruled the little Library Theatre, Grays, for many years and has only recently been promoted to the Theatre Royal, Hanley, where he is attempting to educate the natives in the delights of going to the theatre. Brian had a great charm and if anyone can get bums on seats he can.

'Hansel and Gretel' has toured on and off ever since. It opened at the Theatre Royal, Newcastle-Upon-Tyne to a queue of over two thousand, and made us a pile of loot in the week we were there. Just what we needed. George Johnston, then manager of the theatre, had cottoned on to children's shows, which were something new at the time in the area. He had tried and done extremely well with 'The Owl and the Pussycat'. I, personally, don't like the play, and on many occasions have prayed the Owl would eat the bloody Pussycat!

George Johnston loved 'Hansel and Gretel' and with the money pouring in the box office, actually nine thousand pounds at fifty pence a ticket, and we stayed on for a second week and did as well again. George, nicknamed Georgie Porgie, was a young administrator who had come from Kirkcaldy, Scotland, when he got fed up with the bagpipes. This was a great scoop for him to be running the impressive and grand Theatre Royal. We played the Royal with all my musicals after that.

I wrote and toured a new children's musical each year for eight years, until I got too old for it. We built up a huge following at Newcastle-Upon-Tyne and 'Hans Christian Andersen' and 'Snow White and the Seven Dwarfs' were the only two in the series that didn't play there, but otherwise I had a standing date with Geordie audiences. 'The Adventures of Rumpelstiltskin', 'The Wonderful Wizard of Oz' which starred Russell Grant, and 'The Adventures of Pinocchio' all did well, and helped me get several pieces of merchandise out of hock. Apart from James Jordan who directed the first two, another of our directors was Fernand Monast. 'Fern' as he is to all his friends is a great fellow, a French Canadian, he has an accent which would charm the deadliest of enemies; and a superb director with great flair and attention to detail. Being an excellent singer and dancer himself, he can add great dimensions to choreography which highlights his magic directing.

Brenda Gwyn Williams, at that time the high priestess of publicity at the Theatre Royal, was responsible for much of the record theatre business at Newcastle-Upon-Tyne. She was a striking woman of sixty years, and was a source of warmth and bubbling personality. Everything was either 'wonderful' or 'horrendous'. Her voice and her laughter is very often heard when we are together. She will, one day, fly south and rule a London theatre. Until then we must be content with occasional glimpses of her up north.

George Johnston, however, left the theatre one day to marry a local lass and moved to the southern shores with his family and left theatreland forever, It is our loss.

In the world of the theatre you are only as good as last night's performance, and heaven help you if you only play matinees. The living is never easy, while for many the rewards are fleeting. But the excitement and promise of what could be, is like a carrot to a donkey. Greasepaint lures, seduces, captivates and dominates until something comes along to break the spell and crack the mirror.

Among my many disasters was the day I visited the Ashton Pavilion, St Anne's, where we had played previously. We were to present our 'Wonderful Wizard of Oz' the following Christmas, and in the September, I called there to reassess the place. It was a good, cosy, six hundred seater with bars and a café. We aimed to fill the venue and serve theatre suppers with entertainers at the pianola. Alas, this was not to be.

Russell Grant, who had been touring with us for three years, was to play the Wizard, and all seemed set for a very happy and successful run. I had hired a driver at Blackpool as I was travelling a lot. He was called Len, but we referred to him as Rita, the car burglar. Mainly because every time we passed a jailhouse he gave us a breakdown of each goal we passed, even to the recreation room. I haven't seen him for some time so perhaps he is having a vacation at one of these places now.

I returned to London on the Friday after visiting St Anne's, and on Saturday morning the telephone rang at eight o'clock in the morning and Doreen, my contact at the theatre, told me there was nothing left, but a pile of ashes. Apparently the local amateurs were presenting 'Carousel' there that week and someone had flicked their cigarette into the pit after the curtain had come down. It was unbelievable, and a grave blow for me.

We managed to hire the Lytham Pavilion, another four miles up the road, but it had no equipment or facilities, and was as cold as the North Pole. It was also too far out of Blackpool to pull the crowds, and we had a very 'so-so' season.

On many of my tours and presentations I was fortunate enough to have the help and friendship of David Blair. David came to this country after he had tired of Paul Hogan and kangaroos. He had trained for the theatre as a performer and for a little while the Home Office was not sure whether they wanted him to stay. We did, and mounted a campaign that would have impressed Mrs Thatcher. Meanwhile, he was a first rate assistant, be it directing or managing, and we flew up the highways; down the byways and had much fun while we set up many concerts and weeks of kiddies' fables. David had and has a great sense of humour and a laugh that would wake up the dead or those merely snoozing. He finally took off for a spell as assistant manager at the Town Hall Theatre at Ealing and now rules a new emporium a little further down the road.

His personality is only matched by his beauty and charm – who could say more?

For several years I wrote a part for Russell Grant in each musical, and when he was in 'Hansel and Gretel' for me for a short tour, he was already quite plump. The sight of Russell in the witch's cage, being fattened up every minute for the oven, was a little over the top. Even for a production of mine.

Then we took a tour of 'Rumpelstiltskin' which I mentioned earlier, and Russell played 'the Wizard', a new character who controlled the Manikin. It was a costly production for it contained many period costumes, so we had the entire show's wardrobe especially created by Ray Alexander. And it was magnificent. I was very pleased with the show, but we never did as well as the other musicals with it, sad to say.

The last two shows Russell did for me were 'The Adventures of Pinocchio' in which he doubled as 'Mr Stromboli' and 'The Coachman'. By this time Russell had already got involved in the world of horoscope and tarot card reading, and was prophesying to patrons on tour what they could expect from the Gods. Would that he could have predicted the box office, and we could all have been much wiser! Russell has a tremendous singing voice, and is as good an actor as he is soothsayer.

Norman Thomas ruled 'Radio City' in Liverpool and was a disc jockey of note. Norman did two seasons of pantomime for us when we were at the Floral Pavilion, New Brighton. He is a splendid light comedy personality and his breakfast show had endeared him to thousands. I wait for him to conquer London in the same way. His favourite quip to me was in the year we were doing 'Jack and the Beanstalk' and I really mean 'doing'. We had cast an actor to double as 'The Ogre' and 'The Giant'. The poor man was at least six foot, four inches tall, but on the 'cissie' side so much that he could not bear to be hissed at by the audience. We did not find this out until the first performance. Norman remarked, "With twenty thousand actors out of a job, you had to choose this silly queen."

Too much, indeed!

*****

Grapefruit Productions stayed in business for six years, and then we changed the name of the company to what it should have been in the first place – 'Barrie Stacey Productions'.

I started to present all-star concerts up and down the country with such stars as Bob Monkhouse, the Bachelors, John Hanson, Ruby Murray, Frankie Howerd, Larry Grayson, Don Maclean and many others. With an associate, I started presenting English speaking plays abroad. The times really were a-movin'.

The day had come when I closed the doors of the 'As You Like It' Coffee House for the last time. It was a strange funny feeling, for a whole slice of my life had finished. And the little business that had kept so many of us, through thick and thin was no more. It would take time to realise it was no longer there, but the coffee house would always occupy a soft spot in my heart. The song is ended, but the melody lingers on.

Chapter 12

One Night Stands and the Trappings of Musical Comedy

I did some sole casting for musicals and this pleased me greatly, as for my money, there is nothing like a first class musical comedy. Henry Shirvell and Stanley Willis-Croft, not to mention Emile Littler, were major impresarios in this genre. So was Alexander Bridge, and more latterly Roger Redfarn, David Kelsey and John Dane.

June Bronhill, a superb opera singer and a big star in Australia, joined Sadlers Wells and played many seasons there. I can still remember her excellent work as a sort of singing Betty Grable with Grace Moore trimmings in 'La Belle Parisienne'. Although known to her opera fans for her work at the Sadlers Wells and the Coliseum Theatre in London, Miss Bronhill was virtually unknown to the provincial masses.

Alexander Bridge, after the 'Caligula' episode at Westcliff, sailed out in mid-stream with a full scale National tour of Noel Coward's 'Bitter Sweet' and I was the casting director. June Bronhill co-starred with Barry Sinclair and John Larsen was the third lead. It was superbly staged and exquisitely dressed and I have always felt it was Alexander Bridge's finest production. It had an excellent supporting cast which included Sid Field's son, Nicholas (in one of his first parts), Audrey Leybourne (now a famous Roly-Poly), Barbara Farrell, Anthony Rowlands, Fernand Monast and Maggie Beckit. The tour was a long one and ran into many troubles early on.

There was a particular episode at the King's Theatre, Edinburgh, when the assistant stage manager was having a frantic time trying to restrain two removal men from whipping the piano off stage during the show. It was in Act Two and Miss Bronhill had yet to sing her aria. A little incident such as two heavies trying to reclaim the grand piano was certainly not on for the Australian canary.

"Piss off!" she screamed in a most ladylike manner. "You have no chance until I have sung my aria." With that she went straight into 'Dear Little Café' to rapturous applause. This sufficiently distracted the heavies, reeling from the shock of being spoken to in their own language by the Queen of Song, so that the stagehands could push the grand piano off at terrifying speed to a hidden haven in the wings of the stage.

Never one to beat about the bush, especially an Australian one, June Bronhill was hardly a woman to trifle with. She had the spirit and necessary vocabulary to quell any strike or revolution. She went blind back home in Australia and died just three years ago. A superb nightingale.

I recall another teatime story to your delectation and hopeful delight. The patrons of my café, 'As You Like It', were heavily into tea one matinee day, when a cab drew up outside and the driver called for attention – as it turned out he wanted some service. At the time I was serving twelve 'nuns' from 'The Sound of Music' at the nearby Palace Theatre, who always visited on matinee days. The show was as corny as 'Kansas in August', but bursting with good tunes, and pure delight for all that.

I went outside to answer the cabby's request and found Joan Sutherland, June Bronhill and Alexander Bridge all more than a little merry. They had been to a particularly 'drinky' reception that lunchtime. They were all quite stout – not one under fourteen stone – and the taxi cab was somewhat restricting for three such well-built personalities. They all beamed at me like naughty school children and requested to be served there and then with black coffee and sandwiches.

I could see a twinkling of an eye there was no chance of any of them descending into the café at that particular moment. The taxi driver, a fan of Danny Kaye's, coped with the situation admirably except that the silly fart would have strong tea instead of black coffee. However, the order was executed within minutes and the trio tucked into the finest egg sandwiches they would ever eat. Whether the nuns inside, polishing off the salads and trifles, knew that outside, munching sandwiches, were two of the finest voices in the land, I cannot recall.

The trio relished their tea, and all felt a little stronger, and drove off into the haze of the evening.

Alexander Bridge was the only impresario bold enough to take high class musical and opera to the masses without a large subsidy from the Arts Council, or any other source. With gay scenery and even gayer casts, he toured and captivated the matinee crowds, and sometimes the evening ones in every major town. And more about him later.

When the chorus sang; 'A Bachelor Gay, am I!" from 'The Maid of the Mountains' they could scarcely have spoken a truer word. But what the hell, it was operetta, and it was fun!

Mr Bridge cast June Bronhill again in 'Glamorous Night', with the lovely Olive Gilbert, and then again in 'Dancing Years' and 'Perchance to Dream'. Such well-loved musicals attracted good business at all major theatres and it was a tonic to see the coach parties arriving at such places as Nottingham, Wimbledon and the austere Grand in Wolverhampton. After the show all these old girls, and some of the boys, sailed away for high tea in grand places and over muffins concluded that; "It was just like old times!" And it was.

Much of this has gone from the provincial theatre scene and the loss at the box office is considerable.

It was through Alexander Bridge that I met John Hanson. I was attending a rehearsal for 'The Desert Song', when there was a break in the proceedings. Perhaps they had run out of sand, or red cloaks, but it gave me a chance to speak to Mr Hanson.

I had a little investment in the show. Thus I merited some attention, quite apart from being the casting director. Of course, John Hanson did not need any rehearsal, he knew the part and piece backwards, and every camel by name!

I always felt that 'The Student Prince' was a much better score, but somehow, everyone seemed to pick 'The Desert Song'.

The revival at The Palace Theatre in London was a major triumph for John Hanson. It was all his own work, for he backed the production, putting his cash where it mattered most. Many of the angels had given the thumbs down to bringing 'The Desert Song' back to the West End. The first night was a riot. The audience would not let the company or John go until he, and they, had sung 'Blue Heaven' at least a dozen times. I was backstage delivering some sandwiches to Virginia Courtney, the choreographer, and heard the cries from the audience at curtain call and distinctly remember a man shouting, "This is what we want!" the entire audience then cheered and backed him up. The show had a healthy run and then transferred to The Cambridge Theatre.

Alexander Bridge came unstuck some years ago when his company ran out of money after coming into the New London theatre, Drury lane, with a version of 'Glamorous Night'. With this, and two pantomimes at Doncaster and Hanley, he went down with a thud. Some people threw mud which was very unfair.

They were inclined to forget the years he had kept many artistes in employment, and the theatres he helped to keep open with first class productions. The fact that he had chanced his own cash time after time to support his confidence in others, to put money in the kitty, should be noted. Most people in the business have gone to the wall at some time and as the great CB Cochran went down twice, it must be 'respectable'. With average luck unless you are kissed by the Eternal Gods you are bound to go penniless at some time or another.

The only footnote I would like to add to this is, when it happens, go to the wall in mink, with a glass of champagne in our hand, and retain a beautiful, coloured maid to open the door to the bailiffs. There is *nothing* to beat style!

Chapter 13

Dancing on the Ceiling

In nineteen seventy-six I was just getting started in my concert period, presenting star names and shows around the country. It chanced that Ronnie Scott Dodd, the manager of Wimbledon Theatre, had a spare Sunday and offered it to me. Ronnie, a short, red-faced man, never seemed to be without a cigar between his moulded lips, but he did know how to run a theatre.

The theatre sparkled with his personality, and you were always received (if you were a presenter or a favoured artiste) with an invitation to his office on high for a tipple of your choice. His theatre patrons always received a kind word and a smile. We took the Sunday night to star June Bronhill. I then had the idea of trying to entice Jessie Matthews to be guest artiste.

Perhaps I should explain here that almost everyone with a theatrical bent has one artiste they love, adore and cherish. Many times there are no reasons for this, but one star above all others claims their devotion.

I had an aunt who had a passion for Gary Cooper, she named her first born after him and never missed a film of his until the day she died. He outlived her by three days.

I had been attracted to Jessie Matthews with almost an uncanny affection. It was as if I had known her all my life, and was held by some extraordinary thread. For me, Jessie was the tops. The ultimate and the favourite! Only two others came into the same category, and they were Greta Garbo and Miss Dietrich.

I had followed Jessie Matthews and her career vividly from the time she left Gaumont British, through the period when she was signed by Metro Goldwyn Mayer to make four films with Fred Astaire. Then suddenly on tour, entertaining the troops, she became ill and disappeared from view. Later, she toured Australia with two plays by Anita Loos and opened a drama school in Melbourne. After a while she visited America, then returned home and did a small tour of Peter Shaffer's excellent play 'Five Finger Exercise'.

I first met her when I was stationed in Devon, and she was billed to appear at the old Theatre Royal, Exeter, with the Alan Melville comedy hit 'Castle in the Air'. In this she co-starred with Barry Sinclair and Constance Carpenter.

I slipped into a stalls seat and warmed to an overture of Jessie's hits, even though it was a straight play. After the show I went backstage to ask for Miss Matthew's autograph. I was amazed when I heard her dulcet tones going through the Rodgers and Hart 'Bewitched, Bothered and Bewildered'. She actually recorded this on disc soon after but it sank without a trace.

After her delightful impromptu she came down, signed my book, and I didn't touch the ground for days afterwards.

A short while after I met her again at Jimmy Perry's (a popular author who with David Croft has written 'Hi-de-Hi', 'Dad's Army', and many other hit television series). He was then running the Watford Palace with his wife, Gilda. They appeared in many of the plays as a husband and wife team. Jessie had, at that time, tied the knot with a handsome, young army officer, Brian Lewis, who became her third and last husband.

Jessie Matthews was one of thirteen children and started life in Soho. Next door lived Gertrude Lawrence with her family. Both these girls' fathers were more than a little partial to the good liquid in bottles. After all they did live over a pub. I often remarked, when I got to know Jessie and some of her sisters and brothers, that it was a credit to her mother that all her offspring had done so well in every walk of life.

She was one of the most sought after stars in the world, Bette Davis in her autobiography described Jessie Matthews as 'the biggest star that ever came out of England'. She was as big in the United States as she was here. Her neon sign in Times Square in nineteen thirty-six was larger than Clark

Gable's. She held the attendance record of Radio City Musical Hall, topping everyone, including the Beatles, until the day she died.

She was known early in her career for her short, sharp temper. Later on, in her mid-career, there were certain irregularities and uncertainties especially after the period when Sonnie Hale died. She recovered her earlier form soon after, when she got the part of 'Mrs Dale' in the popular radio series 'Mrs Dale's Diary'. Thereafter she went on to do some sterling work in plays and concerts, and some interesting parts on television.

I had witnessed Jessie turn Bournemouth upside down in my early teens. She was at the Pavilion in a new musical review, 'Made to Measure', which she brought to the town for six days prior to a West End run. Her co-star was Tommy Fields, which, on the surface, was a very strange mix. No matter; Jessie hired an orchestra which was the nearest thing to an American band sound the south had ever seen. No expense was spared on sets or costumes. The juvenile leads were terrific; a very talented boy and girl, Johnny Brandon and Joan Heal. Joan went on to become a big West End star in revue. Sadly, she has disappeared of late. Johnny did some good stage and recording work, then went to America, where I believe he is to this day.

Jessie packed the Pavilion with every show, and was seen in some promotion or other for the production, every day of the week. She was fêted wherever she went. Some days she was in Bobby's Lounge showing off the latest fashions, another day she was signing autographs in WH Smith or opening a fete.

Stars then knew how to woo their public as much off stage as on. Years later she was to buy a house in Dorset, and came back to Bournemouth for a season of plays at the Palace Court Theatre (now The Playhouse) in Westover Road.

One of the plays she was seen in, at intervals, was Terence Rattigan's comedy 'Love in idleness' which suited her down to the ground, and could have been especially written for her. Actually it was written for Alfred Lunt and Lynn Fontaine.

My third meeting with Jessie was at The Palace Theatre, Westcliff when she appeared in variety and was sandwiched between some revue items. These included Marion Grimaldi (whatever happened to her?) and Jamie Phillips (now a top agent and director with Duggie Squires of Trends Management).

Jessie was in great form that night, but unfortunately, her pianist was not. During her act she stopped, turned to the unfortunate fellow and snapped, "Are you with me, or against me?"

Another fond memory was when I was only fourteen and Jessie was doing a short musical hall tour, partnered by her brother, the late Eddie Matthews. She included the old Boscombe Hippodrome on the way. She played to superb business and sang a song I had never heard her sing before, but one which was so apt, 'Wanting You' and we did.

I must return to Wimbledon Theatre to the Sunday night concert, and having what I thought was an inspired idea of having Miss Matthews as guest artiste. I woke up one night with a hot flush, for it suddenly dawned on me I had previously dined with June Bronhill, when I touched on my great admiration for Jessie Matthews. "Belongs in a fishmonger's shop!" snorted Miss Bronhill. The words echoed around my head as I woke up that night with perspiration covering me. The idea of Jessie singing all her songs on stage for the first time for twenty odd years wasn't a bad one, but there again Miss Bronhill was the star of the show. What had I done? The moment we put Jessie's name up beside June's the booking took off, and by the time it came to the actual day, we were ninety per cent sold out. Many of those buying tickets were coming to see Jessie's return to musical comedy.

Jessie's agent thought it a good idea, and she didn't talk in telephone numbers about the fee. This is unlike some of the idiots calling themselves agents today, who put the theatre in the red before the artiste has appeared. The supporting cast included Linda Grant, Keith Hopkins and Toni Harris's singing group 'Blossom'.

On the day of the concert, Miss Matthews was the first to

arrive for the band call, just after 2 p.m. She had a posy of flowers, picked from her garden for June Bronhill. Anthony Bowles was her musical director. They had been friends for many years and he understood Jessie very well. Miss Bronhill arrived wearing a fur hat and long Russian boots and looked like the lead in 'Balalaika'. She was escorted by several young men dressed in similar fashion, who fussed around June like bees round a honey pot. She took one look at Jessie's posy of flowers and the blooms withered!

Jessie opened the show with 'My Heart Stood Still' and even danced a little before going into a lovely little number, written for her by Norman Newell, 'He Needs me'. In fact, she romped through her fourteen numbers like a veteran. It was a great success for everyone, and, ultimately, Jessie scored a hit. The reception from her fans was fantastic. Lots of workers and admirers from her old Gaumont-British period turned up, including several well-known directors, who hadn't seen town for years. Her act overran by fifteen minutes, and the interval went to half an hour. She had the house standing on two occasions.

The queue outside her dressing room stretched round the stairs and spilled into the street for fifty yards. The bars did roaring business and Ronnie Scott Dodd almost died of shock!

The curtain up for the second half was over thirty minutes late. Linda Grant was due on stage as the 'speciality' (a word never more accurately employed than for Miss Grant). She was noted for overrunning, if the tide was with her. This night, as on so many others, she had the audience in her hand. Linda played tunes on practically everything she could get her hands on, ranging from nine feet Austrian horns, recorders, kitchen sinks and watering cans. She was, and is, a skilled musician and a bit of a comedienne. But here's the surprise, she was a 'sex change' and had hitherto been a policeman. Imagine a six foot tall woman, endowed with splendid muscles! You couldn't miss her in a snowstorm.

Her jokes varied with the day and her mood, but that night she was in her bluest form, and the audience were quite unprepared for some of her material. She caressed the flute like a little love affair and what she did with the singing saw had to be seen to be believed. When she told the audience that she had left her horn at St Thomas', Ronnie Scott Dodd fell out of a box, and almost swallowed his cigar!

Things got even hotter when Miss Bronhill came down to see what was going on. She was top of the bill and hadn't been on! It was by now ten thirty. Calamity indeed.

She signalled the stage manager to 'Get Linda off' and proceeded to pace up and down like a prowling tigress. She met her match that night. Linda Grant put two fingers in the air in the direction of the wings and said, "And for my next number…" Her voice was so deep it could be heard in the Himalayas. Finally, we got her off after she splayed 'The Bells of St Mary's on her cow bells. Miss Bronhill strode on. "I think they have just managed to squeeze me in!" she hissed. Of course, she took the whole house and was a terrific success. She did not exactly fall in love with Miss Grant, while her opinion of Jessie was lower than ever.

On the strength of that concert I was confident enough to take Jessie into the West End and chose the Shaftesbury Theatre, which was managed by an old friend of ours, Richard Shulman. He was a great Jessie Matthews fan. This time I chose my guest artiste carefully, and wanted Pat Kirkwood, but Jessie would not have any of this. Then Christopher Gable came to mind as a modern day Jack Buchanan. Whether the agent ever asked him, or whether he was on a tour it was never discovered. I drew a blank and ended up with that fine vocalist, Dennis Lotis.

Jessie thought it a good idea. The two of them got on well, Dennis's act a superb compliment to Jessie. We could do nothing wrong that night, and the show was a fantastic hit. Jessie came on to tumultuous applause as she opened with 'Mr Heart Stood Still' and tripped the light fantastic with Bernard Davis. Her dancing partner, Bernard, was as petrified as any of us would have been. When they came off stage, he asked her anxiously, "Was I alright?"

"Yes," replied Jessie. "But you forgot to smile."

Anthony Bowles was again accompanying Jessie, and the

night ended on a climax not seen in the West End since Marlene Dietrich stopped traffic at The Queens Theatre.

Jessie Matthews' bouquets would have filled Covent Garden. A super lady! Who would have known she was seventy, and had recently had a hip operation.

I booked Jessie into the Theatre Royal, Newcastle-upon-Tyne, the Sunday before. We had done a good press and publicity day a couple of weeks before. On this particular day we picked her up and took her to King's Cross and as we walked down the platform two train drivers recognised her and said, "Good old Jess!" she was very touched. On the journey up we were worried, as we had not been able to book our first class tickets at the booking office, and anyone who has travelled on some of the trains from Glasgow will know how rough they can be. On arrival at the theatres, as I was worried about the return journey, the PA at the Theatre Royal telephoned the stationmaster at Newcastle to ask if he would look for a seat for Jessie and myself, and this he did. When we reached the station for the return journey, probably the oldest porter still around met us on the appropriate platform. He gave Jessie a bouquet and told her that he could still remember her first night at the Adelphi Theatre, London in 'Evergreen' when he was a young man. Jessie squeezed his hand and said teasingly, "You couldn't have been at my first night, you look far too young!"

Another thing that happened was at the reception, arranged by Brenda Gwyn-Williams in the theatre. As the press were sharpening their pencils, and waiting for every word that fell from Jessie's lips, I was summoned by an usher downstairs, who told me someone was asking for Jessie. I went down and saw this oldish man in rough clothes, carrying a large bunch of Dahlias.

"I've come to see 'er!" he said. "And I've come a great distance."

I looked at him long and hard. I could hardly interrupt Jessie's press conference.

"Couldn't I give her the flowers meself!" he pleaded.

"No! That would be impossible!"

"Oh, come on," he coaxed. "I got up at six this morning to come and see 'er, honest I did! She knows me!"

The whole world knows Jessie Matthews, I thought, but that didn't mean that she would have time for them.

I took his name and returned upstairs. Jessie was holding

court from a large chair, and I caught her attention. She was nonplussed and at a loss to recall the stranger we nicknamed 'The Gentleman Caller'. Being the warm and generous person she was, she bade me bring the mysterious stranger up. He came up and immediately conquered.

"I know you, Miss Matthews, and you should bloody well know me!"

"I know I bloody well should! But I probably don't see as well as I did, so you must bloody well enlighten me!"

"I lit your first show in New York when you was with Mr Charlot."

Jessie studied him for a moment and then said, "So you did! And we haven't changed that much, have we?"

"You speak for yourself!" came back the reply.

They chatted for a good twenty minutes, while the press waited in vain and got slightly high on the spirits with which Brenda was plying them. Then Jessie resumed her audience.

At the show that evening, the same man, wearing the finest suit you ever saw, came with his wife. I fancy he was as much captivated with Jessie this night as he was all those years ago when she replaced Gertrude Lawrence.

After that, I became much closer to Jessie, and we spent many lovely evenings at her home in Hatch End. We did more concerts, and another terrific evening at The De La Warr Pavilion, Bexhill.

Later, Jessie opened a season I was presenting at the Buxton Playhouse. This was situated in the heart of the gardens. The Buxton Opera House had not then re-opened. Following the show at Buxton, we entertained Jessie to dinner at the Sandringham Hotel. There they did her proud with a sumptuous meal at 11.00 p.m. We were presided over by June Donlevy, known in the trade as 'Coo-ee-darling! She greets you with this on every occasion, followed quickly by a request for 'A double brandy, darling! Coo-ee-darling!'

A superb hostess and vivacious personality. June could drink the Thames (and I fear frequently does) and still be up at 7.00 a.m. for business. She was a short, stout woman with blonde hair in a June Allyson fringe. She could have seduced

Oscar Wilde and was a great favourite with the men for miles around. All fifty guests were joined by members of the repertory company, of which June was the director. The wine flowed, as did the conversation!

I was relating what I thought was a witty bit of dialogue to Sister Florence, who had become Jessie's constant companion since her hip operation, when Jessie leaned over and said, "Thank God he's getting a bit bawdy at last! What fun!"

While I was in Newcastle, the local radio station asked me to do a radio hour for them, spotlighting all the musical comedy stars. I outlined a most ambitious programme and asked them to get certain records which I wished to feature whilst presenting the programme. Among the records were collectors' items such as Alice Delysia singing 'If You Could Care for Me' and Jessie singing 'Hold My Hand' (from the show of the same title, which had played at the London Pavilion in the twenties). I also included several records of Fred and Adele Astaire, Bea Lillie and Jack Buchanan. Rumour had it that Adele Astaire could run rings around Fred, so she must have been something! The radio station also found another of Jessie's older records, 'I'm in Love Again', which was delightful. The broadcast went well, and we left Newcastle on a very good note.

Jessie Matthews, like so many of us, made some disastrous decisions during her lifetime. One was to turn down the lead in 'Charlie Girl', which was especially written for her and Tommy Steele. The fact that she didn't try just a little harder to get the lead in 'The King and I', was one of her regrets. This eventually went to Valerie Hobson with Evelyne Laye as second choice, and Jessie third. How different her latter years would have been had she captured this plum.

A little while after Newcastle, Jessie asked me to arrange a charity show in which she would star in aid of the local hospital. This was voluntarily run by nuns, and was the hospital which had restored her to health after her hip operation in nineteen seventy-six. The hospital was badly in need of funds, and funds Jessie was determined it would have.

I had played pantomime the previous Christmas at the

Watersmeet Theatre, Rickmansworth, and the manager kindly loaned the venue for the charity show. It was an excellent evening and Jessie was on top form. A goodly sum was raised for the hospital.

I had dinner with Jessie three months before she died. She had just had a fantastic reception in Los Angeles, where she appeared in concert. Jessie was fêted by half of Hollywood and lots of close friends like Roddy MacDowell and Anna Lee. (Older moviegoers may remember Anna in 'How Green was My Valley' and more recently as the neighbour in 'Whatever Happened to Baby Jane?'). That evening, after the meal, Jessie sang all her old songs, and seemed relaxed and warm to the world.

On another occasion she was clearly unwell and rambled at length about the bitter moments in her life, and the many disappointments. Her mental illness was known in the trade long before I got to know her well, and some repertory companies had tragic moments to recall when Jessie was in a production for them. But through all this she had managed to keep her end up, and never disappointed audiences. It was a great pity that I had to cancel the last concert she was doing for me on a Sunday. She was taken ill on the Saturday with a greatly swollen neck, and it would have been impossible for her to sing, even if she managed to get out of bed.

It was then that the cancer started to show which would call the final curtain on one of Britain's brightest stars. Her greatest sorrow was that her adopted daughter never really accepted her, and gave little love in return for Jessie's devotion. In fact she ridiculed her mother on many occasions and caused much sadness and torment.

Jessie loved her garden, and spent many happy hours in it. Her views were strong on many subjects, and when I asked her pertinent questions, her answers were always most definite. She adamantly declared if she had her time all over again she would not have chosen the theatre. I enquired who she thought could play herself in a film and she warmed a little. An obvious choice, earlier on, would have been Ann Miller, but Jessie would have none of this, and declared Miss Miller would have been far too common! She thought, as many of us do, that Greta Garbo was the greatest star of them all. Alas, Marlene Dietrich did not get her vote!

I was included in the radio tribute to Jessie Matthews on London Broadcasting Company, Capital Radio and other radio stations. I was honoured to give the address at the Memorial Service held at St Paul's, the Actors' Church in Covent Garden. I spoke for ten minutes, following Dame Anna Neagle into the pulpit. I hope in tribute I did justice to the lady, star and friend I loved so much.

In nineteen seventy-eight I teamed up again with Quentin Crisp. After his sojourn in the West End, from which London had never really recovered, I booked him up and down the country in places as far removed from each other as Chipping Norton, Mold, Newcastle and Maidstone. Even New Brighton had the pleasure, but then nothing like Quentin had arrived in New Brighton since the Ferry. Mind you, the administrator of The Floral Pavilion was an understanding man, and I was presenting pantomime for him. He booked Quentin more out of politeness than enthusiasm.

This was how Quentin was booked to give his lesson on lifestyle to the Merseyside following. Surprise! Surprise! Without Cilla Black we played to over five hundred enthusiasts. This delighted me, and stunned the management. Patrons bought Mr Crisp flowers, presents, tokens, messages and kisses. His reception was sensational. Quentin, in his usual relaxed style, said, "Isn't this cosy?" and continued receiving the rapture from his public, as if it was his due, and it surely was. Quentin never addressed anyone by their Christian name. It was always Mr, Mrs, or Miss, and with those in doubt, Madam. He lived permanently in the Hollywood heavens, with such movie queens as Bette Davis, Katherine Hepburn and especially Joan Crawford. 'Mummie Dearest' held no terror for Quentin.

Every evening we were doing a show, and kind-hearted Brian Cooper usually drove us, and I would enquire from Quentin where he would like to eat. His reply was always the same, "Whatever you want, I want." One can hardly quarrel with that. I was asked on a radio show how I would describe Quentin Crisp, and I said, "He is the godfather of hope," and I really think he was.

Quentin had been struggling for many years to give his message to the world. His book, 'The Naked Civil Servant', first appeared in the sixties as a novel. The book, through the faith and judgement of the late Philip Mackie, was sold to television. Philip could see the enormous potential that the subject would command, but could not have known the success his work would enjoy in practically every country. Certainly, it was never envisaged that Quentin would take the stage of theatres all over the world. After all, he had taken the stage of life for many years, spreading his messages and philosophy to all who would listen. He played to packed houses and excellent notices everywhere.

After an initial try-out at the King's Head, Islington, when Quentin addressed a few 'gay blades' at lunchtime, sandwiched between a beer and a steak and kidney pie, Richard Jackson persuaded Quentin to take his 'message of hope' into the West End. So he sailed in to rule at the Duke of York's theatre for a few months, before transferring to the smaller Ambassadors Theatre.

He went on chat shows as if there was no tomorrow and thoroughly enjoyed being in the limelight as much as he knew he would. Equity got uptight and yelled "Mr Crisp, is not a member of our flock!"

Quentin was quite bemused. He thought the entire affair quite amazing, and continued playing to his audience with abandon – Equity then issued his card in desperation!

During his West End run, I telephoned Quentin about doing some provincial dates for me. "How are you fixed, work wise?" I enquired. How bloody silly of me, knowing Quentin!

"I have no idea. You had better ask my agent."

The agent turned out to be a large bear of a man. Hungarian to boot! His vocabulary was extensive, and his delivery flamboyant. He was a literary agent with more wit than most of his writers, and if he ever takes to touring his own show, I would have to manage him. His name is Richard

Gollner, and he would give Peter Ustinov a run for his money. We met and agreed on terms which were more attractive than the pittance Quentin had received in the West End. He always said he had only made three hundred and fifty pounds out of the television version of 'The Naked Civil Servant'. So he couldn't retire to the Sunset Strip just yet.

I fixed up thirty dates without delay, and with no trouble at all. A young lady named Kate, extremely attractive, and wonderful (when she was awake, for she slept an awful lot between meals and performances) joined us and became Quentin's personal assistant. Together we travelled the hills and dales, delivering the message to each and every town astute enough to book us. Most performances were sold before we got there, and every one of us had something to smile about. You may wonder how Quentin coped with all of this, and I can only say, superbly.

He took to the stage, made the audience his subjects and they worshipped him. The audiences throughout the country were made up approximately sixty-five per cent of middle-aged ladies, twenty per cent of men that they dragged along, and the rest were 'gay' curious, or both. The middle-aged ladies were all dressed for the ball, avid and restless to get the message and learn what makes little boys 'tick' and big boys 'tock'.

One old dowager said to her escort as she poured a Bloody Mary down her voluptuous throat, "Whatever do they do together, dear?" Unluckily, that particular day four 'queens' were taking the waters nearby and nearly collapsed with laughter and hysteria, as they tried to tell her.

Finally he settled in the United States, and just a few years ago left us for the world beyond. I, for one, will never forget him.

Many years ago music halls had flourished with revues carrying such titles as 'Soldiers and Skirts' and 'Call Us Mister!' and many talented artistes such as Louis Hayden, Alan Haynes, Lee Sutton, Tommy Rose and Mark Fredericks were talented lads (or lassies) who threw on frocks like things possessed, and entertained the masses when they needed to be

226

cheered up. And the audiences left well pleased that a gay lad could be up there with the crème de la crème when it came to entertainment.

Russell Grant – during his "Wizard of Oz" days

Chris Barrie – one of the newer stars launched by Barrie
Stacey Productions

Keith Hopkins

"Barrie Baby" winning Holsten for ladies race Doncaster
10.3.93 at 16:1 odds

Friend Bill Kerr with the late Danny Kaye and Rob
Murray at the London Palladium

A virgin at twenty-two years old!

Alexander
'Momma'
Bridge

Quentin Crisp relaxing with us on tour

ALASTAIR GORDON IN ASSOCIATION WITH BARRIE STACEY PRESENTS A CABARET-STYLE REVUE

TODAY AND TOMORROW

STEVEN COLE · BARBARA FARRELL · IAN CALVIN · ANNE LANGFORD · GRAHAM JOLLEY

MAY FAIR THEATRE
Stratton St. W.1.
2 minutes Green Park Station
TEL. 493 2031

produced by
T. LESLIE JACKSON

Sunday evenings
6.15 and 8.45pm.
Commencing JUNE 11th
Tickets £2, £1.50, £1 & 80p.

The late Dr. Alastair Aitcheson and I staged the first
official Sunday Variety Show in London

Jessie Matthews and Dennis Lotis

Chapter 14

Some Stars Twinkle, and some are Top Heavy!

In the world of which I am a member, values can be deceptive, allegiance can be known to waver, especially when under siege in the rat-race.

The whole game is made worthwhile because fortunes can change overnight, and while you might be on the floor in the morning, the heavens could be yours by nightfall.

Such turning of fortunes is really the main attraction in the world of show business. There is always room on the swing. With a little bit of luck, drive, timing, good management, or even talent, you could make the big time. That magic castle in the sky!

How many lovelies have flown to Hollywood to 'make it' and ended up as waitresses, models, seamstresses, hookers or just plain librarians? Some, however, realising they were not going to make the big time perhaps because of their paucity of talent, or run of bad luck, have found themselves a man or woman of substance to love.

It is much the same in the world of an agent or impresario. They are human, have to eat and pay rent. The fallacy that 'Mr Ten per cent' is loaded, is not necessarily true. They have highs, lows, periods of confidence and downers. An agent has the tax man, the value added tax man (known to many as 'VAT Lil') and the rates man to deal with. Then there is the return of hundreds of thousands of pounds one may have spent getting one's starlet known, talked about and invited here, there, and everywhere. Suddenly, there's a recording contract for the artiste, and all at once you have the rent, the VAT, the tax and the 'cream in your coffee'. It is never too late, and an eye must be kept on the ball; a goal is always possible. At least that's what I think. On the matter of stars, some have it and some don't. I have worked with most of them.

For comedians you really have to go no further than Bob Monkhouse, Frankie Howerd and Don Maclean.

Bob was a natural. Forget the junk on television. Here was a man who was the supreme master of comedy, with the skills of Danny Kaye, the magic of Charles Chaplin and the timing of Jack Benny. He could not go wrong if he were drugged, drunk or raped before he went on. The pity is, that when Bob played variety, and I have been fortunate enough to present him in a dozen shows, he would come on and wallop the audience with such impact that the poor onlookers would be punch drunk for the first few minutes.

"I never knew he could be like that."

"It just shows," said her mate, "it really does!"

And there are many that agree as they were carried away on waves of hysterical laughter. If they don't get the jokes, the tremendous pace of the act does. Bob was like quicksilver and the gags were fired at an amazing rate. One is apt to forget that Bob Monkhouse did his apprenticeship in summer season, cabaret and repertory, long before television. I can remember him giving a superlative performance in an early play by Neil Simon, 'Come Blow Your Horn' at the Prince of Wales Theatre, with Michael Crawford as second lead. And like the dynamo he is Bob had the thing running for an age! If he ever went to America, and one wonders why he hasn't, they would probably have to open up a new channel to accommodate him!

Bob's knowledge of films would give Barry Norman a sleepless night. He was sensational when Alice Faye came over to guest on his programme. Alice is a leaf of the tree that was truly Hollywood, and was one of the finest vocalists in the world. She can still provide a very lovely dulcet tone on the rare occasions when she sings, she manages to look a million dollars, and of course she always did, and has guested on several star-spangled spectaculars on American television.

All the women manage to look superb on the all-star carnivals, while the male stars from the thirties and forties (with the exception of the late Cary Grant and the late Paul Newman), look as if they have one foot in the grave and stumble like old buffalos.

Betty Grable was the other lass working from Twentieth Century Fox stable of lovelies to make it big. She had been working since the Boer War and really knew her business. But unfortunately she never made the Bob Monkhouse Show or any other of our top programmes. But more of her later.

Frankie Howerd was another cup of tea. He was the master of timing and the head of the class in mimicry. He was a serious, testing professional, never really pleased with his lot, always strived to conquer new mountains of mirth. He seemed to be forever searching for new heights of fame. He was superstitious and fussy (and there are many of us about), and colours affected him markedly. He worried over publicity, over ticket sales, and had been known to tour a town he was playing to make sure a theatre publicity manager had done 'what he ought' which, believe me, in some of the areas we have played, is not a bad thing. Like most stars in the business he knew many lows and highs but made it all and was firmly placed at the top of the ladder. If the Gods are kind, he will never fall again. Although I was paying his salary he rarely spoke more than a dozen words to me, except when he heard I was also touring Quentin Crisp, then he was most talkative. A true English star, if ever there was one.

Don Maclean is the man on the outside looking in. Brimful of talent, wit, drive and personality, he has been waiting in the wings for a long time for the ultimate accolade. He has something of the quick-fire Monkhouse attack, and his quips come thick and fast. He has a smile as wide as a water melon to front his artistry, almost defying one not to laugh. He is often on television, but never in the right programme at the right time, to make him a big star. He must have his own series for he has the harp, the party is there, dying for him to play.

I once had Don sharing the bill with an excellent impressionist, Paul Melba, who is as tall as a skyscraper and as wily as a fox. The two men would never be lovers. Mr Melba thought he should have top billing, and turned his act from a cascade of clever impressions into a stand-up comedy one for much of the time and just sprinkled an impression here and there to seal some of Don's thunder. But happily where Mr Melba spat, no green grass grew, and the night was all Don Maclean's.

I got myself involved in a national tour of a Dave Freeman comedy called 'A Bedful Of Foreigners'. In this Don Maclean starred with the comely actress, Mandy Rice-Davies and Tony Scott, (Terry Scott's younger brother). Mandy Rice-Davies and I had met before at my office, four years previously, when we were both contemplating some play or other. She climbed up my three flights of stairs and when reaching the top, puffing her lungs out, said, "If you can survive this, you can survive anything!" And this was true!

Kathy Kirby was another talent bent on self-destruction. A slim, most attractive blonde, she had a voice that could shatter windows pleasantly. She had more managers than hot meals, and agents were not far behind. With a temper that could cause a mutiny and a quick right punch, she had rejected many a pair of arms that could have helped her and guided her back to the top. On a good day she was terrific. She died a few months ago.

One evening in October in nineteen eighty-one, I had for my sins taken the South Pier, Blackpool, for a concert. Blackpool is a town that has never been kind to me. It was a bitter evening on this particular night and there is nothing sharper than a cold, eastern wind to your bum when breezing along a pier in Blackpool, believe me. The South Pier is not a popular one with the promoters and punters. It is large and spacious, but is given little care, either with management or amenities. Kathy was coming home to a theatre where all those years ago she had topped her first season as a big star. She sang 'Secret Love' as if she meant it, so that every boy and girl in the country were with her. Her record sales had given Doris Day a bad night.

This was my first show with Miss Kirby, and bookings were not at all bad. We had plastered the town with handbills and the box office was showing an agreeable enthusiasm. Adam Daye, an impressionist of note, was on the bill with 'Golden Brandy' two sisters and a brother, who were the

240

children of the well-known 'pickpocket' Mark Raffles. Band call went well, although there was still no sign of Kathy Kirby. When six o'clock arrived and went, I rang up my old friend who happened to be staying with Tommy Trafford in Blackpool and asked him, if all failed, if he would stand in for Kathy Kirby. Of course he would.

By this time the famous Blackpool illuminations were in full swing and the town's promenade was packed with cars from end to end. Movement was therefore extremely difficult and it was just coming up to half past six. Then I received a message that Kathy was being escorted through the town by motorcade. It was like old times for her, once again.

She came through the stage door with her musical director, Bob Barter, at six fifty. It seems they had broken down somewhere near Birmingham. Miss Kirby threw a few pieces of paper at my musical director, David Carter, who did a noble job of deciphering them.

By this time the crowd of patrons was gathering in the foyer. There was no one there to welcome them, the café was closed, and the only staff to speak of was an old and somewhat deaf commissionaire. Everyone was freezing, with nothing to fortify them against the bitter wind. Some wit was heard to say, "No wonder the theatre is dying! It's because of inefficient fools like the young manager, that's why!"

We finished Miss Kirby's skimpy run through at seven twenty and let the audience in a moment later. We eventually went up ten minutes late! This was a miracle, under the circumstances. Kathy Kirby was singing some sixteen numbers, and one of them Don Maclean used to end his act with. I asked Kathy if she wouldn't mind dropping her version of the popular song, and was given a veritable cold shoulder and heave ho. So both artistes sang the number.

But the show ran very well. Kathy had come on like a whirlwind, in a very good voice and I started to relax.

It was through Jess Conrad that I met his good friend, the late Diana Dors, whose birthday was the day before mine. Perhaps we shared some of the same temperament. A lady never heavily favoured by fortune, but regularly crossed by fate, she had an upward battle to become the sex symbol who graduated to make the acting awards. Her ample measurements were later matched by her many talents; she toured the music halls at one stage and her act was very clever, never attempting more vocally than she could give and her flair for mimicry and accents were given full vent in several compelling point numbers. She made Hollywood sit up and when the world thought we were all very sedate country types and gave the big busted lovelies in Hollywood something to think about. Her career developed far more impressively than her earlier films had promised. Being a 'Scorpio' she suffered many battles with the authorities and her savings were depleted more times than Mickey Rooney has had wives. But Diana came back again and again, and gradually made a fortune. Along the way she was a lady to be reckoned with; a tough, plain spoken woman. She asked for her fee in cash at the theatres she played, even before she went on to do the act, and a man with arresting looks and a large carpet bag was her minder. On the last particular night we worked together she arrived in a hurry at five thirty and immediately asked me what colour briefs I was wearing.

"Black!" I replied.

"Excellent," she said. "I have forgotten to bring any, and as my stage dress splits up the side, there may be more to see than is fair, and if that's the case, we had better put the ticket price up."

I always carry a spare pair, and Diana went on respectively clad.

Diana Dors' beginning was as inspiring as anyone could have wished, and if Dennis Hamilton had not fancied her when she was an usherette at the Blue Hall Cinema in the Edgeware Road, way back in the sixties, Britain may have lost its answer to Marilyn Monroe.

I had a male model friend who liked 'a bit of what you fancy, does you good' in the afternoons, and was a terror for a pretty face. He borrowed my flat in Earls Court on many occasions to entertain a lady of his choice, and when Diana Dors' house caught fire at Maidenhead, he was at the party to throw Diana through the bathroom windows as the fire raged. As she was heavily pregnant at the time it could not have been easy. Nevertheless, my friend did it. Alas, he was burned alive, and all we ever found after the fire were his car keys.

With plans to present a stage version of 'What Happened to Baby Jane?' in the West End with Noele Gordon starring in the Joan Crawford part and Diana Dors in Bette Davis' footsteps, their demise is all the more tragic, for this was casting on an inspired note. Recently Greta Saachi and Anita Dobson portrayed these very same names at The Arts Theatre in a camp send up of 'Betty And Joan' and scored a tremendous hit.

That Diana Dors found a man she could love after several runs, was a bonus. He might have been a handful, but Diana liked men who were not perfect, and she gradually found the key to Alan Lake, who found love at the same time. With Alan's suicide, so ends another era, though her son, Jason, could easily carry on the family tradition with his strength and good looks.

With summer seasons in this country going out of favour, the star-laden one-night stands, are gradually replacing those annual performances and pier shows as we know them. It is a great pity, as concert parties and summer shows were the backbone with pantomime of the English provincial theatre scene. They were the place where most of us cut our teeth on the way to the top. So many household names today owe so much to impresarios like Ronnie Brandon, Jerry Jerome, Bobby Pett, Terry Cantor, Duggie Chapman, Tommy Trafford, Ronnie Parnell, Robert Luff, Lisa and Bunny Baron, Aubrey Phillips and many, many more.

You may hear people scoff about the end of the pier shows, but if you put all the artistes who have made it to stardom from this entertainment, end to end, the line would run the length of the Charing Cross Road.

Stalwarts, like Ken Dodd for example. Ken goes on for so long with his act that the buses and cabs have all gone to bed, and you just get home in time to meet the milkman. Frankie Vaughan, The Bachelors, and many others, still star in shortish summer seasons when given the opportunity, but the odd one, two or three night stands in summer are here to stay. It could be that the summer season has not kept pace and grown up with the public, not nurtured on glossy nightclub routines with breasts a-flying, and the boy dancers showing most of what they can boast. Performers are not much younger. Stars are maturing at thirty and publishing their memoirs at forty. Stage shows have had to keep pace, and some have not made it. Hence the exodus from the seaside resorts to the packaged starlight roof and nightclub game.

Adelaide Hall was a truly great jazz singer. She was a plump, comfortable woman who came here in the thirties with the famous 'Blackbirds Show', and lived here on and off all her life. She displayed a voice of pure gold and a personality that would put most artistes to shame.

Tommy Trinder and I only met and worked together three times, but I found him a great Cockney personality, as uncomplicated as you would expect him. His face was his fortune. He did a great week at the Kenneth More Theatre, Ilford, for me with that super lady Rosemary Squires. She works steadily through the years. If you like the radio on, as I do at night while having my cocoa, you will surely hear her singing with one of the radio bands as the midnight hour approaches.

Years ago, as a young scribe, I had been invited to meet the legendary Gene Autry at a grand splash at the Savoy Hotel. Gene was exactly as one would picture him. Acting every minute, as if he were still on his horse, the wonder steed. But it was his wife that caught my attention. With a room full of at least five hundred people, she managed to greet everyone. She looked and could have been Claudette Colbert's sister. She spoke in a lovely South Carolina drawl and was true magic.

Gene Autry was always very lucky and made millions from everything he touched and must have been one of the wealthiest men in the United States.

It was also at the Savoy Hotel many years ago that Charlie Chaplin was partaking breakfast one morning, when Paulette Goddard, whose jewellery collection was one of the finest and most valuable in America, arrived in evening dress in the breakfast room. When asked if she had just come from a very late party, she replied, "Oh, no, on the contrary." She looked at her ex-husband, who was shovelling eggs and bacon down his throat and continued, "I just want to show that bastard there what he's missed!"

My role of impresario continued throughout the seventies with one night concerts becoming more and more numerous. I was heavily in favour of this sort of presentation, for apart from the fact there was no risk, we always made a few bob. I had retained a particular fondness for the vaudeville scene, probably from my early beginnings on the music hall circuit, and still find immense pleasure in this form of entertainment.

After a long and arduous but immensely pleasurable tour with 'An Evening with Quentin Crisp', I looked around for a similar attraction to tour the length and breadth of the land. For the first time I had made money and kept it, and everyone had butter on their bread.

I chanced to see the television play based on the life of the 'Spend! Spend! Spend!' lady, Viv Nicholson, and wondered whether she could deliver enough for a one woman show. We approached her and she was as vague as Billie Burke. But she wanted to talk about it. She came up and had supper at my flat, and half the press in London trooped round to interview the lady. Viv was her natural self, swore like a trooper and was more outrageous than Hermoine Gingold, in a down market way.

I liked her from the start for she called a spade, a spade and seemed stunned I had bothered, when one evening I cooked her a meal. We then had her skipping along the Charing Cross Road early one evening in a skimpy nightclub costume, showing her legs and a soupçon of flesh to titillate the scene for the newspaper photographers who were shooting the scene. The passers-by seemed to enjoy it also.

The idea was to present Vivien in a try-out concert, and I managed to get a booking at the Tameside Theatre, Ashton-Under-Lyme in Manchester. As the lady came from Castleford, this was not too bad. She needed some vocal tuition, as well as movement, and we got her lessons from our friend, David Keller, at the Wigmore Studios. She came up to town three or four times a week and did the scales and a few steps, and although it was obvious she would not set the world on fire, she might do.

A backing group of four were booked, and the concert announced. A few days before the show, Viv was suddenly on every radio station from Cheshire to Corby saying she was doing the show, and that she would be telling all about her sex life on this very night – between ditties. Oh my God! I thought.

The house manager of the Tameside Theatre took the night off and accompanied his little boy to see 'Dumbo', which was quite a difference from the attraction playing at his theatre. The police were in the back stalls sitting like ten little maids all in a row, to watch this 'News of the World' special. The audience was a mixture of dirty mac devotees, some camp followers, and very middle-aged voyeurs. The remainder of the audience were just plain curious! I had two supporting acts, Adam Daye who, at the time, was courting a widow of substance, who declared she could not have her talented Adam on the same bill as this notorious woman. After a while I literally pushed Adam on while she was in the toilet. He went well and at the end of his act the widow collected him in her butterfly net and they swept off to the unknown world outside.

Vivien took the stage for her act in a reasonable dress and was not all that bad. She did let out an oath here and there, which was clutched at immediately by an audience praying for a 'bit of the other', and for a consolation prize she put in a little dialogue that would have excited the magazine 'Forum'. But her numbers were all standards and catchy and she remembered what David Keller, the singing teacher, had taught her. The audience warmed to her. The policemen relaxed, save one, whose truncheon was almost out of control.

Vivien held court in the bar afterwards talking to all who cared to listen, and she was a warm, vivacious creature. An acquired taste maybe, but definitely a flavour on some people's lists.

The concert was not a mistake, but the takings from the

box office were poor, so the theatre lost bread, and no one rushed to book this startling act for further sessions. Vivien did a few clubs, then vanished from view for a period, and has now reappeared on the circuit, knocking at doors in some towns as a Jehovah's Witness, to impart a message of a somewhat different kind.

Not the follow-up to Quentin Crisp, I am afraid.

*****

We did a week and a few one nighters with Larry Grayson. He is a very different type of comedy man to the others I have mentioned. He was very much a character comic and his character never changes. It extends the way you expect it to, with the same friends being touched upon as the act progresses. Larry can only deliver a thirty minute act. After that the impact fades. Larry's moods do vary but he can be a feast of merriment, especially when one gets on to the movie questions and answers. His background of the clubs is a vast one, and it was a stroke of fate that he was booked for the 'Birds of a Feather' revue that Paul Raymond put on at the Royalty Theatre, Holborn. The show was rich and luxurious as any you would find in Paris. The costumes were out of this world and it had a great cast. 'The Mime Timers', a very fine drag act, scored a big hit, but it was Larry Grayson who came out a star. He whipped the first nighters into a frenzy, and the critics reached for new superlatives to describe his talent.

These days we have talent programmes by the score. They are cheap for television companies to present, but do occasionally come up with real talent. Always on the other side there is the outrageous, the pitiful, and the no-goers brought in to fill the time, and amuse the judges. On top of all this we have the monumental screaming studio audience, making it difficult to understand anything. Hardly vintage television.

I feel we cannot leave this chapter on variety stars without mentioning several Americans. Betty Grable was a joy when she came over to do 'Belle Star', a saloon musical based on every Western you did not see. It proved to be the only flop of her long and spectacular career. Although it had an excellent cast with the fine Blayne Barrington supporting Miss Grable, it was masterminded by the movie actor Rory Calhoun. He stalked around in a large cowboy hat and boasted that he had made love to ninety-eight movie stars of which Miss Grable was one. This naturally did not make him flavour of the month with anyone. Betty Grable was excellent, but with a so-so book and no tunes of consequence the show only lasted about twenty-five performances. Around the same time Ginger Rogers was arriving to star in a musical the other side of town and the red carpet was extended from Southampton. She had the boy with the bugle and every newspaper in town. It was almost like the Second Coming. Betty Grable came off very second best. Luck again plays the major role in everyone's career.

Ginger was always a great favourite of mine, however, and I was one of the few who thought she put up a good show in 'Mame', a very under-estimated musical, full of good tunes. Sadly, the film version buried Lucille Ball for good, for she was shot through gauze and chiffon so much, she almost came out distorted. 'South Pacific' you may remember, although not shot through any sort of fabric, did almost the same for the delightful Mitzi Gaynor. Ginger was always a superb comedienne. She could dance the light fantastic so well, that practically every shop girl in the world copied her. Her true glory was always her split second timing, detail and delivery. What a pity she did not have the vehicle later in her career to drive this home.

While I was running the 'As You Like It' I was asked to supply Betty and Ginger's meals on matinée days and I had long conversations with both of them about Hollywood and the early movies back in the 'good old days'. Betty Grable lived mostly for her racehorses and on reading her biography I was astonished at references to crudeness, for I must confess I never say any of it. She died very early, and we were robbed of a great 'hoofer'. Darryl F Zanuck once said, "There are two reasons why you are in pictures, Betty, and you are standing on both of them."

Chapter 15

One Up for a Mug's Game

On a wet Sunday in nineteen eighty, I chanced to see on the racing page of the 'Daily Express', an advertisement announcing a quarter share of a spirited horse in a stable at Newmarket.

I have always, with my brother David, nurtured a fondness for the turf. I noted that the horse for sale was a descendant of that superb racer, 'Roman Warrior', who had won over a thousand races. So that could not be bad news.

As a follower of the sport of kings for most of my life, I telephoned a friend and we put in a couple of grand each for a portion of this nag. I rang the breeder concerned, who said I was the first that morning. Two days later, after he had said that, fifty-two fellow spirits had rung the breeder, who was also a trainer. So it was a good thing I was up with the lark.

The trainer, Patrick Haslam, and I made arrangements to pop down to Newmarket and view the spirited animal without delay. The following Saturday we climbed into Brian Cooper's lovely green Capri and sallied forth, eventually arriving at the stables. Patrick Haslam lived in a fine, sprawling old house, which was in the middle of a series of clusters of stables, housing horses of every description, temperament and breed. Patrick turned out to be around thirty-five and of a countryman's complexion. A gentleman farmer type, he was desperately conservative, and true to Margaret Thatcher through civil war, famine and beyond. He ushered us into his spacious lounge and bade his lovely lady to bring us coffee and brandies without further ado. He assessed, and quite correctly, that we were a little at sea so he did most of the talking. He could see in a twinkling of a blue eye that we really didn't know a horse's ass from its elbow, but learning is a tremendous gift, and by God, we could learn. As it turned out, we didn't learn fast enough.

After downing the coffee, we had a brief chat about the health of the horse we had come to view, look at his credentials, and learn a little about our co-partners in the venture. We then departed with Patrick across the maze of paths which led to one or other of the stalls, to look at our new purchase. And what a purchase he was!

He made 'Black Beauty' and 'Flicka' seem like peasants. As tall as a chimney, our horse was a beautiful chestnut, with his head high with pride, and with legs that Betty Grable would have admired. He stood, for all the world like a champion, or so we thought. He was approaching two years old, still growing, but would he take to racing? Or was he merely an ornament of beauty, and the epitome of decoration?

He winked wickedly at my partner, and we were done for. How done, we would realise later. The Gods were not going to smile on this particular deal.

Patrick Haslam looked the part to a tee. Curt Jurgens could scarcely have played it better. He was tall, handsome and rugged, from his checked shirt and old school tie, down to his riding breeches. He asked me what else we would like to see. The previous day a filly by the name of 'Mink Coat' had won a handicap race. It was her third in as many outings, so we asked if we could see the horse.

After the grandeur and radiance of our horse, whom we christened 'Barrie Boy' without delay, we expected a horse of perfection, quality and manners. The creature that faced us was similar to a scruffy donkey. 'Mink Coat' was mostly black with a dirty stretch of white here and there. She stared at us as if we were nurses from a madhouse. Not very tall, and certainly not well built, she was not a pleasing sight. We spoke to her in dulcet tones, to cover our astonishment, and not a little disappointment in her general appearance. All she did was snort with venom and turn to look at the back of her stall and toy with a random piece of hay.

As we showed no signs of going, she decided to expedite our departure, and very ungraciously relieved herself without further ado, as if to express her utmost displeasure. Whoever had named her 'Mink Coat' was obviously a customer at the wrong furrier. Or perhaps was short sighted. After this, we were shown 'Black Mike', a stallion, who also had won that very week on the course. This animal was altogether different, and showed an excellent set of teeth to bid us welcome. His smile was a joy. Again, however, his appearance would not have excited Billy Smart's Circus, for he was a tall, rangy creature with a lack-lustre coat. At least he was well named, and had been to charm school. Unfortunately, and I hope it was not laid at our door, the poor beast has never won from that day to this. He is now with another trainer, and is awaiting a change of luck.

We accompanied Mr Haslam back to his mansion, where we renewed our brandies and got to know each other a little better. Enough, that is, to part with the necessary bread and announce our racing colours, for we were to have the head share, my brother and I. all was understood.

After the brandy and the excitement of the morning, we were not anywhere near sloshed, but had certainly downed enough of the wicked spirit to think we had achieved a good morning's work.

Three other clients owned certain parts of 'Barrie Boy'. Which parts we never ascertained, but we had the head and therefore he would race in our colours, which is what it is all about. Black and scarlet. Pure 'Wicked Lady' country. We never did meet our other business partners.

We left the stables and Mr Haslam's empire, in a merry mood, and moved into Newmarket proper for a little shepherd's pie, washed down by some ale, in a nearby tavern.

This was our entry into the world of the turf.

Brian Cooper, who would give pessimism a bad name, was dubious. Brian, thought much and said little. "I should wait and see," he muttered, "before behaving like the Aga Khan." So we finished our sherry trifle and returned to London without further delay. After all, we had passed our money over, so what was done was done.

After three months again we paid a visit to Patrick Haslam and 'Barrie Boy'. He had grown some more. As Al Jolson had said, "You ain't seen nuthin' yet!" No truer words were ever spoken.

Patrick expressed opinions on suitable race meetings for this speedy son of 'Roman Warrior'; quite overlooking the fact that the poor thing had not achieved any training.

We shook hands with the stallion. My friend kissed him twice, and the stable boy once. Again we departed for refreshments in nearby Newmarket.

Soon afterwards with the summer sun setting in the heavens, I got a characteristic twitch in my left buttock that told me all was not well. Shortly afterwards we got a telephone call from the Haslam stable. Mr Haslam was in Morocco looking at some other beauties. The caller, however, said they wished to geld our horse to stop him growing. I hastened to my co-partner and over a lengthy gin and tonic, reviewed the situation. To lose one's manhood at any time is a total disaster. I was convinced that the swish of the shears or whatever else was the severing instrument, was torture most Gothic!

The more we thought about it, the gloomier we became. Monica Dell, our singing friend, who is always a source of information on any major problem, was sympathetic. She, too, had ventured into the world of horse ownership, and also suffered total despair when her horse had collapsed and died without even a warning. She was not too keen on the knife, be it kitchen, organ grinder or decoration. Apparently, the other shareholders had given their permission, and we came to the conclusion that Mr Haslam would not advise such a 'chop' if he didn't think it wise. How stupid can you get?

This was the beginning of the end of us and 'Barrie Boy'. After surviving the most painful of operations, he got over his indisposition very quickly, but grew with abandon even quicker.

We went into utter gloom about the entire incident, and I changed from Wincarnis to neat brandy to waylay the mood of despair. I then learned what I should have done in the first place after chatting to sages in the racing world. It was their considered opinion that Patrick Haslam had far too many horses, something like fifty-eight. He was a little like an overworked schoolteacher, and could not give the required attention, patience and love to each and every one. We felt, and I fear we could have been all too right, that 'Barrie Boy' needed a lot of love. As there was no sign he would run well on even the Haslam greenery, let alone the race track, I again consulted the wise Monica. She had a friend in a Yorkshire stable, and this kind gentleman recommended a breeder called Robert Urquhart, who ran the 'Hunsley House Stud'.

This gentleman was truly Jockey Club material, and with little fuss said he had a stable free, and we could bed and board 'Barrie Boy' for a period while he convalesced, and started to discover some of the delights of Yorkshire.

This worked wonders, and our horse responded to the love and care the Urquharts gave him. He became even more beautiful and striking. He stayed with them for four full moons. Then after a depressing early spring, my income deteriorated to such an extent we reluctantly decided to part with this unfortunate horse.

Bob had a vivacious wife, Jemima, who started off as an actress in repertory at an early age, when she played such leads as 'Nancy' in 'Oliver' and other little acting gems. We spoke the same language, which was a distinct advantage. She was dark and trim and should have played the lead in 'International Velvet'. A touch of Susan Hayward and Vivien Leigh also emerged from this volatile lady, who spoke her mind with force and didn't care a damn about it. She rode with speed and style rare for a comparative amateur. Her capacity for life and the bounties were boundless. I was most impressed.

We left 'Barrie Boy' in his large hayloft – and never met again. It was all too sad. He was sold to a very rich racing fraternity in Limerick. He was growing taller still and now nearing four years of age – so was almost in the backward class in the world of horse racing. He fetched only one thousand, six hundred guineas in the sales, which was truly a measly sum. But without a 'how's your father', he wasn't really that useful until he appeared on a race course and showed his worth. My brother David, who knows more facts and figures than possibly the later Prince Monolulu, with or without a turban, said that 'Roman Warrior', our poor horse's ancestor, never raced until after his third birthday, as the whole family were giants, and needed much growing space. This clearly was the case with 'Barrie Boy'.

So we really did not do well on the deal, what with the weekly stable tab. We had parted with five thousand pounds or more over a period which included stable bills, and the low selling price, recouped very little.

'Barrie Boy's' half-brother, having held on to his private parts, had fetched nine thousand guineas in the same sale, which angered us to the verge of violence for our stupidity. The moral is never go in for the 'chop' for any reason if it can be avoided. And I don't think it is advice for horses alone. One thing is certain, that one day 'Barrie Boy' could, with the right tutor, show an aptitude for jumping fences. With his large frame and stalwart legs he may appear in the 'Grand National' or other over-the-stocks jamborees. I do believe he has retained his name, which could be a drawback or a bonus. Who knows? We may not have seen the last of him yet!

*****

Now everyone knows what backing horses and theatrical ventures have in common, You can lose the money, or your knickers, with no trouble at all. On a visit to the Urquharts' for lunch – we were presenting the 'Wizard of Oz' at a nearby theatre – Bob Urquhart mentioned that he had brought many foals into the world, and at this moment had one filly, 'Rowley', who was particularly captivating and had won everyone's heart with great ease.

'Rowley' had been born prematurely to a married lady, and was as frail and sickly as a filly could be for the early months of her life. The fact that she was eight weeks premature was not good.

Bob Urquhart persevered and gradually 'Rowley' began to fill out and become a very good looking filly. He suggested if I had a bit of money to spare, we could both own 'Rowley'. So I paid Bob the necessary cash and we both became partners of this delightful filly. She would be in my name at the Jockey Club, and I enquired if we might retain my colours from 'Barrie Boy', which we had never used, and they generously consented.

In January, nineteen eighty-four, 'Barrie Baby' was registered with the Jockey Club and at Weatherby's, and the name 'Rowley' was forsaken forever. The fact that she was out of 'Import', a most useful horse, and 'Evensong' meant it was not a family tree to be ignored. A relation, 'Night Nurse', had done us all a good turn several times when she came up with the winning recipe. She also lived on the farm, as we called Bob Urquhart's plantation.

In the next stall to 'Barrie Baby' was 'Teapot', another horse who provided the cream for the peaches many, many times when gracing the race tracks. Altogether, the scene was much more pleasing than pastures old.

A trainer of repute, Mr Charles B B Booth (I have no idea what the B B stands for) was suggested. He arrived for tea at the Urquharts', and was the life and soul of the party. A large man of at least fourteen stone, he could have made a living, I'm sure, as a light comedian. He has a dry sense of wit, and a little of the circus seems to be in his large and jovial frame. I had never heard of him until that day when we had lunch, but then on the other hand, he had never heard of me either.

This season he has saddled many horses, and has had winners, including some top notch horses, so his standing in the racing fraternity is good, and he is obviously a trainer to watch. He agreed to take our chestnut lady, and this proved to be a fruitful union. 'Barrie Baby' trained religiously, taking to the preparation like a duck to water, and all augured well for the future. All my friends said, "Stupid sod, he'll lose all his money again – just you see." For once they are wrong, and I didn't.

Bob Urquhart said little in the way of conversation that day, in between desert and coffee, but he was obviously pleased about the state of affairs. Jemima, with a continuous flow of conversation, took the stage, and Bob was content to be a good listener, only coming into the arena when we got back to the subject of horses. He is a man of the turf and very dedicated.

I was telephoned by Mr B B Booth one Saturday in April '83 to say that our horse was in danger of running at Beverley, then his idea was to run her at Redcar, then York. Alas, the rains came, and for thirty-two days we had nothing but more and more rain. Would our horse ever make an appearance in public before we were all relegated to mature character roles? As it turned out, we didn't have long to wait. 'Barrie Baby' had, after all, only been training for fourteen weeks, and to think she was ready for the thrills and spills of the race course was unbelievable – at least it was after our first experience in this neck of the woods.

With baited breath we waited for the chosen day. After all the delays and non-appearances our friends thought the horse was a myth! But even a flood has to subside some time. Waterlogged courses gradually began to drain before every bookmaker in the country had ulcers. One day the sun came out, just to show that it could, and everything looked good again. The swirling waters were all forgotten in the rush to get a tan and look healthy!

It was then conveyed to us that 'Barrie Baby' would definitely run on Friday June sixth, nineteen eighty-three, making her debut as a racer. Leicester race course was the chosen venue.

Friends and I made our way to Leicester via British Rail and there she was, looking every inch a champion – or so I thought. The sun had come out and all was well with the world. The race was the four fifteen and there were sixteen horses in it. 'Barrie Baby' was not in the betting so I put twenty pounds each way. Betting gives me the 'heebie geebees', it's all or nothing.

Disadvantages were many, the course was still soft from the weeks of rain and our horse hated rain and soft going, as did her parents before her. She had drawn an unfavourable number in the draw for positioning, and finally, the course started on a hill, so it was downhill at the very beginning. All very perplexing for a filly who was taking the air for the first time. We had all told our admirers of the situation, but it was agreed that caution was the keynote.

I stood on the bridge near the Champagne Bar and looked at the breathtaking scenery with Jemima and Bob. It was nearly as quiet as the hush before the Charge of the Light Brigade and Charles Booth was as restless as a native, and I swear crossed himself three times before they were off.

The favourite was 'Irish Slipper', a leprechaun as plain as a pikestaff, with little to recommend her. She had been placed fourth and then second, so she was the favourite, and the rest of the field were 'never wuzzers', meaning this was their debut. And this included 'Barrie Baby'.

The off!

Our excitement mounted as our horse did us all true justice, and won easily by eight lengths. Clearly an outstanding victory! Was I dreaming it, was this all a movie?

Her price was thirty-three to one, which would keep anyone off the streets for a few days. Champagne was the beverage we sipped to toast our victory!

The filly was as cool as a cucumber, not even sweating and clearly she was a horse to be reckoned with. Her 'finishing school'. Mr Booth's dormitory, had been worth every penny. In the Winners enclosure we posed for every kind of picture and the horse took it in her stride, giving a few smiles every ten minutes while the camera clicked. The journalists buzzed around and many lines were told for 'The Sporting Life' and 'The Sporting Chronicle' as well as all the other newspapers. The Urquharts were in seventh heaven, and Jemima took over the winners stall like a veteran, as she told the crowd about this new and most promising of horses.

'Barrie Baby' ran again and came second, then took a powder and came back in form by winning the 'Holstein Stakes' at Doncaster at the St Leger meeting in September. The day was a mucky one, with rain pouring down, so that the course was a veritable waterslide. We had learnt however, that our horse, far from disliking rain, took to it as well as Esther Williams had, long ago at Metro-Goldwyn-Mayer. She flew down the course like a thing possessed, taking her time in the early stages. 'Barrie Baby', when asked by Jemima to respond (it was the Ladies Amateur Race that day), obliged, and flew to the winning post!

In nineteen eighty-four she did not do well, whether out of sorts or ridden badly one will never know, but she did manage to win for the young apprentice, Simon Hodgson, giving him his first win, on his first ride. This, for Simon, will no doubt be a memory for him to cherish. But our filly did put up a super race to come sixth in the world famous Cambridgeshire in nineteen eighty-four and no one could ask for a better effort.

After a brief appearance at Chantilly in France in October, 'Barrie Baby' retired to mate with a recommended stud, and commence another career as a mother.

Obviously we have made money with this super little horse, so to all you sceptics who believe racing can be a 'mug's game', think before you smirk, if you please!

Chapter 16

Back on the Road

By now we had got to nineteen eighty-three, after five Swedish seasons and countless one night stands. In nineteen eighty-two I had done over forty star concerts, and I was beginning to wonder where next my caravan would rest. 'Handbag-wise' the going was tough, and more than once I thought I may have to seduce the bailiffs, but I always maintain that if you find yourself going to the wall, make sure you go in style!

Life was still a carnival, although some of the acts were changing. The world that was entertainment was always different from month to month, year to year, with a rhythm all of its own. A production that cost you a fortune last year will suddenly astound you by coming up like a gush of oil. A case in point was the current tour of 'The Rocky Horror Show' which John Farrow and the lads of the Theatre Royal, Hanley had masterminded. Six or seven years ago you couldn't give the damned show away if you tried – two impresarios did, and were seen returning to London with their tails between their legs.

Only a couple of years ago, the West End was wearing black, as if the plague had arrived at all its theatres. The current year it had been a record year and the West End is humming a different tune, coining useful dollars on the Great White Way! The provinces in contrast were for several years doing excellent business, now suddenly they are hardly taking a bean. So you can see that the living can be easy and then again sometimes downright miraculous. How can one gauge what is to come up trumps? The cards never lie, but my God, they can be temperamental.

So one asks will the train stop for success, change rails for adventure, or crash on the skids for me and my kind? Very trying if you have a lover who does not appreciate when they are playing your song. Theatre people have been called an acquired taste. If you do not have trouble with indigestion, they can be the salt of the earth, or at least the condiment of the day.

The profession is composed of many different mixtures and talents, some are as different as chalk and the highly praised cream cheese, but they all wear make-up, and are all entertainers, of one kind or another. I remember with warmth the case of the stripper in Sweden, who was hauled into court for unpaid taxes. The judge summed her up in more ways than one. In that fair city the money you make on your back is tax deductible! The old boy enquired of the maiden's assets, and without a murmur she lifted up her skirt and said, "There you are Judge!" So even in a tight spot, dialogue is not *always* necessary, though smelling salts sometimes are.

A day in the life of an agent or impresario holds unbelievable promise. The contacts you meet, enjoy, or spat with are comparable to a game of roulette. Everything is possible, as long as the dealer is not a magician. You can be broke one morning and clutching a million dollar contract in the evening. Your star 'most likely' may disappear to the world beyond in the afternoon without even a note, while the girl you chanced to meet in the grocery store captures the part of a lifetime when you send her to have cocktails with the latest American casting director. Who knows?

It is said that if one lives over again, one never makes the same mistakes. I say you make exactly the same ones, sometimes even quicker. Learning is almost complex business for many, and only the very gifted learn by their mistakes and refuse to dance to the same tune twice.

"The world is full of married men," says Jackie Collins, but bigamy has always been so much more exciting, and the snake of temptation is indeed a club member. So what is the message for tomorrow?

The message for tomorrow is to make merry and indulge in whatever takes your fancy. You will be criticised and talked about whatever you do. Thank God. But the way you really live your life is really up to you. I was asked what was the burning difference between life in the sixties when the 'As You Like It' was sparkling – and today. I told the radio reporter that there was a vast difference. Then you had nothing to worry about. But today if you don't develop AIDS, or cancer, you get mugged, raped or find yourself run over by a steamroller. No way can you win. It is truly later than you think.

So many names rush through my mind as I wind up the roundabouts of my carnival. In that now far off period, two boys whom I think will stay and rule the skies in the world we worship are Rupert Everett and Limahl. Rupert used to sit on my office floor on many a busy day before he became well known. He, like many other youngsters, was eager to be discovered, be it on film, television, stage or a mature star's slumberland. He was the chicken and the older person the mature hen. Rupert has the elusive charisma that haunted James Dean and will be a name on the marquee for many years to come. How right I was. Limahl is another child we commissioned into the profession, from whence he has stormed the heavens. The top ten, the million dollars singing to the youth of the world has paid off – he is rich. With his hair spiked with a thousand treatments of peroxide and even after he was sacked from Kajagoogoo for a misdemeanour or two, he soon acquired his wings and flew to the top of the tree, leaving the boys in the band grovelling to find a little bit of tinsel to make ends meet. He has subsequently disappeared to lands unknown. Another question unanswered.

The press are, as ever, ravenous for spicy items. They owe Boy George so much. Whatever has happened, and much has to Little Boy George, he has a quick and witty brain, an assured voice and the nerve of Arthur Scargill. He sings for his supper, and his potential is enormous. He cohabits with whom he chooses and the newspapers are avid to know the colour of the sheets on his bed. He is news when in town, and a serial when not. He is built to stay, and life lifespan could be lengthy. That is until George Michael becomes a movie star and Will Young marries Madonna.

Comebacks are never really successful. Perhaps only Gloria Swanson turned the rapids of yesteryear into the triumph of tomorrow. If you have been there once it is rarely as satisfactory when you return. Better to change the act, the image, the wardrobe and the mask and come back as an epidemic.

Rape is commonplace and yet millions write to Clare Rayner, who does her best. Why do the wrong people get the treatment? It is all a matter of luck. It governs us all our lives. True, some people court disaster, some misadventure. And in our world, jealousy reigns supreme.

We all have our favourite, here are two of mine.

Elizabeth Taylor, it was announced, would give a one woman recital of Shakespeare in New York. She had just bewitchingly confused 'Cleopatra' and mesmerised Richard Burton along the banks of the Nile, and the whole of Broadway was screaming to be present to see this pupil of the great company, Metro-Goldwyn-Mayer, give Mr Shakespeare a grilling!

Zsa, Zsa Gabor was there, loaded with diamonds, the weight of which nearly killed her. In the second act, when Miss Taylor had amazed her critics and taunted her rivals with a most entertaining rendering of the Bard, Miss Gabor rose to her feet. She, with her tiaras, gathered her mink around her shoulders and said in a voice loud enough to wake the dead, "My God, if she's not bad soon, I'll have to go home."

Ant *that* almost ended the lesson!

If it is not jealousy, it is power. Hedda Hopper once sent Joan Crawford a birthday present. It arrived in the midst of a party for five hundred, carried by two well-built native lads. Unwrapped, it revealed a skunk with a less than enchanting perfume and carriages were called early that evening.

"It was all *too* amazing!" said Quentin Crisp when questioned on the affair.

Tallulah Bankhead stunned London with her use of four letter words – beginning with f and working her way through other gems of the alphabet.

After the tour with Quentin Crisp, I had a meeting with

Jimmy Young. He was a middle-aged, almost nondescript man in appearance and he greeted me cordially. He was as cool as a cucumber at the harvest festival and mellow beyond belief. He had after all, done most things, and what he had not done, he had surely booked! He enjoyed hit records when we were still listening to Radio Luxembourg in the evenings because the BBC had not grown up and he had developed a congregation to hear his gospel, which extended from the Hebrides to Land's End. And probably into the jungle as well.

He seemed to me never to strive to get out of his closed circuit. He knew his goldfish bowl well and there he would swim. We discussed doing some one night stands when he would deliver to the stalls his message of life, sing a song or two, backed by five musical birds, and then answers questions at the font. Alas, alack, Jimmy either became too busy or didn't fancy the strain. A pity, as I feel he would have done so well, and I could have paid the milkman. Jimmy, these days, writes a column in the Sunday Express, on anything from politics to world affairs, a long way from crooning to the masses. A nicer man I have not met in a long time.

*****

Of all the world stars, there are three that stand out as beacons of light over the seas of mediocrity. The legendary Garbo is mentioned in almost everyone's lists as one of the most beautiful women of all time. An original, if ever there was one. She hit America with a 'Svengali' and then played the checker-board with such dexterity that even Louis B Mayer reached for his Alka-Seltzer. Greta Garbo was known to everyone living this side of the moon, and her fan mail was destined to be answered by over a hundred minions every week! She didn't need words. One look from her eloquent eyes and a thousand fables were told or demolished! She knew when to get off the train of tomorrow and if the station was not there, she created one!

She is alone in a field of poppies, a film star with the courage to wave it all goodbye at the height of her career, and retreat into the shadows she so adored. She did do a test for 'Anastasia' which would have been right for this ageless, ethereal, royal character. But although the rest set alight a million forest fires, she changed her mind at the last minute, and Ingrid Berman was brought back from the roasting at the Cross, and given the role which returned her to favour in America after an age of ridicule for her Italian misdemeanours.

If Garbo is a legend, what of Dietrich?

Both ladies leaned their craft when film making was a 'two and eight', but they braced themselves with the script for the woman they were to portray. They also learned the camera angles and accompanying know-how so that in later years they could direct a movie better than most!

I met Marlene Dietrich several times, and each meeting was more surprising. There is a lovely story which I believe to be true, that Miss Dietrich would appear on no stage that had not been scrubbed the very day she was to appear. In one Midland town the stage had not been swept, and with her opulent and expensive stage gowns, a nail or dirt would either rip them or cause irreplaceable damage!

Miss Dietrich got to the theatre around two o'clock, learned the state of affairs, gathered all the stage crew and house cleaners together, and made them stand for an hour while she scrubbed the stage on her hands and knees. You might say that you have heard that Marlene Dietrich had a fetish for housework and scrubbing in particular. That may be, but the lesson went home like a bullet to the lazy crowd posing as stage staff at that theatre.

Miss Dietrich believes that age comes from within, that if you feel young, you are young! And I wholeheartedly agree with her.

In her later stage concerts, Marlene came to sing more sad songs than happy ones, but her mesmerised audiences were so rapt and totally devoted they pretended not to notice. She toured as a solo attraction for many a year when her Hollywood star had finally waned. I am looking forward to reading her autobiography, one day, which I understand is written, but the publisher is having palpitations getting it into any shape or form. Miss Dietrich, with twenty thousand dollars advance, lies on her cushions nibbling an After Dinner mint and hardly opens her eyes to her agent's pleading.

Falling in love again is a national pastime. It was always so and not sponsored by the News of the World. All right, we are moths around a flame, but how powerful the candle that was Marlene Dietrich, and how eagerly we absorbed the colours and the aroma. Truly a great cabaret star. (I can still recall the twenty-eight curtain calls after only one performance). My last memory of her was possibly in the film 'Judgement at Nuremburg'. She was taking Spencer Tracy around Berlin to see the ruins, and after passing a half knocked-down club, we hear the strains of Lilli Marlene on a solitary accordion. Miss Dietrich turned to Mr Tracy and said, "You should have seen the old Berlin!" How true, and perhaps only Christopher Isherwood saw it all. I *wish* I had been there.

Alas, Marlene has gone, but how the memory lingers on!

*****

Mae West is the third flower in my daisy chain. She was before her time and was probably one of the cleverest and wittiest women alive. Stories abound of the lady, from the rumour that she never made love to anyone, let alone a man, to crazy suggestions that she was a hundred years old. Her four bodybuilders who back her stage act were there just to incite the audience. And for her? She only looked?

My favourite story of Mae West was when she was coming off stage at Las Vegas after an evening of complete bliss, when her coloured maid rushed forward (Butterfly McQueen had become a star by this time and was through with one liners), and said, "Mae, there's ten men waiting to take you home!"

"Send one back," said Mae, languidly. "I'm kinda tired tonight."

She stoked manhood when the seeds of war were being sown, and studs from here to China forgot Adolf Hitler, Mussolini and other clockwork oranges and longed to 'go up and see her some time'. That they might have been disappointed never entered their heads. The invitation was magnetic.

She brought Cary Grant to manhood, and made W C Fields love children. Mae West ruled an empire, and yet was never crowned Queen Oscar. Such are the rewards in the tinsel town. She rules another heaven now, but God knows where!

Live theatre and the cinema have been pronounced 'dead' or 'ailing' since the Boer War, but happily they will always succeed while they give the public what they want, for the poor fools have got to go somewhere when the permanent squint from television finally settles upon them. To see an adored player in the flesh is always one card up on any other.

The star system has come and gone and I, for one, mourn its going. But it must be said that many movies have got by without stars and that the movies have grown up. They are now fine and intelligent, studious and dedicated, where in the days gone by they were merely gay, workmanlike and stylish. Style is one commodity we do not have in abundance today.

Chapter 17

A Different Scene, Perchance

After I had been 'had' under the animal tent, as it were, (and I do mean more than once), it did occur to me it was time, perhaps, to move my carnival to another town. Or was it? I had been living for over twenty years in Central London, but better a province you know than one you don't and had life been that bad to me? I had become a native of London West Central 2, ratepayer of a district known as Camden. Not one as reasonable as Westminster, but then it does have more prominence and more majesty than poor old Camden. Westminster rules the left-hand side of Charing Cross Road with a much higher council tax and all the other trivialities that come with an area of London Town. However, we were located on the right-hand side of upper Charing Cross road near an area with an infamous record bordering squalid King's Cross, (although apart from drug peddling, drunkenness, begging, betting and fornication, King's Cross railway station is a pinnacle of virtue).

A period of adjustment, or possible reflection, seemed somewhat sensible. I had spent the seventies touring with a mixture of theatrical creatures, from Quentin Crisp to Mandy Rice-Davis, June Bronhill on a Tuesday to John Hanson on a Sunday. Wayne Sleep would be teaching Darren Day to pirouette. Our concerts encompassed everything from a touch of Ivor Novello to a medley with Kathy Kirby. I was still as stage struck as C B Cochran or Sylvia Young. So many people owed so much to Sylvia Young ('Who is Sylvia?' Indeed). She could spot talent even if it was passing on an express train. She coaxed, guided and moulded many youngsters who, without her genius, patience and strength would have probably been working in a biscuit factory or, if the Gods were good to them, slicing the best ham in Fortnum and Mason's. Recently Sylvia

Young opened her new school opulent and a joy. Students will feel 'posh' and Sylvia the Queen Of The May. No one deserves it more, for all the wisdom, encouragement, and advice she has given to so many over the years.

Yes, I was stage struck and could be still. But life was changing. It never stands still and neither does the world of show business, which seem to come along on an endless conveyor belt from the provinces, had grown up, knew a thing or two, and were not to be trifled with as in days of old. No longer was there a nubile body offered on a platter to anyone posing as an impresario, producer, casting director, or actor with connections as had happened in days gone by. No Siree! Would-be Maggie Smiths were more adult, perceptive... and that's only the girls! Even in order to get a lingering rope one had to offer at least an audition or meeting for a play, revue or pantomime on offer. And pantomime it invariably was. Boys also were nobody's fool. Some, we are told, might sell their body for a trip to the moon, though the price was more likely to involve featuring as a walk-on in some Scottish play or showing a flash of muscle in the musical 'Hair'. Midway through the eighties, revealing cameos became the province of the show 'Let My People Come' and you can take that anyway you like! When George Clooney calmly says he slept his way to the top and Rupert Everett swears he was a rent boy, nothing is sacred – even for a famously randy producer casting 'Snow White' in Rotherham.

There were some straight fellows around in my office with the most astounding stamina. They could please at least two would-be starlets before breakfast, helping to calm the middle-aged slags who always swear that the theatre is littered with queers. These chaps could recite Miller, Williams, or even Shaw whilst in the throes of a heady embrace. However, although I have always decreed that a kiss on the hand is quite continental, much further down can be treacherous.

Women, superior to me in matters of strategy, can always suss out the butch from the bitch and seldom waste time on a gilded lily who cannot get his cock up in a snowstorm, going instead for the real thing. The casting couch may be a thing of the past, but the ritual is as powerful as ever in its many changing disguises.

I had a girl on the books of the agency, Alice, who was the most amazing **** in the universe. Forever playing 'Snow White' (or 'So Shite' depending on the town), she would invariably, after putting the seven small perverts to their various pursuits, put on her hot pants and vanish with the man of her choice to an inn, lodging house or other guest room and fornicate until it was time for the Wicked Queen to take her heroin. After a while, Alice gave up the stage and married into the holiday business. She is still 'at it' in various countries whilst settling in her clients. Never very particular about which sex attracted her, she is still going strong and brings to mind that lovely old song of Noel Coward's – 'Alice is at it Again'.

Several drama schools send me a flow of students who, after three years' training, are sent out into the wide, wide world, having been taught to fly with precision. They select me principally as I like helping new talent, and many is the boy or girl I started off that has made it. Many agents do not bother with newcomers. They scream that, unless they make at least £200 a week in commission, they are not interested. In order to get on some agents' books, another racket that goes on involves having to pay a fee upfront for the privilege.

Still an agent, at least a theatrical one, I pressed and clamoured to stage and produce further concerts, revues and epics in more prominent and larger venues. As a producer, some fading stars and some new potentially attractive ones beckoned. Some friends of mine were not pleased. They argued I had toiled for ten years or more as an agent and had only made a living, not a fortune. Surely there were other avenues to follow that would make more gold pieces, for who knows what tomorrow might bring!

So there I was, like Fagin at the crossroads, reviewing the situation. If you get to the point of saying 'When I grow too old to dream', you possibly ponder on religion, or selling English tea and cream cakes on a faraway island. You never want the industry to think you are too old for the game. Oh, no!

I think I was on the verge of early sixties (I am never magic with figures – as my accountant will tell you), but in the end I re-joined the treadmill that is the entertainment world and started offering my wares to the theatrical managers. When you have been around for a year and a day this is not a problem. You know the manager of a venue personally enough to boast to him of the magic of the project you are suggesting. With a telephone call to this man who you know as a friend, business associate or a bloke that likes a gamble, you get a date for your show. The man is not a fool and knows you always deliver even if the stars you are presenting as the impresario (such a posh name) are mostly on the wane, although still attracting many loyal fans. The flavour of the month names are, naturally, with the bigger boys and play the grand marquees.

There are, of course, impresarios and then there are IMPRESARIOS, all of varying quality, texture and reliability. The manager of a theatre has to know the wheat from the chaff. One who does not is not long in the position of 'God Almighty', and, believe me, there are many charlatans on the road who are masters of deception and get away with murder. I knew one such fellow who, rather than hiring a spacious van, packed the whole of the scenery for his productions in the back of his car.

So here I was in the early nineties, once again contemplating many tours and concerts. Surely there were other ideas to follow. I had pondered on this more than once. But when you always eyed the big boys that had made it, or were on the verge, there was always tomorrow. Take Cameron Mackintosh (people are always amazed he did not come from the confectionary dynasty), whose meeting with Andrew Lloyd Webber changed the West End forever. Hitherto an empire which belonged to Binkie Beaumont of the great H M Tennant dynasty, now the whole look of London's theatrical offerings are an entirely different scene. If we talk of Lord Lloyd Webber, then we soon come to Tim Rice. I always remember him bobbing about as a musical director. He did a show for one of my clients called 'Salad Days' which always pops up somewhere or other and never paid his commission to me for the introduction. The interest on such a small offering must be gigantic in this year of grace.

Still a major player in the world of great West End theatre at that time was Harold Fielding. A very ordinary chap to look at, but what a career! He is remembered for all his many musicals from 'Gone With The Wind', 'Half a sixpence', 'Singing in the Rain' etc, through to his last show and perhaps his one total disaster 'The Great Ziegfield'. He died, an old and sad man as 'The Great Ziegfield' emptied his handbag and he had nothing to remind him of all the great shows and great successes. His death was almost unnoticed by press and TV. Talk about being only as good as your last show! Stage wise, this man was the nearest thing to Sam Goldwyn this country has ever seen. Yet the newspaper ignored him. Such is life on the seesaw called show business.

Another interesting man was Paul Raymond. He toured in the 40s and 50s and didn't have two halfpennies to his name. You would find him on a bill with Phyllis Dixey. His experience in the music halls taught him the value of a girlie undressed and, after a few naughty and nude revues in which the girlies were not allowed to move, he graduated to town with all the money he had saved and set up shop in Soho, opening an emporium for nudity and lovely girls. Called 'Raymond's Revue Bar', he got the lease for very little money and, with his profits, gradually bought up half of Soho. He died with scores of millions in the bank. A quiet and almost remote man, he was not a lot in conversation (but neither was Gypsy Rose Lee) and looked to all and sundry like a head waiter. Greying hair and a moustache, I knew him to speak to as we went to the same moderately-priced restaurant for supper.

So here I was in the valley of decision, a location frequented by so many for a variety of reasons. One thing was certain, I had to make a few bob. I needed a new scheme to open up the 1980s and beyond. Should I open brothels and become a 'madam'? My good friend Cynthia Payne had made quite a living at that and became a celebrity at the same time.

A nicer gal one could never meet. "Decisions, Decisions," as the nun said to the vicar as he lifted the cane. I must say at this state that one hates to say goodbye to anyone. Happily they disappear, or most do, without ceremony. We all have to go and I, for one, visualise a tremendous gathering up in the heavens for my arrival as so many of my friends had departed early. I can see them all plotting dates, tours and screaming "Where the hell have you been?" I believe that when you are born the day you die is decreed. So when I go I shall know the scene. One hates to say goodbye at this stage to either professionals of theatres (and a few of them have kicked the bucket). The only goodbye I have ever advocated was Miss Garbo waving farewell in the final scene of the movie 'Queen Christina'. Who could follow such an act as hers?

I always think the role of an actor is akin to a minister of religion. They have to wow the crowd every Sunday from the pulpit (without some of the equipment we have on the stage), and do very well. They have to delight the mixed crowd they attract from spinsters, queens (not royal ones), married couples and those just curious. They live on a pittance and are always on the lookout to make a few more bob in other ways during the week. My parish vicar was very helpful in letting us store scenery in the local hall adjacent, though he would not have been so happy if he had seen the shenanigans the ASM got up to with the students. Vicars are all younger these days, and know more. Everyone knows collections are not what they were and staunch churchgoers have long gone to the organ loft in the sky, so we miss their contributions. Also choir practice is not what it was. Young men used to fondle ladies of their choice behind the curtains at the end of the hall, where the curtains obligingly used to hide the carnal sins. In my day one used to hide behind the tombstones for a little hanky panky, but this seems to have gone out of fashion. I always remember what a splendid vicar Spencer Tracy used to make with Walter Pidgeon a good second.

Prior to our adventures up and down the country in the eighties, we had managed to get ourselves a secretary, or rather a PA to sort out our many tangles.

Angela Graham-Jones was the name. A tall, striking miss, with a cascade of blonde silken hair that went beyond her shoulders. Angela, straight after her teens, had met and fallen for a tall ballet dancer called Sebastian, which was fine as it went well with the Graham-Jones that followed. He danced like a thing possessed, did the ballet pointe with aplomb, and altogether was quite a dish, and a dish that Angela went for... and how! Then Sebastian pined for foreign parts (meaning locations) and after a while the romance had retreated from the marriage. Sooner rather than later, Angela was on her own and a divorced lady. Angela's mother was not at all amused. Jacqueline Lacey was a natural for shopping at Harrods and having lunch at Le Caprice whilst wearing (almost every day) a most becoming hat, with veil. She dwelt in a very fashionable area in town and, although at this time busy on her own career, her plans for Angela did not include a marriage and divorce in double-quick fashion.

Angela became a most indispensable creature at our offices in Denmark Street and much of my success at that time was due to her sterling work, excellent memory, and personality. She warmed to one, even on an initial meeting, and artistes who were clamouring to come on my books were very taken with the flaxen-haired miss. She immediately came to mind when I was casting for a fairy and she took her wand to parties and revivals of Hunt Balls, what was more natural than that she played Fairy in one of my seasonal operas, after all her wand was something to behold! Thus we got our office into some kind of shape and our productions of a quality that might get them properly noticed.

The eighties has arrived and we had already made plans to stage shows in Sweden. However we were to meet two Liverpool gentlemen who were to change life for me once again and hurl us back to the pawnbroker whom we should have married many years ago when he first became a fan of ours.

We had enjoyed presenting pantomime at the New Brighton Floral Pavilion for six years and this would have been our seventh, but the council suddenly realised we had made a reasonable profit for two years and when we broke even, quite forgetting the four previous ones, and desired a change of management and several stars for their yearly escapade into show business. New Brighton for the uninitiated was then a curious shanty town, with shops and houses almost desolate as if the Pied Piper had driven his rats through. It was a perfect setting for a movie thriller.

The top dog at the Floral Pavilion at New Brighton in those days was a most amiable gentleman called Ray Wood. Aged about fifty and not a fool in any way, he made our years at that venue very worthwhile and enjoyable. He was aided by his assistant Paul Halliday, who these days runs the joint since poor Ray succumbed to a disease and left us for other palaces in the skies. Paul has proved a most capable and excellent manager for the old Pavilion. Latterly in this year of grace it has been tarted up and renovated to the tune of over a million and has moved up from a Number Two theatre to very much a Number One.

During my six years presenting pantomime at the theatre, on one of the last days of the run, I always staged a party for the cast, staff and helpers, in fact anyone who had contributed to the show. At the party, over a hundred guests feasted on a mammoth spread, with everything from vol-au-vents, turkey legs, chicken of every variety to sandwiches of the highest order, all washed down with endless punch and wine.

It came about that the Royal Court Theatre, Liverpool, attracted our attention. Ray had hinted that the council was possibly looking to change the management for their pantomime productions in the coming years. That is how we came to look for a Liverpool theatre, just far enough away to still attract the fans we had made in the six years we had been at New Brighton. We had already noticed that the once great Royal Court Theatre in Liverpool was empty and deserted. A formidable palace in days gone by, it belonged to the famous chain of theatres for Howard and Wyndham.

We made contact after enquiries with the two gentlemen who, it transpired, had acquired the lease, or so we thought. I always held the feeling that they had driven taxis for years and had suddenly won the pools. They knew fuck all about the theatre, but that really goes for little, as many profess to be thespians of vast experience and also know nothing.

Clearly they had come into money or sold their bodies to a rich bidder. One was short and looked like Bob Hoskins, the other was more trendy, wore trousers that were skin-tight and showed off his attributes superbly, and was altogether smoother. We were now into November and these two jack-the-lads knew that pantomime and Christmas was something that made money even at a dark and neglected theatre. So after a discussion and a lot of thought, we all agreed it could be a good idea to invite that old harridan Snow White to gather her little people together and delight the kiddies of Liverpool.

A deal was struck giving us a generous percentage and Angela and I set about collecting a cast that would do us credit and would be easy to work with. This turned out to be a very wise thought as the irritations that hit us later on were massive and would have thrown all but the dedicated. Thus we acquired ourselves a cast for this forthcoming mammoth production at The Royal Court Theatre, Liverpool.

An army of goblins, gnomes and camp homing pigeons were sent up to Merseyside to spread the message and get all the mums, and grandmothers round to the theatre to book for the festive attraction.

Wheeler and Woolsey as we called the Liverpool owners who held the lease, had arranged a press reception. Their helpers ran a duster through the stalls and dress circle, someone polished the brass – probably two rejects from Coronation Street, lovely girls besotted by Ajax and the spotless results it achieved. Suddenly we had a fearful turn, something like the one you experience when you hear that Cilla Black is announced to sing a song. It hit us hugely that the theatre was freezing.

Apparently heating was not on the bill. At the dress rehearsal the place was so cold the mice were frozen and if the four stage hands were not on cocaine then they were certainly customers of poppers. Wheeler and Woolsey were of little help, wallowing in their new role as impresarios. They spent their time wining and dining their many new pals and showing off, just stopping to murmur that all would come right... we would see. And this was only the heating. The electrical wiring was like a maze and the lighting board as old as Barbara Cartland. Perhaps we should have sat down and thought a little, but at least we had a theatre and didn't grumble at all. We got through the dress rehearsal unscathed. Never was there a moan that the joint was colder than a polar bear's nose. Sometimes one would wonder whether the scenery was in the right place at the right time, but as everyone knows pace is the thing and everything must run like an express train.

Simon Browne, a superb comedy actor who was originally trained in mime, starred as the Wicked Queen. He made his costumes himself and they would have delighted Danny La Rue and astounded Ceri Dupree (the new headliner who arrived at that time in the world of female impersonation). Simon was assisted in the needleroom by ten nuns and a lesbian with nimble fingers. All were adroit at the art of threading needles and riding the sewing machines as if it were a nag in the Derby.

Mr Browne was a dame majestic and in the league of Les Dawson, Tommy Trafford, George Lacey, Rogers and Starr, and the newer dames and sisters at that time of Nigel Ellacott and Peter Robbins and Simon Bashford and Mark Two, and Keith Hopkins.

Simon Browne never made Buckingham Palace, but toured a few noble hostelries. His last major success was the sergeant in several productions of 'The Pirates of Penzance', then he vanished forever and probably works for the Salvation Army.

Another in our company was Anthony Donnelly, a handsome lad by any standards who played the prince. It said male on his equity card, but what Errol Flynn would have made of him I could not hazard a guess.

The advance bookings were superb, something like many thousands of pounds. Wheeler and Woolsey were visible every evening up to the 22nd December, basking in the praise of their new admirers. Even the Gods were with us, as the weather changed and it turned really mild. So, we never worried about drawing monies for the salaries from the box office takings since we were seeing so many punters at every show.

Our official opening was on a Saturday (after two previews the day before) and Sunday we had the day off. Angela and I arranged to draw some cash and with that in mind, we both tripped back to town to answer the mail and feed Maud, the cat.

We returned to the Royal Court, Liverpool on the Monday before Christmas and Wheeler and Woolsey were nowhere to be found. The box office ladies were busy though. I enquired what the advance was like and had to sit down when they told me; Twelve thousand. We had to find Wheeler and Woolsey quickly.

Angela made a cup of the strongest tea you could imagine and we paused... and thought... and paused again. Where were the two comedians? All their telephone numbers were disconnected and we were fucked. Ambushed! They had done a runner with all the money. Twenty-five thousand quid.

I looked at Angela and she looked at me. Whatever were we to do? We quickly went through the friends, lovers and ex-lovers who had a few bob, but, on the eve of Christmas, finding everyone was not easy. If you had a few bob, you were probably lazing away in a province far from Britain. Angela made another cup of the strongest tea imaginable, got out her packet of cigarettes and tried to calm both of us down. We decided that nothing was impossible, the Royal Court was a large house and bookings were coming in at a tremendous rate. We decided to keep cool and this is exactly what we did.

We visited the box office where both ladies were selling tickets with abandon, quick as lightning. We questioned them intently, but they had only been engaged three weeks before and obviously knew as little as we did about Wheeler and Woolsey. They were as much in the dark as we were. It was madly important that the cast of this operetta knew nothing. We were petrified in case any of them walked. As several had asked for an advance in salary, to keep them quiet, we dipped into our handbag and gave them what they requested.

Fortunately, Lady Luck and the Royal Court were faithful and we achieved takings of some stature over the course of the run. We were able to pay decent salaries to everyone and could close our chronicles of pantomime at the Royal Court, Liverpool, with style. Angela and I learnt much from the episode and think that we shall meet with Wheeler and Woolsey to do battle, one day or another.

After the show ended, Denmark Street seemed not a jot different and our usual routine started to return with the New Year. I passed around our robbery to the many shady boys I knew, promising great rewards for success, but alas Wheeler and Woolsey seemed to have gone for the border and are now probably running a brothel with an adjacent bar in faraway Mexico.

A few months after our trials at the Royal Court, Liverpool, I was recommended during Lent to a showman who was an impresario and gold prospector by the name of Neils Wenkens (a name not to forget in a hurry). Neils was Danish and had presented shows all over Europe for many years and had even masterminded many tours by major artistes in this country, so he knew how many beans made five like a veteran. Many big names owed much to this sandy-haired Danish gentleman; Glenn Miller and his Orchestra, Liza Minelli, Lorna Luft, The Platters – just to name a few. He looked not unlike Herbert Marshall, a fashionable actor in the days of Garbo and Dietrich.

He ruled Copenhagen, his native city, in more ways than one and I was excited to meet such a guy. Playing the Tivoli Gardens, part of his producing empire, had long been a goal of mine and I had always wanted to know whether Hans Christian Andersen was gay or not! As we later knew of Danny Kaye's dalliance with our own Sir Laurence Olivier, it was a matter of great importance! Neils presented a superb trio called 'The three Danes' year in year out and they paid for his breakfast regularly. He was a salesman in the great tradition and I often wondered whether his papa was a travelling salesman, a breed so long lamented in the world of country fairs and certainly in show business.

Many publicity agents I know couldn't sell their own bum in a famine and they are not the only ones I know. I will tell you about certain press agents later on and that will take many pages. However, Neils Wenkens was a superb publicity agent and could persuade the Dutch to buy tulips.

Mr Wenkens wanted to present English plays in English in Stockholm. Why, I have never known, but I was delighted to be involved as it was work for me and my actors. I had been suggested by a piano player in Copenhagen, one Tom Howard, whom I met when he worked in summer season for several years in Newquay for Ronnie Brandon and Dickie Pounds, great summer season specialists who are long gone now to the home in the sky. Tom was tall as a mountain and sturdy, but possessed a ready smile and wit, and played the old Joanna like a thing possessed. The upshot of his recommendation was that a ten week season was planned in the spring of 1982 which was to prove so successful that we stayed on for several years at the old Jarla Theatre in Stockholm. English plays were much sought after and proved to be a sensation with the Swedish masses, especially high school students and scholars in places of high learning. The youths and adolescents who were the hard core of colleges and convents in the Scandinavian climate, turned out to be beautiful, knowledgeable and into sexual matters like none else. They were far slower in the bed than our own sixteen year olds, and one eruption in four hours was, I fear, the norm, but they could make hay like a whirlwind and were beautiful with it. Their complexions were indeed kissed by the sun and, whatever sex you fancied, it was all pure gold. And did they appreciate good theatre? Oh yes, be it Jane Austen, Agatha Christie or Ray Cooney!

As an agent and sometimes casting director, I had a nucleus of good players to adorn a strong play be it in Stockholm, Athens or Istanbul. The initial idea of a season appealed to me greatly. I liked the man behind it and a deal was struck. We would be guaranteed enough shekels to rehearse, transport and stage the agreed play season and I quickly assembled the cast, producer and a set market to put together a production. Then I had to seduce a ferryman and take the bloody thing over without charging too much. Richard Franklin, an old friend and most accomplished actor, came in to direct our first piece, an Alan Ayckbourn play called 'Relatively Speaking'. It had several things going for it. A light comedy piece by one of our most popular playwrights, it has only four in the cast (which helps greatly when totalling up your employee costs), and a set which is not too difficult to construct or too costly.

It came to pass that Swedish producer Tommy Iwering came on board. It is always a good thing to have a native as part of the set-up and so this was the case. Neils was short and stocky, Tommy was as tall as a steeple, well made, and looked very much like a rather large mountain bear. His thin glasses were always perched on his large nose and he looked very much like a musician of the operetta. Indeed, Tommy had a father who was well known in Sweden as a violinist of repute. Tommy knew his hometown like the back of his hand. Neils set the scene and Tommy captained the ship.

'Relatively Speaking' went down a storm at the Jarla Theatre. Neils and I cast come splendid players from my agency, proven actors with style and no grand airs. Simon Clarke was leading man, a strong type whose parents had him in the autumn of their days, which made sure he was never a teenager. Neil France and Maggie Ryder were a joy on and off stage with personalities to admire, plus ready wit and panache (always helpful when one is selling a show). They were complemented by the fourth actor, Suzanne Peveril – a spinster of the parish, who has since absconded to the land of the Kangaroo and the uncertainties of Melbourne.

Neils was a past master at marketing. Along with Tommy, he circulated the news that an English case had landed. The schools and colleges tipped in. the production being in English by a renowned English writer convinced many teachers that here was a splendid chance for the students to test out their language skills. The play and cast were a swift hit in Sweden and a good time was had by all, not least Messrs Wenkens and Iwering who got some gold pieces in their pockets. 'Relatively

Speaking' paved the way for many more play seasons at the Jarla Theatre. Soon after, Neils Wenkens had to bow out to pursue his many adventures at the Tivoli Gardens, Copenhagen, and other outposts. Unfortunately he passed away suddenly earlier this year at only sixty-one.

In the several other seasons that followed, we had a variety of different directors working for us. One, a certain Richard Jacques, decided to set up an opposition company and later romped off with Tommy's PA to open up across town. If Tommy had owned a shotgun Mr Jacques would have been in serious trouble.

With an agency to run alongside our conquests in Europe, life was never dull and occasionally proved to be very exciting.

Back in central London, in Denmark Street (known as Tin Pan Alley in the business as its main trading was selling musical instruments of every kind, mostly guitars, for pop stars), we rented a whole floor at No 4. We had six desks and so were able to hire four out to help meet the rent. Eventually, we shared this office with three other associates. At one desk were two friends we had met and shared pie and chips with one dark evening. They now decided to enter show business as producers and started plotting tours as if they were Zeigfield. Young and ambitious, Mr Philip Permitt was small, Jewish and excitable. He could sell a bucket of sand to an Arab. His partner Nick Ranceford-Hadley was tall, handsome and laid back. Cautious, astute and not carried away by either a gold rush or monsoon, he only believed an idea after a ten minute meditation and then he still had to be wooed. He was a perfect foil for young Mr Permitt. They plotted, schemed and interviewed actresses by the ton, especially the ones who were pretty, witty and haveable, and their first tour was set. 'Two and Two Makes Sex' was always a winner and so it was once again. That lovely actor Henry McGee was starring and the boys could not have wished for a better actor or more faithful friend. They toured the hills and dales and made some really lovely gold.

A second and third tour followed, again with the solid and helpful Henry McGee. Once more the tours showed some profit for the boys to build their sandcastles on. Then they got more ambitious and launched into a tour of one of the large scale musicals, 'A Chorus Line'. There's nothing wrong with 'A Chorus Line' except too much dancing and not enough melody, but, with a fairly large cast and an even larger handbag required to pay them out of each Friday, their fortunes dwindled and they ended up much poorer. Then they moved further along Denmark Street and shared an office at the top of the house with a personal manager who kept getting his throat cut from old admirers. La Permitt now is out of the scene and the guarded Mr Ranceford-Hadley works for the reputable Noel Gay Organisation.

A friend of the Permitt – Hadleys was Anthony Blackburn. He was carrot headed, small and sharp and assisted me on several tours up north with such delicacies as 'The Wonderful Wizard of Oz' and that pair of strumpets 'Hansel and Gretel'. We did a couple of seasons together escorted by another friend, a muscle boy of great determination by the name of Howard, but known to all and sundry as Muscle Pete! He gave a massage a complete new meaning. He was from Lancashire and had three wives to my knowledge. Muscle Pete was a masseur before Boyz newspaper and The Pink paper were born and he could teach those lads something!!! Howard was a great pal and did much work as an extra, a model with muscles and then as an assistant stage manager with small acting parts. He was doing quite well until a tour with Ken Platt where Howard was booked as ASM. After disagreeing with a bumptious stage manager, he decided enough was enough and kicked the guy straight in the balls. Muscle Pete went back to being a masseur seeing to his clients. From then on he was busy in the hotel trade with the baby oil!

Another friend who worked with us at the Denmark Street abode was Marion Haywoode. Marion was a black lady of great stature and an agent of much spunk and attack. She represented mostly musicians of every shape and size. Her husband, Don Haywoode, was very much a star in his own right. She had two devastating daughters, Sidney and Emma. Sid, known as Haywoode, had a big number one and earned masses of shekels for a time. Her sister Emma has done several most pleasing records and waits for her turn to go to the ball. Marion is a plump and weighty lady, not unlike Ella Fitzgerald. A toughie, she makes Annie Oakley look like a Sunday School teacher. She knows her music backwards and her musicians even more so. A friend in every way, we still meet occasionally and discuss the gossip of the day. I always assume she will pop up with one or both her daughters on TV and then history will be made.

From our fortress in Tin Pan Alley we went forth through the years doing what we did best, producing shows and managing our stars, though always with an eye out for a new opportunity.

Chapter 18

Every Stage can be Different

We had travelled through the eighties in rapid style. I seemed to have encompassed already a passage of time as long as one of Cecil B De Mille's spies. I had witnessed the death of the music hall, the touring revue and the stationary nude model was no longer the most dating of attractions. Impresarios, a mixed bag at the best of times, had been and gone, clutching mink if not sable, but many with barely the train ticket to return home to an ageing mama.

Being a showman of versatility, I grieved for the many old timers who had left us, whether to present epics or delights in some distant heaven or to light the torches for many more who would follow them, I know not. It seemed that life had seasoned and changed, especially in the world of cinema, as what was caviar in the forties was merely ham and eggs in some movie marquees in the eighties.

Many of the starlets from the seventies had graduated to full-blown stardom in the eighties, becoming household names and attracting vast crowds at movie premieres. Some had given up the trail, a few had taken to working for charity, others entered politics and some had realised the might of the pen and become gossip columnists of wit and truth. Several chorus girls I knew became nuns and pursued religion as fiercely as once they had courted opportunity and fame.

Television had become even more powerful and created characters so well loved and revered that to flit to the pictures and miss their favourite TV soap was unheard of... so great was the power of the box. No longer would drama students crave part of the year in the theatre, the magic of a starring role in 'The Glass Menagerie' or 'All About Eve' or some equally well-loved epic. No, it was to the small screen their attentions graduated and, to many, the idea of gaining stage experience before TV exposure was anathema.

Life upon the wicked stage can be eventful. Promiscuous, uncertain, possibly disappointing... and sometimes a delight. Mothers had for many a year spurred their children on to try the magic of the greasepaint, the lure of the spotlight, and the glamour and glitter that would accompany such a debut. Sometimes the enthusiasm of Mama engulfs the child for, in so many cases, Mama had failed to have a go at this most desired of professions herself and hoped to bask in the success of their daughter or son. By the nineteen eighties boys were openly encouraged to go into the theatre, for no longer, as in the forties, was a life upon the stage for a lad regarded as labelling him permanently as being 'a bit the other way'. Young ladies, as in preceding generations, dreamt of becoming a star, a leading lady in movie land or possibly the wife of a superstar with wealth untold, or even perhaps as impresario of quality.

Some parents, on the other hand, still declare a stage career a most risky proposition. A kiss on the hand is one thing, but a finger or two on one's thigh is another. In this business it is widely known that being a virgin can be quite problematical, in more ways than one and what goes on occasionally in the wings of a theatre certainly confirms that sex is possibly a four letter word. Some, of course, decree that there are only four safe trades to follow; the undertaker, baker, the candlestick maker and the brothel keeper. All demand dedication and a certain flexibility of timetable, especially at weekends with the latter profession.

If all else fails though, one can always go into the church. Most of the training in this most arduous of trades involves the learning of lines for the sermons. To captivate the congregation, from those confirmed religious churchgoers to those hordes of middle-aged women who fall in love with the vicar, is a most necessary thing also. Regardless of his status in the marriage market, these female devotees pander to him and his every request as if he was the most spoilt creature on earth. It is no wonder where a vicar gets his confidence from. Women, in the middle of their lives, scream to prepare tea for the vicarage, sandwiches for the choirboys and jumble sales for charity. For them, being granted the privilege of ringing the bells on a Sunday is the pinnacle of fame.

Now however, we were in a different time. Drama and stage schools were building and enjoying reputations, some of the best including Guildford School of Acting Mountview and Webber-Douglas. RADA still had the reputation of being 'stuck up' and 'superior' which did not go down so well with all the students' parents as drama grants had not even been invented. Feeling myself to be of Variety extraction, I personally think a couple of months on the road with a play or musical (or possibly a season in repertory in such a town as Newquay or Weston-Super-Mare) can teach you more in five or six weeks than three years taking in the histrionic arts for which you would have to pay.

Nowadays though, I do have several good friends who run most worthy establishments in London and across the country and carry out this essential training work in the drama schools. Some are commendable, some haughty and some just adequate, but they do disgorge a steady stream of youngsters who leave the village and, joining in our carnival, provide The Stage newspaper with flourishing sales. If you are one of these aspirants, make sure you have a quick brain to learn your lines or else stick to a career in haberdashery.

My agency was popular and thriving. It catered for the students who pour out of drama schools each year and I have been able to point so many of them in the right direction. David Easter is still starring in soaps. In between romances, Darren Day is earning a hefty fortune in pantomimes and soaps. His hefty fee is heightened still further by coverage in various newspapers of his courting of society's favourite young ladies. Dick Condon, an impresario and manager of the excellent Theatre Royal in Norwich, rang and begged me to help Darren, whom he had seen in a local talent competition. Dick had signed him on the spot and then had thought on reflection that he might not have the time to launch the boy, whose impressions were first rate and could rival Beryl Orde, an impressionist of quality who toured the halls in the 1940s. Some of my older readers may remember Beryl. Dick Condon knew I was as busy as a bee making honey on a Friday, but Darren Day had talent coming out of his arse and I assured him I would start displaying Darren's talents in my weekly variety shows without delay. A very talented impressionist with a cheeky grin, I included him in a Frankie Howerd special without more ado, and gave Frankie Howerd something to think about.

Agents are a funny breed and much depends on their horoscope, but a good manager in any age is hard to find. I have never wished to be a personal manager, much too demanding and restricting, at least for me. Alright, there is more money for the manager in this game. Ten per cent is certainly not his fee, more likely thirty per cent. I, myself, have never really got upset when a talented and ambitious youngster, whom I had raised from birth as it were and guided through the minefields of the business, leaves me. I say this, although it is a bit of a lie as the first child to do this to me caused me to sit down and cry like a baby. It cured me and I never did it again. Now they come and they go, but so does life.

Being an agent is a gruelling job and time consuming but, when you get a good day with a victory and your endeavour results in a magic job, then the irritations go overnight and life as an agent is bliss.

Like every business, there are sharks and alligators out to prey on unsuspecting newcomers. They pounce, ready to promise the earth and riches galore in return for a joining fee of something like fifty pounds or more. The piece of paper they produce is worth analysing with great application, as you could be signing your life away. Efforts have been made from the powers that be to curb such practices and licence only legitimate and worthy individuals.

'The Stage' newspaper is a journal that has been around since Jiminy found his inner Cricket. It is informative and carries blocks of advertisements announcing vacancies of every description. The people required are varied; chorus girls, dwarves (one has probably absconded from the troupe), vocalists with amazing tones, musical directors who can conduct a thousand violins, stage managers with expertise. The paper's layout has broadened with experience. It has grown from being the fledgling it was in journalism and can now register as a most necessary periodical, very helpful and essential for people in the trade, especially unemployed lap dancers. Many years ago there was another periodical 'The Performer', but this went the way of all flesh or print in no time at all.

Another avenue to success in the world of twinkling lights is that of commercials. They come on incessantly on TV channels and it has been rumoured that many are more entertaining than actual programmes. It is a most competitive world and commands a different type of professional. The odds are a hundred to one to land a contract, but if you are paid for the actual shoot you can then look forward to either repeat fees over a lengthy period when the commercial is aired regularly or a buy-out of stature. Many artistes have made a career out of a single advert and become household names, forever afterwards wearing mink instead of mackintosh. A great example is Lorraine Chase. One big advert and she moves on and develops into a stunning actress of the television screen in such shows as 'Emmerdale'.

Fringe theatres have been springing up, some of them good, some of them horrendous. In the eighties I wrote a lunchtime frolic called 'The Dressing Room'; three separate stories in one bill. We opened the Bush Theatre, Shepherd's bush and ran for several weeks to very good business indeed. We had a husband and wife team starring (who meant nothing to anyone but were superb in every way), Joe Cook and Jo Beadle. Very well known in the one and nines, and complete strangers to the dress circle. Joe was small and dapper and Jo was a pretty looking secretary type. The third is this triangle was a youth we discovered called Ian Kellgren. Ian was an excellent juvenile lead and I was lucky to have such a team. Ian went on to many good parts in repertory and eventually became a producer. The fringe has grown from its early days and recently has achieved many successes, in some cases with direct transfers into the West End. The King's Head, captained by Dan Crawford, is a pub with a large back room and most uncomfortable seats, but has featured many current star names and some on the way down. Sadly, Dan Crawford died but the pub and theatre has been taken over, better seats installed and we look forward to a new exciting chapter in its history.

As ever in the business, there are performers who will not consider fringe theatre. Too tatty or provincial they scream, but many a star approaching obscurity had been glad to be offered a role in fringe, perhaps in a strong revival to remind theatregoers they are still around and capable. On the other hand, many a novice has seized a chance to be on stage in a fringe production and gone on to greater things from there. For every artiste that takes up the profession and becomes an Equity member, only one in ten remain on the book when middle-age sets in. Women especially are very active in the theatre in their twenties and thirties and possibly drift away after years in turbulent waters with fragile remuneration... but they do look back to their 'bookable' period when their figure and their beauty were the rage and height of adornment and the world of entertainment promised wonderment of every kind in the profession known as show business.

A girlie must know her onions and how to look after her jewellery. After possibly a wedding or two and a few small roles in tours and festivals, a girl has to look ahead to the future and possibly seek a position and something more reliable in some other profession. As one always says 'nothing ventured is nothing gained', but luck plays a large part in the world we are discussing.

Naturally, one should really know which part of the profession to aim for, be it as a dramatic actor/actress, soubrette, chorine or cabaret artiste. Each has its own rewards, but it is always a good thing to know one's capabilities. Variety again has different demands and one always imagines nubile young ladies being pursued by a gaggle of old men, but this image has been updated and, although many butch men go after the most immature actresses, sex is not the four-letter word it was made out to be. These days youth is not at all vulnerable and it knows how many beans make five. So, a quick pass by an over-zealous male is usually spurned. Mind, here there are many in the business who fornicate like rattlesnakes, and it has not hindered their careers one bit. Another factor to consider is that some men may be gay, bent or queer… whichever title you favour. It is possible for women to travel down the yellow brick road and not be hassled too much.

Many artistes play themselves… I am a good case in point. They adapt their personage to the character they are playing. If they have a distinctive voice, they become as well known for their speech and personality as for their so-called acting. They just play themselves in various forms and way to complete the picture and become possibly better known as a star than a character actor. This is very common in the world of films and television and the names I put in this category include Basil Rathbone, C Aubrey Smith, Margaret Rutherford, Errol Flynn, Hugh Grant and Joanna Lumley. This principle can apply to the stage as well as the screen.

I am always conscious of living another year, but still forget that everyone else is a year older also. Some show it, others manage to remain the same, a shining example being Joan Collins. Time waits for no one, but it travels so quickly that one scarcely realises where it has gone and how. I always think of the beautiful one liners from the great Marlene Dietrich dealing with the passage of time. To grow old is natural but to show it is unforgivable.

Chapter 19

There's more to Change than Trains in Crewe!

It is the year of 1983. After a spring of discontent where bookings were sparse on the theatrical production front and the casting of soap operas a little thin on the ground, I thought I spied a new opportunity in the profession's theatrical bible, aptly called 'The Stage'. Published every Thursday, 'The Stage' is a newspaper read by has-beens, never-wassers, hat check girls, waitresses and the merely hopeful, but still it is nevertheless a trade paper of distinction and topicality. I chanced to see an advertisement for an administrator for the Lyceum Theatre, Crewe – thereby announcing that there was something else in this Cheshire town apart from a station and trains.

The Lyceum Theatre was a small, lovely old Edwardian Theatre which had, in the past few years, enjoyed a most chequered career. Closing more times than a Jewish matron's lips, the last occasion had been merely two years before when the Arts Council, playing one of their favourite games, (Eeny, Meeny, Miney, Mo – who shall be the next to go?) gave the poor old Lyceum the chop so that it closed without even a firework display.

I knew the joint having played it a couple of times, firstly with John Hanson the musical comedy actor (on that day the heavens were definitely not blue) and, secondly, with my children's show 'Tales From Hans Christian Andersen'. The latter performance must have been in the late seventies and it certainly did not slay 'em. The theatre was at that time administered by an old friend, Leslie Parker-Davies. Leslie has an insatiable sense of humour and a temper to rival a thousand foxes when given the slip by a solitary hound. He is nevertheless pure 3-D and an entertainment not to miss. Once a friend of PD (as his fans and enemies alike call him), he is utterly faithful and as dependable as Marks & Spencer's.

I first came across Leslie at the Gateway Theatre, Chester, otherwise known as Fort Knox due to the fact that the building, pure cement surrounded by a walled fortress, is most unattractive. One particular day I had been summoned to the walled city to see their current attraction: 'A Funny thing Happened On The Way To The Forum' (and the Forum had nothing on the Gateway Theatre on this particular night). Keith Hopkins, the Welsh singer, our favourite juvenile lead and a close friend, was playing the sex symbol, Hero, in this tale of Roman fornication. With his legs so dolly, he would have given Dorothy Ward a bad time. He was a raving success, and the production was a delight. It was directed by Julian Oldfield, a producer of note, who later moved on and became a casting director for Thames Television. Among the inmates of 'A Funny Thing Happened On The Way To The Forum' was Matthew Kelly, in a small part playing a eunuch with ideas. Matthew later burst upon the West End scene as the backward and gormless son in the smashing play 'Funny Peculiar', which was berthed at the Garrick Theatre. He shot to fame from then on and quickly became a well-known TV name in such trifles as 'Game For A Laugh'. Matthew was and is a smashing chap. He often stayed with us when we lived over my restaurant, the 'As You Like It' in Monmouth Street, when starting his career. I last saw him wedged between two fat titted madams in a joint called 'Peppermint Park' in upper St Martin's Lane, eating dumplings with abandon.

Leslie Parker-Davies was the house manager at the walled city that was the Gateway, Chester, and he was my host this particular evening after the play. To say that he was about to enjoy a rush not seen since the Gold one was the understatement of the year as everyone seemed to develop an unquenchable thirst at the very moment when 'time' was called. The barman, a camp little cross between Mischa Aeur and Billy de Wolfe, was still serving cocktails when suddenly Leslie hurled a bottle through the air, which landed with a plonk on the wall in the lounge, spattering at least three vestal virgins from the show with red wine. If you had been under the influence, sad to say, a nun in the corner was, it appeared like blood was flowing everywhere and all hell broke loose. That was my first meeting with Mr Parker-Davies.

*****

Back to Crewe. The advertisement in 'The Stage' announced that the Crewe and Nantwich Borough Council was seeking an administrator for their lovely old Edwardian theatre, the Lyceum, and applications were invited. It was not clear, however, that the council were not offering a penny to run the joint, but this was made plain soon after.

Everyone, from a defrocked vicar to a Butlins flunkey, sent in replies and they were duly sorted. Sixteen lucky sods were selected to appear before three wise men. They were Mr Wood, the borough solicitor (who obviously had a way with words), the top dog of the pack, Mr Bamford (whose conversation was meagre), and Keith Burton, a stalwart of the parish, who was the director of Leisure Services and other delightful pursuits. He got the picture from the other two and usually did all the talking. In my opinion, Mr Wood was by far the peach in this particular fruit salad.

I was amongst the chosen few summoned to appear for inspection. I immediately called a friend, Martin Wenner, who, misguided youth that he was, longed to enter the portals of this particular profession. As it turned out, the Gods were to smile on Martin and he has made it, with lots of solid television roles and impressive parts on the boards. It could not have happened to a nicer fellow. Anyway, Martin arrived without delay in his jalopy to convey me to yonder town of Crewe without further ado.

I presented myself in Mr Wood's office on the stroke of twelve midday. I wore a suit of Emerald Green. Martin, nicknamed Golly-Wolly because of the affection he had for 'The Wizard of Oz' and all the munchkins fluttering up and down the Yellow Brick road, seated himself outside the chamber with a pencil, pad and vigorous ear to relate the dialogue that was to come from this illustrious meeting. The fellow was indeed a great consolation.

The three wise men were charming, gentle and inquisitive. Like all applicants who really did not mind if they got the job or not, I looked something like Joan Crawford in her glossies from the silver screen. I mean in my manner not appearance, alas! I had written my application tongue-in-cheek. I was relaxed and natural, which somehow collected stares from the gentlemen who were obviously perplexed, astounded or at a loss as to how to deal with the fugitive. If I had really needed the job, they would probably have biffed hell of me and I would have likely ended up on my arse outside contemplating either a piss-up of the highest order or the lyrics of 'God, I need this job', which is the chorines' lament from the musical 'A Chorus Line'. They asked me all about my background, from my time at the monastery to Borstal and beyond; what I had been doing, who had I been doing, and what could I suggest for the Lyceum Theatre. Now I am a little older and know more, my replies could have been so much more entertaining!

I told them, as well as I could, the facts I thought they were desperate to hear whilst glancing out of the corner of my right eye at my scribbled notes on the back of 'The Sporting Weekly'. I spoke of my proposed programme of ideas for this palace of varieties until it became abundantly clear that I would have to have a handbag laden with gold pieces to fulfil the dream they were longing for. It hit me between the eyes that a benefit or two and a succession of Poppy Days would have to be arranged.

I told them I was interested in the role or what the fuck was I doing there? It suddenly all became very earnest. Eventually, Martin and I ran outside as the councillors tucked into their lobster lunch and gave themselves chronic indigestion comparing the various victims they had just screened. I jumped into Martin's car and we drove down the M6 with style.

Martin related his notes on the interview. There were like a cross between 'A conversation with Joan Rivers' and 'The

Nine o'clock News', and he declared that he had pissed himself laughing, which was more than I did, then or now.

*****

After a week-long heat wave and a full moon of promise, four recall interviews were arranged by Mr Keith Burton, of which I was to be one. I rang Golly-Wolly, who was currently having a love affair with an Equity card, and we again journeyed to Crewe.

Preparation was vital. I knew what I wanted to say about how I would run the damned theatre, but could I wrap it up into a bouquet that would please? They might even ask for a profit or loss sheet, which would fuck me up for a start. How could one possibly forecast what one could make at a venue that might have a farce one minute, a shit show the next, a carnival, a peep show, a parade of willies from the local 'Dream Boys' or a triumph? The wide range of product to programme was endless... and disturbing. On top of that, how could you gauge what the demands on the attached restaurant might be? It could serve four, forty or seventy lunches according to the day, the weather or the whim of the oversized cook. With a little help from my friends (mainly Brian Cooper between drags on his fags) I composed a précis of figures and fables which showed I could put two and two together to make five and we arrived for the interview.

I had prepared folders for six members of the committee, all singly and nicely packaged, naïvely thinking six would be the total number needed to set out my background and list my backers for the initial venture if I was fortunate (or unfortunate) enough to be appointed the job. I then listed the many shows and theatres I had played since I had got the bug in 1970 and presented the Welsh soap opera 'Under Milk Wood' to an unsuspecting public. I also thought it might help my cause that I was a younger member of the TMA (Theatrical Managers Association), a clique most revered in the world of theatre councils and management. I again dressed with care, which meant I wore clothes, including a tie left by a chorine when disturbed on Guy Fawkes Night, and I presented myself to the main boardroom of the town hall in Crewe on the stroke of two. I have enjoyed a few strokes in my time, but that clock really had a dong. The day was hotter than a whore house on May Day and fried eggs could be cooked in the streets.

Martin again sat outside the inquisition room, rather like Elsa Lanchester attending Charles Laughton in 'A Witness for the Prosecution', and he managed to take in a few keyhole notes. Although prepared as I was, the flock of councillors that sat around the long table when I flew in the door was indeed formidable, and rendered my quota of folders prepared for the committee totally inadequate. The Last Supper was not in it. There must have been sixteen councillors presiding, again headed by the three wise men. This time though, they had a guest artiste, Mr Richard Digby-Day, an eminent theatre director and an administrator of repute, dressed from top to toe in white (a suit, not a bridal gown) who looked for all the world like an angel from a movie 'Heaven Can Wait'.

I first clapped eyes on Mr Digby-Day when he was an inmate of the Palace Court Theatre, Westover Road, in the mellow town of Bournemouth. It should be a city but someone lit the plans for a cathedral with a De Reske cigarette. The Playhouse now has developed ecclesiastical urges every so often and entertains the wicked, the wanton, the poor and the plain neglected as a house of salvation. How long ago the 'Band of Hope' seems now. In my role as a theatrical agent I had acquired a season for one of my striplings at the lovely Northcott Theatre in Exeter when Mr Digby-Day was the reigning chief. He had left the Nottingham Playhouse after a madly successful season there and was riding on the crest of a wave. I was not always sure of what he thought of me, but on this occasion he was most cordial and supportive. Whether this was because he had seen some of the credentials of the other victims who were interviewed, I had no idea.

Strands of evidence drifting around later revealed one of them had been in the clink more times than I had enjoyed proposals of marriage and another had achieved total chaos in every venue he had set foot in. Whether these findings may have swayed Mr Digby-Day's affections or he had better things to do elsewhere, I could not tell, but he was nice.

I handed out the six brochures I had prepared like a Salvation Army lass at the Mission – picking out the councillors most likely – and steeled myself for their reaction. Some had glasses, one a lorgnette, and two possibly a squint. The committee seemed impressed that I had catering experience (running the 'As You Like It' coffee house in Soho in the sixties evidently counted). Obviously I knew who or what to put between two slices of bread, but was this enough? One spinster of the parish on the left-hand pew asked me what fillings I had in mind for the Lyceum Restaurant. I rattled off such a selection (cream cheese and prawn, egg mayonnaise, smoked salmon, tuna fish and chives, and other delights) that her mouth and tongue twisted outrageously in an orgasm of expectation over the forthcoming banquet.

The second councillor told me that the council would like the theatre reopened at the beginning of October. A long period is always needed to book worthwhile attractions and the opening looked problematical since we were already in July. In the main, it was agreed by all and sundry that the theatre should be a receiving house, staging touring productions initiated elsewhere, with an occasional in-house production in the season. Mr Digby-Day concurred that it would be a feat of the supernatural to entice shows into the Lyceum in such a short time, especially without a guaranteed sum of money for the producer. (The mere thought of offering a guarantee to a producer sent the three wise men into a trance!) Consequently, only a percentage of the box office take would be made available to the visiting promoter. Bearing in mind that many folk who lived in Crewe all their lives had never set foot in a theatre, let alone their local hostelry the Lyceum, much financial risk would be involved for all. As one bright theatre promoter said when taking the waters there: "Who wants to bring in an Agatha Christie to Crewe and fucking well lose money? There are many more delightful towns for a wake."

It was also made crystal clear that the council did not intend to choose their new head boy straightaway. I told them, in what I hoped were seductive tones, that it was imperative that they made up their soddin' minds that very week, otherwise no one would be able to book in a fucking thing... except Snow White and her fucking Dwarfs.

Looking every inch the dead spit of Margaret Courtney during the run of the musical 'Mame' in Drury Lane (and if you don't know who this lady is, go and stand in the corner), a lovely lady councillor addressed me head on.

"How do you propose to entice the school children into the Lyceum Theatre, when for a long period they have got into the habit of going elsewhere?"

Christ, I thought, what did she think I was, the Pied Piper of Hamelin? I came back immediately with my reply. "I shall endeavour to charm the headmistress off the trees."

"Indeed," she mused, "but most of them are headmasters."

"It makes no difference to me, ma'am," I replied. A few heads turned.

After a lengthy barrage of questions which seemed to go on longer than 'Les Misérables', my interview concluded and I was given leave to go back to the real world.

To say I was exhausted was putting it mildly, but I knew that I had done well. The ladies' votes were mine, that much I knew. I grabbed Golly-Wolly by the hand, which seemed the thing to do, and we ran from the hall. Golly-Wolly insisted the whole thing was funnier than watching 'Oh, Calcutta!' the famous nude revue, on a cold day.

We flew like things possessed into a pub called The Cheese Mill on another corner of the square. There, I ordered brandies without delay.

Golly-Wolly strode around to find two seats. Normally he would have got the drinks as that was the kind of chap he was, but this day I did the collecting. I had my wallet clutched securely in my hand, a lovely old wallet given to me by an Egyptian prince, a great personal friend, and I took a couple of quid out to pay the hired help. I took the drinks over to the table Martin had selected, leaving my wallet on the counter. We quickly gulped down the brandies and Golly-Wolly sped over to the counter for reinforcements and related to me his version of the interview that had just concluded. Martin said that the whole thing sounded hilarious and, apparently, the council had laughed long and loud, which made me think that perhaps I was the cabaret act between interviews and that I would therefore be regarded as not more than a joke.

After half an hour I was more relaxed and we walked out into the sunshine of this quaint Cheshire town and jumped into the car. I had not even sat down when I realised my wallet was no longer with me. Fear swept through my body, for not only was there at least a hundred quid (not a fortune, but I had long been rumoured to be Jewish in my thrift), but also all my credit cards were in the wallet, including my much prized Gold American Express card which had been acquired after great perseverance. We searched the car and each other, but to no avail. The bloody thing was missing.

I swept back into the pub, but the barmaid insisted she had not seen it and was most indifferent. I did notice a lady hag sitting on the window seat who did not take her eyes off me for an instant whilst I was questioning the staff at the bar. Perhaps the cow had pinched my wallet and stuffed it in her knickers – what then? From the look of her it would be the safest and most undisturbed haven in the country. There was no doubt about it, I was completely undone (which should have been an omen about Crewe, but I am always madly optimistic). There was nothing for it but to go to the cop shop, situated in a posh new building on the other side of the square, and bemoan my loss. The police were most helpful and it appeared that a male customer at The Cheese Mill, who was having a sly drink with a nun of the parish, had seen a woman pick up a wallet, which must have been mine. Why the silly sod had not intercepted the bitch was not clear. Perhaps his companion, Sister Teresa, had screamed, 'God is Love!' or perhaps he was fey or just not courageous, after all, if you are beaten to death or raped on an underground platform, precious few people will come to your aid – this has been proven a million times. "Do not get involved," say the wise old sages… not until it happens to you!

The fuzz promised to comb the district thoroughly and we had no alternative but to find our way back to the motorway

299

and race back to London. This we did.

Now it was obvious that I could be in the running of the Lyceum in Crewe, but then I got to thinking. Did I really want the job? Did I want to be head flunkey for the three wise men? Would the money last out for the first season? Could the local bank manager be bribed? A thousand thoughts cascaded from my mind and spattered like snowflakes on the poor driver, Golly-Wolly. And what of my London office with fifty haglets screaming to have the chance to play Saint Joan? I had to get back and consult Angela, my factotum and solace.

Angela, my PA was quizzical and very eager to hear what had transpired. I told her of the whole fucking affair; the three wise men, the hesitant chap with Sister Teresa and the cop with his promise of finding my wallet from the Nile – everything.

One morning, in my office where Angela was brewing strong tea. We had just got through the mail, which usually consisted of nine bills and a cheque for £2.68 (a repeat of some long-forgotten BBC TV saga, sold to the natives in Bucharest), and I was shoving down the prescribed three shredded wheat into my hungry mouth. The telephone rang at four minutes past nine and it was Keith Burton, the third of the wise men from Crewe. He told me the job was mine. Angela jumped ten feet and caught her left breast on a lamp. I choked on the bloody cereal, told Keith Burton he was too kind and put the telephone down. What had I done and how would I do? Only Mrs Thatcher and Russell Grant could tell me that.

I talked it over with Angela, who almost did herself a mischief planning the opening night. I had already raised eight grand from two associates and with our own handbag it would indeed start the proceedings off. Angela rang the third wise man and said we would take the job. How it would take me was not to become evident for at least six months.

*****

After Angela and I had got over the shock, I telephoned my friend Brian Cooper, who was as guarded as hell and more pessimistic that Molly Picon on a good day. He always spoke with a quiet assurance and puffed cigarettes constantly through a middle-class cigarette holder. He screamed that I would need at least £30,000 to run for the first six months and that I was really as mad as a hatter or at least temporarily deranged.

The theatre had agreed on a peppercorn rent (the sods should have given the whole thing rent free), but further rates were added on afterwards. Other financial burdens included having to lease the cutlery. If you did not dob up, the patrons would not have the necessary utensils to eat their lasagne. This was hardly an attitude conducive to promoting business. The final degradation was being charged £2,000 a year for customers to use the downstairs toilets. These opened to the theatre on one side and to the markets on the other and were owned and staffed by a lady of middle years in a turban, which was actually a large coloured scarf that originated from an Oxfam in Bournemouth. Obviously this arrangement should never have been tolerated. But, with the excitement of making the place work, it was relegated to the back of my mind until the day of final reckoning with it stuck in my craw like a Labour councillor at a Tory picnic.

I pooh-poohed the idea put forward by Brian Cooper that the handbag would have to be far larger to encompass the expenses for this midlands home of entertainment. Instead, I insisted that as the young, the brave and the demented would do that hard work, initiative and a dollop of luck would see us through. How many otherwise sane creatures have said this and ended up on their arses in a field of debris?

The next step was to advertise for staff. I had an elderly relative to help me called May, who looked and sat like the old Queen Mary on a chair in the corner of the office. When she spoke it was something akin to Bette Davis addressing Errol Flynn in 'Elizabeth and Essex' (a popular Warner Brothers film at the height of the success of moving pictures in the thirties).

An advertisement was inserted in the local papers and we journeyed up and down the M1 to interview haglets in the office at Crewe. We had sixty-six applicants, the picture of a depressed area quickly emerged. Most candidates either had not worked since they threw away their baby rattles or were on the verge of being made redundant by the current firm they worked for. When asked to name the sort of wage they might expect for their labours, most mumbled something in the region of £50-£60. This caused May to fall off the regal chair that housed her rather large arse and she sat on the floor, stunned beyond belief. For a couple of minutes, only a fire or Richard Gere could have brought her back to the land of the living.

The applicants were met by my luscious friend Tessa Wood, a sometime actress. (It was not that she was not offered many acting jobs, but she had the tendency to place work in the theatre second to the males she favoured, and, as they often came from wealthy backgrounds where limos and visits to The Ivy were the norm rather than the extraordinary, her dazzling talents for the stage were not seen that often). She had a marvellous profile. With a strong jawline plus short, beautifully tressed dark hair, she looked like a young Mary Astor. Who could ask for more in an assistant? Long eyelashes framed her large eyes while her wide generous mouth (a feature so often responsible for seducing the men) hid a superb set of teeth, white and gleaming in their excellence. When the workers arrived for their interviews, they were so astonished to see such beauty in their midst that they forgot to be nervous. As a result, when they met me, (never the least bit average even on a grey day), I got their full attention and replies before they were conscious they had said them.

The big question mark hung over filling the position of house manager. No one was anything near what I was looking for, except Margaret Stone. I had asked two splendid house managers of my acquaintance, with the permission of their current bosses, to consider the job. Alas, they opted to remain where they were in case the new adventure did not last. How wise they were.

I did not set out to engage a woman (something many men have said after being skilfully manipulated by a woman they hoped would serve them). With the way of the world as it is and the devious skulduggery of many women, the fair sex achieve untold victories in the field of business and male domination. I have always been of the opinion that women are three times smarter than men and have three times as much style when proving it. Everyone knows a girl about the house does infinitely more variable things than a man, whether it be in the fields of cuisine, theatre or knowing where the master puts his slippers.

One particular day, Margaret Stone arrived. With a twinkle in her eyes and seduction in her movements, she knew how many beans made five and how to throw the dice in her favour. Although not ravishing, her appeal was total. She had full red lips and dark curly hair. In fact, generous red lips. To hell with the hair, that came for free. She came in and crossed her legs like all good girls and we laughed like hyenas for at least ten minutes whilst I got her answers to my questions. She was thirty-five going on forty and nothing like the Ms Stone in the 'Roman Spring' of Mr Tennessee Williams. She had a natty black suit (so suitable for wakes, audiences or interviews) with a grey blouse allowing just a quick peep at her fulsome bosom. She had worked for Mecca (a dancehall and leisure industry company for those not in the know) who were strong in her native area of Manchester. She looked married, as indeed she was, with a husband who was rarely seen, a wayward daughter from a previous marriage and a little son of nine years old. The daughter (fifteen going on twenty) proved to be a problem, having discovered the delights of sex a little ahead of schedule, pleasures which she had no intention of giving up for Lent, or any other time. Despite the family trials, Margaret looked as strong as a donkey, which is just as well as I work like a steamroller. I think nothing of an eighteen-hour day, but still I do not want to kill the poor cow in her first week. We took to each other as a knife would to butter. All the other waiting females were dismissed and relegated to poppy selling duties for Armistice Day.

*****

Margaret Stone agreed to come in as my house manager for a measly sum with prospects and a great problem was solved. We had already obtained the services of one Eric Sanderson, a first rate manager recommended by a great friend of mine, Russell Hills, of the Empire Theatre, Sunderland and, later, of the New Theatre, Hull. Mr Hills ruled his theatre with precise military mind and I was always in great awe of him for the expertise and knowledge with which he ruled his particular empire. Eric Sanderson was small, plump and as quick as a nun on roller-skates when discovering Lourdes. He wore a badge which declared he was one of the 'little people', which indeed he was. He quickly engaged an electrician I had picked up (not literally) from the Cromer Pavilion (a venue near Norwich boasting excellent fish, a few hundred residents and many splendid seagulls) when we were reviving 'The Desert Song' and 'Blue Heaven' with John Hanson on hot Sunday afternoon in August. A tall, well-hung young man called Mark was also taken on and he completed the trio of full-timers backstage at the theatre.

I had one piece of luck when a lad from Scarborough arrived to apply for the post of box office manager. He was 23 going on 24, with Harpo Marx blond curly hair and a smile like a watermelon. He had had a box office grounding and, although he seemed a little bowlegged, taking money on the productions I had planned would make him walk and dance like Astaire, of that I had no doubt. I engaged Peter Saxon, for that was his name, without delay. He raced up the main street and booked a bedsit with pretensions without further ado. Peter is still with us, but has changed his occupation a little. He is a puppeteer for the Sooty touring show nine months of the year. In between, he was a marvellous Mayor of the Munchkins (when Russell Grant gave up the role), and toured the hills and dales with my circus as we played once again the well-loved 'Wizard of Oz'. Peter a little later on worked as a puppeteer to off sales gentleman and made so much money he has flats in several towns. He was cautious with money – a strong worker and liked a pretty face (male or female). A good friend to this very day.

Two ladies were to run the restaurant, called Elsie and Dolly (or Lil and Rose – I cannot recall their exact names), along with a very good barman who was a projectionist in his spare time, Anthony Owens. He was cheerful, efficient and altogether good news. Two young male PA's completed the staff and we were all ready to open.

Or so we thought. After La Sanderson and his men made an inspection, he declared there were weeks ahead of cleaning, renewing, and minor alterations before we could sign a contract for the opening night. This was most disappointing and he ran away with the small handbag we had assembled at great speed.

But I had to work on. Margaret started ordering all the beer, spirits and wine that were necessary and the two ladies did the same for the restaurant. The market people outside on their stalls took no notice whatsoever as they had seen it all before many times. It was just a rerun to them.

Back in Denmark Street, Angela and I had a talk and decided we would have to engage an assistant as I would be spending much time in Crewe and she was ever hopeful of a theatre job or strong exposure on television. We found a youth called Jürgen. Tall, laid back, his mother German and his father English, he did what he was bid. He was truthful, hopeful and reliable. What bliss. With Angela making arrangements we felt the launch was well underway.

*****

The Lyceum opened in a blaze of publicity (although the glory was yet to come) with the William Douglas-Home play 'The Dame of Sark'. Marius Goring, usually cast as the Hun, arrived to play the Nazi Commandant and a splendid girl called Janet Hargreaves coped with the role of the eponymous Dame. She was far too young, but managed somehow to age up and please her public. It really called for Dame Anna Neagle, who had graced some important theatres with her presence in the play, but there we are. The show was well received and my friend David Kirk, who had toured the provinces since I stopped singing as a child star, was the impresario. Other plays I booked followed with very good results indeed. Paul Darrow came in a piece called 'Joseph and the Amazing Technicolour Dreamcoat' (then featuring Jess Conrad). There was no court case to decide his sexuality and the crowds tipped in. Rodney Bewes ended the first run of plays in a new comedy, 'Relative Strangers'.

Between these plays, I presented top stars in variety, Frankie Howerd, Syd Lawrence and his Orchestra, Frankie Vaughan, The Bachelors, Showaddywaddy, and many others. Almost all of them made money and started to get the theatre talked about. I had at least proved that the theatre could take money and be a winning, multi-purpose proposition.

*****

The two ladies who started the restaurant lasted a couple of weeks then opened a tearoom for frustrated spinsters, so I took over much of the running of the restaurant. On Fridays and Saturdays we had four waiters scuttling about to serve the customers and we always had a queue for lunch on Saturdays. In the corner, in return for a free lunch, I gave aspiring cabaret performers the chance to wail the latest hits and provide an atmospheric background of some sort. This we later extended to Sundays also. I stayed open after the show and one could get sandwiches, desert or a bowl of goulash long after the performers had fucked off. Cabaret nights on Fridays went on until late and the buzz after the show upstairs in the bars and restaurant was vibrant and exciting. I engaged a superb musician and musical director called David Carter to play in the bar with his trio during the evenings at weekends. He delighted the Crewe clientele with his masterly playing. Since then, David has played for many stars including Frankie Howerd, Bob Monkhouse, and Don Maclean. He still works with us and is as much a genius as ever.

'The Wonderful Wizard of Oz' was the Christmas attraction. It was my own touring production, of course, and starred Yana, a siren of the 1940s, whom I had found serving in a Boots shop off Baker Street. Although neglected by life, she was still a handsome woman and one could barely believe that at the height of her fame she was the most beautiful woman in the world (press opinion) and had enjoyed many romantic episodes with top stars at that time (or so the papers declared). Anyway, she was a 'hot' lady and a star. That she had an army of admirers, I would think perfectly true. I always remember her as a smash hit in 'Cinderella' at the Coliseum with Tommy Steele, and she was in 'London Laughs' with Jimmy Edwards and others at the Adelphi. Now she was my Good Fairy in 'The Wonderful Wizard of Oz' at the Lyceum theatre in Crewe, and we were glad to have her. We hired a limousine as long as the Thames to whirl her around the area so that the press and television cameras could get a look in and help promote the show.

We previewed the piece at the little Civic Theatre in Chesterfield (now called The Pomegranate, probably because the reigning mayor owned a fruit stall). It is a lovely little venue that I had played many times and was presided over by one Derek Coleman, a tiny man with a twinkle in his eye and a most pleasing disposition.

Everything went fairly well at the dress rehearsal. A Brighton girlie, who went by the name of Gayle Ashley, was Dorothy and we were fortunate in finding a little Scotty Terrier to play Toto, Dorothy's dog. Toto only tiddled on matinee days to show he was human. Otherwise he would have given Lassie a run for his money.

On the Monday we were scheduled to open at two o'clock. All seemed well until the choreographer, an amicable chap called Poppy (nobody knows why, but he did wear the colour red a lot) came to inform us of a calamity. Rupert, who was playing the Tin Man was missing. He was nowhere to be found. Had he been seduced, offered a role to advertise cod liver oil for rusty joints, or had he just pissed off back to London unimpressed with Crewe? It was an almost understandable reaction considering I always felt the fish in the market was several days off.

Poppy looked at me. I looked at Poppy. We both knew

what had to be done. I would go on as the Tin Man, although it is one thing writing the bloody piece and another going on to play it and getting the lines where they should be.

The cast got me into costume. It was grey and so was I. Nevertheless, extra make-up had to be applied immediately. I was given a defining circle of pink around the cheeks. I was also sprayed with grey paint from every quarter. Trust the stage management to overdo it and coat my glasses too. Renée, the deputy stage manager, always knew everyone's lines as well as her own. She threw me some titbits and pushed me in the right direction on stage. She only played the wife of the Mayor of the Munchkins in this, but by Christ she guided me along the Yellow Brick Road and beyond. I watched her lips and then said the dialogue. Sometimes it was okay, sometimes it was cheeky and sometimes it was a mess, but I was getting through it. It was easier to bluff in Act Three as the Scarecrow had much to say while the Lion screamed and rustled his animal skin. If I just grinned and occasionally watched Renée miming some more of my lines we would get away with it, and we did. The next thing I knew, we were all in the finale belting out 'Over the Rainbow'.

Later on that evening, we got hold of old friend Betty Crane, who ruled Norwich and always had a coterie of out-of-work thespians at her boarding house. She sent me a lad named Robin Wright, who coped admirably next day and knew a few more lines than I did the day before.

Yana played her part as if she was a different character each day, but she flashed her wand with style and abandon, and got through every show. She had many scent bottles in her dressing room, so it always smelt beautiful. Towards the end of the run the perfume was replaced by Vodka, so occasionally the running of the performance was not as smooth as before. The wicked witch (one Virginia Graham) hated Yana with the ferocity of a viper and one matinee Yana screamed her dress had caught fire. The wicked witch cackled and said, "Let her burn!"

Simon Fricker, a musical director of tender years, was dispensing music. Simon had arrived when we first restarted

'The Wonderful Wizard of Oz' in 1978. He had been a choirboy at the Cockney Tavern in Blackpool, which was run by an old friend, Maurice Moran, and he played the organ and many other things there as well as managing a few vocals. Simon arrived for our first rehearsal in London, which was masterminded by Ronnie Parnell, a director from Blackpool, and one half of the well-known Blackpool production firm, Trafford & Parnell. Tommy Trafford, a Northern star for 30 years, was his partner. We had long been friends and I cast many of their shows. They presented first class summer season all over the country, a form of entertainment which has more or less faded away. Ronnie smoked like a fire that engulfed Chicago all those many years ago and moved like a panther. He had one pet hate, Equity, the actors' trade union. If ever a chorus member even mentioned this firm of labour leaders, he flew into a rage and was not seen for two hours. If the offending chorine did not apologise in triplicate, he or she was dismissed and never seen again.

Simon fitted our bandwagon well and has since matured to play for most of the reigning stars of today, although he does accompany us on tours of our latest creation, 'The Jerome Kern Songbook'. Now sporting a small moustache (which is a little reminiscent to the late Teasy Weasy) he is slight and laughs like a hyena. But, if a chorine does not hit the required crochet or quaver, he can be inconsolable and is known to use the lash from a great height. His Ma and Pa used to rule Nottingham and the Goose Fair. Dada was the headmaster of the local grammar dormitories, and, when he retired, the family flew to the Isle of Wight to bask in the sun. Simon now has a houseboat there and plays his organ in the bedroom as the seas and the seagulls dance to his rhythm.

*****

There was a band of supportive lady volunteers who, from time to time, arranged little fetes and raffles to help bring in the gold pieces and provide a better class of toilet paper in the loos. They did this in return for various concessions to shows at the theatre. Radio support in the area was extremely good. In those days, before making it at a higher echelon, Bruno Brookes was at BBC Radio Stoke. Signal Radio was also so-operative and keen at all times, as were the press. Unhappily, the banking chiefs in the area did not have any enthusiasm for the theatre in Crewe or for the striplings newly arrived in their midst to present the world of show business.

*****

As I had moved my costume department from London to the outhouse at Crewe, I thought that a New Year's Eve Ball was a good idea. We costumed everyone (who bought a ticket for £12.50) free of charge. We sold out in no time for this most noble soirée and must have made two grand in profits on the night. At the ball, Simon Fricker came as the Hunchback of Nôtre Dame along with our puppet master or, in this case, mistress who was dressed as Joan of Arc (an apt choice as she said she had been hearing voices in her head for years). It was three hours before we uncovered Mr Fricker, such was his disguise. Two boys came as 'Beauty and the Beast', but had to be reprimanded when caught playing Happy Families in the dress circle. Angela came as Lady Godiva, but the horse bolted, so she put on a shift and was recognised as Mary, Queen of Scots. One of the wise men, Frank Wood, came with his wife, which must have excited the council as did the presence of Peter Barnard, the Chief Architect, who couldn't give a fuck what anyone else said. Everyone had a great time and I made pennies for the theatre.

A little while after the masquerade party, the Scouts' Gang Show has a sell-out week. The bar made so much money we could have had the brewery around for a free lunch, but I still had to start thinking quickly about how to make great profits. I dreamt of the pawn shop with regularity and one night had a hot flush when a nightmare vividly convinced me that I was running a brothel after time at the back in order to raise more ready cash. We did have the local dance school in for their annual week of dance, but sixty Shirley Temples have their drawbacks, although once again the brewery received a cheque as part payment of their large outstanding account.

So, I dreamed up the idea of a repertory season and assembled four weeks of plays. Audrey Leybourne (more of her in another chapter) came to do a play, directed by John Chilvers. Before returning from the Welsh Valleys, John had run the Swansea Grand Theatre for 30 years and I had got him out to Europe to direct some plays for Terence Young and Tommy Iwering in Stockholm and elsewhere. He directed the show 'Entertaining Mr Sloane' with venom. For my money, Joe Orton was the English Tennessee Williams and one of the best writers of all time. Fuck Shakespeare and all his sonnets.

The council were keen on rep, but the punters were not. We only played to twenty per cent capacity, which was a shame and proved to be the first nail in the coffin. Two stars of expertise and glamour, Simon Oats and Pearl Anne Turner (now an agent), revived Neil Simon's 'The Last of the Red Hot Lovers'. Alas and alack, this too simmered on a gentle flame.

By this time Martin (Golly-Wolly) had consummated his love affair with an Equity card and was a practising married man. He had the good fortune to meet a talented writer, young and spicy Debbie Horsfield, whose conquests on the TV screen had already aroused much attention. They fell in love and life was a ball. Martin began appearing in several TV series, including 'Brookside'. He attracted much attention and began his TV career.

An old friend arrived at just the right time. By the name of Anthony Royale, he had sailed the high seas doing stage management for the entertainment departments of cruise liners. His main job was to create the lighting for dancing nymphets on board these ships for ageing madams and frustrated widows. The cast of these theatricals is invariably gay, but the ladies don't mind. They are satisfied with a kiss on the hand, knowing bloody well that, after dusk and when the lights are out, many games of lust are played out in the crew quarters.

During my time at the Lyceum, I edited and brought out a newspaper called 'the Lyceum Times', which was printed by Mr and Mrs Ball of Hanley, Stoke-on-Trent. The Balls charged for advertising space and this helped pay for the periodical. By editing the paper myself for free, we could afford to print 10,000 copies each month in order to spread word of the theatre and its entertainment to every Tom, Dick and Harry. The Balls made back their running costs and a few bob extra for chicken and chips. The paper itself was a great success from the very beginning in the second edition followed the raves of the first. I felt my efforts were really being supported and so in the early days I did not worry too much about the future.

All the time, I persevered in trying to obtain some sponsorship for the theatre, but this proved an uphill job and I was running out of time. The theatre scene in general was watching me. Opening and attempting to run a theatre without grants, subsidies or sponsorship was practically unheard of. Only probably two theatres in the whole country had succeeded. It was so deranged that I was regarded as something of a curiosity, to be monitored closely. I was always an optimist, but, like many a captain, I found that you cannot run a ship without oil, however passionate you may be. During this time the council were marking time, taking notes, and gathering forces within to cope with the fallout, if and when it came.

*****

'The King and I' did much to help finances in the remaining month and Alexander Bridge, a master in the world of musical comedy, did a great job. Unfortunately, it was to be my swan song. The financial backlash was collecting momentum and I wrote to the three wise men stating the position and asking for a loan to cover me until the autumn. I had no idea how my request would fare, but, on looking back, many others had.

I was summoned to the inner office for a private consultation with Frank Wood and the treasurer and we all went over the scene carefully. They gave no inkling either way as to their feelings or thoughts and asked for a rundown on takings plus a profit and loss account sheet for the coming six months. I had booked in a most alluring galaxy of attractions. The plays included: 'Sleuth', 'Children of a Lesser God', a new play with Diana Coupland called 'Comic Cuts', and the Ray Coony farce 'Run for Your Wife' (perhaps it should have been renamed 'Run for Your Life!' with all the expensive star names in it). Also, I had scheduled a concert with Louis Armstrong's band (dear old Louis had departed to pastures new some time before) plus return visits of Syd Lawrence, Showaddywaddy and God knows who else. The autumn therefore looked good and marketable. Mr Wood was most helpful and referred me to the Policy committee and I was asked to make an appearance in the large council chambers which were in every way similar to those of a high court. Was I on trial? Could I be facing a charge of murdering a theatre or possibly gross failure to make gold? It was all very worrying. Over forty members of the Policy Committee quizzed me from all sides and asked me to account for the expenditure of what had been my own monies (and those of my friends) in the running of the council's establishment.

I must say that they, mostly, seemed cordial and grateful for the results I had achieved. Ninety-two per cent returns in the first season were not bad for a theatre that had been closed for two years and that had a decade-long record of opening and shutting down. Just one or two councillors were sceptical, believing that I had been unable to make the theatre commercially viable. Again, they stressed they were not willing to pump the ratepayers' monies into the Lyceum. The message came over loud and clear that a fair majority of the council wanted the theatre, but only if it did not cost them any brass. Already, two large and luxurious centres, the Meredith and The Oakley, were running shows on certain occasions and losing over £1,000 a week of the council's money. This was common knowledge and food for thought.

The matter was referred to a sub-committee set up for this very purpose. On the following Monday I attended with Brian Cooper (puffing his long cigarette holder even more viciously), which I felt would add a little stability to my side of things.

313

Graham Steane, a bookkeeper of repute, had worked arduously and prepared a profit and loss accounts. Although it was agreed I had done much for the theatre, bookkeeping and accountancy were not my major assets. Of course they were not, as funds for a first rate secretary and bookkeeper were not included in the wage breakdown. These tasks had to be dealt with by my PAs and myself.

A step in the right direction came the next day when a sum of £20,000 was approved by the sub-committee. This was to be awarded immediately and a further £30,000 would be made available for the next year should the need arise. This was a grant not a loan. Someone, somewhere out there, had a heart after all and chivalry was indeed not dead, merely ailing.

Brian Cooper was so surprised that he puffed at the cigarette holder long after the fag had burnt itself out. He had presumed we would be dispatched out of town on a fast train to the metropolis from whence we came as a failure of a dream is, generally, not to be encouraged. The sub-committee closed with the recommendation approved and remitted to the main council meeting two days later.

When it was presented to the main assembly, it was kicked out with the speed of an Intercity train on football Saturdays… and that was that. Afterwards, the local newspapers hinted a political meeting had been held privately on the day after the sub-committee recommendation had been made.

The news was relayed from my spies at 10.30 p.m. in the evening. I closed the theatre next morning and put on a black veil and returned to Charing Cross Road. I was driven by my good friend Peter Saxon, who had toiled long and hard as the box office manager. We took all our wardrobe with us, so we looked something like a fleeing peasant in 'The Inn of the Sixth Happiness'. I was not so lucky with my tens of thousands of pounds worth of scenery which was housed in a council warehouse up the road. That disappeared when the new licensee took over and is probably still being used for pantomimes up and down the Yellow Brick Road.

A little more than twenty-four hours afterwards, the telephone rang. By this time I was dressed in sackcloth and seated on a pew drinking Wincarnis. I was informed that the council had appointed a new tenant for the theatre and that details were not available of the deal. As the libel laws in this country are still stringent, I will merely say that I felt this deal had been brokered long before I was appointed to the Lyceum Theatre and that the new fellow had been already earmarked to take over the job as and when I went down the plughole. It was intimated that the new licensee would be funding the theatre. This was not true, as, later on, a huge grant was awarded and it was this that funded the Lyceum Theatre until a few years ago when this fellow, leaving a theatre unloved, neglected and the total opposite of how we handed it over in 1984, pissed off! So, really, the wheel had come full cycle and the poor old Lyceum was again abused and abandoned. If you looked into the credentials of the new management I fear you would catch a fever.

*****

However, as Mr Micawber says, "Something will turn up." On occasions like these a strong pot of tea is not only necessary but compulsory. I was naturally devastated, having to relinquish a dream and a band of hardworking people who were my friends, plus kiss goodbye to many thousands of pounds of my own money. I did, later on, repay my good associates so that they were at least not losers in this nefarious project.

Naturally, I could say more, but solicitors are so expensive. So, I will merely close the file on this chapter. "Into each life a little rain must fall," goes the song, but bugger an avalanche without an umbrella.

Chapter 20

Snippets

In the eighties a young man came along called Anthony Royale. He had been driver and PA to ageing comedian Charles Hawtrey. Having had a battle of wits with the 'Carry On' series star, he decided to elope with his limousine. By hook or by crook, he arrived on my doorstep. Tall, very country and with a ready smile, he called everyone 'daughter' regardless of age and sex.

Someone had suggested he called on me and sort out lunch if not a living. He was awarded both. I liked him and his country manners and signed him on the spot. He stayed with me for nine years and I could not have wished for a more reliable and talented assistant.

I christened him 'Smiling Mary' for his lips always had a smile on then and, as he counted all friends as 'daughters', this seemed somewhat a good idea. He got on with all the artistes I was presenting, the timing of his duties was never an issue and, when I ran the Lyceum Theatre in Crewe for a few months as administrator, he picked me up at 6 a.m. on the dot each morning and brought me back each evening, reaching my flat on the stroke of midnight. Devotion was never as constant.

We were presenting Kathy Kirby one summer in Blackpool, together with Elizabeth Dawn, Linda Grant and George ('I'm not well!') Williams and I was getting a few tips from veteran comedian Tommy Trafford. Anthony rang the doorbell of the Trafford residence and Tommy opened the door and said, "Oh, you're from Barrie Stacey. You must be 'Laughing Alice.'"

Anthony was a PA to be treasured and my mixed bag of artistes at that time (John Hanson, Frankie Howerd, Ruby Murray, Yana, Don Maclean, George Williams etc) could be temperamental, difficult or merely trying. Anthony took it all in his stride and outbursts of temper were never allowed to rankle him.

Anthony left me to get married to a lady agent. Whether it was love, passion, blackmail or superstition, I never knew, but I don't think the union was made in heaven. He committed suicide and hung himself several years ago and it was a source of utter regret to me that the funeral was held on a day that I was up North on a one night stand. It was a theatrical gig, of course, so please do not get the wrong idea.

Kathy Kirby came to us by way of a young actor, James Harman, whose path had crossed mine on the Yellow Brick road. She had also been suggested to me several times by one Lena Davis. Lena was a forthright and hardworking lady who worked for several charities. A woman of character, energy, enthusiasm and wit, she rules today in the North Hants area. She was a strong supporter of blonde nightingale Kathy Kirby. Kathy had been adopted or seduced by Ambrose whose orchestra was a top name in the world of quickstep and waltz. He saw in Miss Kirby a talent that was powerful and a voice that would delight the angels. Slowly and surely she climbed the ladder of fame and became a big name while he guided her into the big time. I always likened her talent to Dorothy Squires, sadly so neglected in her later life by Roger Moore.

Kathy had a marvellous run for a few years. Then Ambrose died. She gathered a motley crew of admirers and (not unlike the late Judy Garland) slowly began to sink, unsure of her talent, her fans and where she was going and with whom.

Incidentally, a book on Kathy Kirby entitled 'Secrets, Lovers and Lip Gloss' hit the publishers a few years back and is a worthy tribute to the singing star. Written by that same actor James Harman, who has been in love with her for a year and a day, it follows her career very well. Although more or less a recluse in this day and age, there are plans to possibly turn her story into a play and maybe even a film. One cannot tell what might happen. Kathy Kirby died recently, lonely and forgotten, which makes a very sad ending for such a lady.

George Williams was a popular comedian in the days of

'Variety Bandbox', a very popular radio feature. In the forties and fifties, when radio was the main source of amusement, George became a household favourite with his droll comedy. A small figure with a cloth cap and a long, long scarf, he always came on with the immortal line, "Eeee, I'm not well. I've got a going off feeling coming on!"

All through the fifties, sixties and seventies, George was booked in variety along with such favourites as John Hanson, Ruby Murray, Dorothy Squires, Don Maclean, Elizabeth Dawn and Benny Hill. He was popular at stage doors, signing autographs and talking to anyone and everyone and caring very much for his own fans. He was a brilliant painter and artist and made quite a living with his talents in this profession. I have a large portrait of the singer Josephine Baker. A present from George, it hangs on the wall in my lounge and is admired by all.

Chapter 21

Back Again in the Footlights

When I first moved into 132 Charing Cross Road (known as Shaldon Mansions to the carriage trade) everything was regular and as it should be. We had a caretaker who lived at the top of the house. He was strict, calling a spade a spade even when it was a shovel. He permitted no indiscretions such as all night parties, natives wandering about the house in the dead of night or hobbies such as drug taking, exceptional boozing or perversions of any kind. The latter, if at all popular, were rehearsed behind closed doors.

The house was council run and had been since the Dutch invaded Holland. Some older hags had been there for generations and looked on newcomers with more disdain than interest. Dogs were not allowed, not even pedigrees with pretensions. Cats were popular though, with little bags of excrement usually put outside the front doors for collection.

Some strong professional bodies inhabited a few of the best apartments. Over in Flat 4 we had a GP, whose practice was masterminded by a bastion of femininity who would have frightened Mrs Danvers from 'Rebecca'. Appointments were discreet and punctual, and Dr Kildare (as I named him) when on his rounds after a fortifying lunch, which usually consisted of some ham from Fortnum & Mason's partnered with some delicious, crusty raisin bread that was invariably topped by a cheese of high repute.

When the learned doctor retired or faded away in the early 1980s the flat was purchased by a European young man who, every so often, flitted in and out with gentlemen friends. I still refer to him as 'The Mute' since he so rarely speaks. Instead he grimaces tensely as if he expects you to start discussing a local election. Latterly I have managed to extract a "Good morning" out of him plus a slight smile, so not all is lost. He is, according to rumour, as rich as the heavens and owns flats in New York, Rome and one in Paris. Whether he entertains his guests with a strong quartet, harp or flute is not known, since no music escapes very strongly from his flat.

In Number 4 we had two dentists of strong recommendation. On the list was Mr Branston, named by me as 'Branston Prickle'. He was fifty-ish and looked like a businessman of astuteness, selecting his patients carefully and with great discretion. He chattered like a monkey so rapidly and expertly throughout the whole half hour you spent with him that you rarely felt a damned thing as he corrected your smile or took an occasional offending tooth to the cleaners. His receptionists came and went as frequently as a chambermaid changes her knickers, but all were poppets. Then suddenly in the 1990s he announced his retirement. He popped in a month after the announcement, saw all was well (I deal with Mr Rafel, his partner, in a moment) and was never seen again.

Mr Rafel, a different kettle of fish, took over the whole shebang and became the reigning star. A quiet and most observant man, no doubt he owes much to his upbringing in distant Cape Town where oranges and peaches go for a song, and, we are told, crime rages like the Crimean War. He weighs you up and down with great detail and slowly unwinds into the business of the day. When one gets to know him better, one finds he is a kind and helpful man and many old hags have much to thank him for when he prepares their ageing molars for the world outside. He has been the salvation of many a film and music hall star and he treats everyone the same whether they belong on stage or in the gallery. He knows his empire meticulously and can tell you what you owe his treasury with an accuracy that would entrance a Jewish bookmaker. He continues trading in Flat 4, Mondays to Fridays, pursuing his sporting hobbies at the weekend. Whether he goes to Mass or not, I have never yet found out. However, it is always more fun to leave something to the imagination.

Often you come across the surgery's clients lurking in the stairwell. I recently bumped into Joan Turner, a nightingale of yesteryear, on her way to have her teeth polished. She recognised me without hesitation as I helped her into the lift. Joan screamed, "I love you!" in her highest soprano, which was very gallant as she last saw me in her Marble Arch flat at least 30 years ago. At that time, she was a little pissed, so I was amazed at her memory. A woman of great talent, over the years she has been replaced on many an occasion. I recall hearing about one incident at the Wolverhampton Grand. She apparently came on stage at the top of the bill and sang a few songs, hitting at least 3 to 4 octaves in style. Then she took her applause as if it was the end of the evening. We are told that a large woman with titties to rival Pamela Anderson jumped up in the front row and screamed, "Is that all we are getting?" Joan sauntered down to the floodlights to have a closer look at the harridan and replied, "Yes, dear, that's it. Now fuck off while I have a gin."

The lift at 132 Charing Cross Road is the smallest in London apart from the lift at The Gielgud Theatre, formerly The Globe, on Shaftesbury Avenue. It is more temperamental than a woman in mid flow and has a period each month when it refuses to go up or down and you have to resort to climbing masses of stairs to get to your garret. Luckily I am on the second floor which is not too bad, but bad enough for an ageing chorine nevertheless. Galaxies of stars, haglets and wannabe thespians have ascended in this lift over the years to come and see me at Flat 8. The best of these was a prima donna of light opera who just managed to squeeze into the lift, but as her large tits took up so much room, suffocation, for her, was almost total. If she travelled in the lift or came by the stairs she arrived totally out of breath and found it difficult to sing a nursery rhyme on arrival. Let alone an aria.

Once I was trapped in the lift with a buxom wench who tried to have her wicked way with me. Silly bitch, she should have known better and not wasted her energies and time. But it was an interesting twenty minutes.

On the third floor was a well-off patrician of excellent means. He decorated his flat annually as a showcase for his exotic guests. Then the following spring he would change everything again with a different colour scheme altogether. We assumed he was something in the fashion business, as his shirts would have delighted Savile Row. I was not included in his circle of intimates, being more a patron of the village dance than the Hunt Ball.

A few of the other flatlets were bedsitting rooms, with toilets and bathrooms adjoining. They were small enough for a single haglet who might extend accommodation to a lover at the weekend. On the fourth floor was a swarm of Chinese who seemed to specialise in mediation and keeping themselves to themselves. I always assumed their lives were governed by cards, and, believe me, their cards are vastly different to ours.

In the basement, however, it was another world. I supposed that the several rooms were occupied by strangers who came and went. The briefness of their visits always suggested a service – what service, I cannot say, only imagine.

Our flat was spacious and light with windows opening on to the Charing Cross Road. It was home for me and my special friends who came and went with rapidity according to the demands of the theatre. One of our regular inmates was Audrey Leybourne. A buxom nightingale, she had a tremendous range on a good day. The famed comic Les Dawson, after she appeared with him, got the idea of establishing a speciality act of six fat or buxom ladies who would tap dance and sing. They became very much in demand, both with Les Dawson and the television public. Marie Ashton was one of the Roly Poly girls along with Audrey Leybourne, and the two became great friends. Marie was previously married to Ronnie Parnell (half of the management – Trafford and Parnell) and did many pantomimes and much choreography during the seventies and eighties. Audrey was a Welsh lass with a great passion for falling in love with gay boys. She gave them adulation unequalled since Anthony gave Cleopatra the old one-two. She started back in the stone age with Donald Wolfit and progressed to repertory seasons on stages such as that of the Grand theatre, Swansea (in the days when John Chilvers ran the joint). Her favoured boys would be plastered with gifts and mementoes daily, if not hourly, so even if they had possessed some ardour for the Welsh actress initially, it soon faded away.

Audrey worked her way through five or six repertories and a few musical tours. Eventually, she saw little future in her pursuance of the gay world and started to go in for vicars. Always a staunch churchgoer, she was devoted to their every need and would ring their bells on a Sunday. Unfortunately, vicars in general are known to favour a well-toned chest or masculine splendour. The fair sex only gets as far as the prayer books. I fear ladies who court the gay person will go to their maker unopened.

Keith Hopkins came across me when I ran the 'As You Like It' café in Monmouth Street. He was introduced to the joint by a producer who had worked several years for me, one Jim Jordan. Keith was not too smitten with the café and the mass of would-be stars who frequented it, although it must be said that various customers whom I looked after got their names in lights in no uncertain way if you list Simon and Garfunkel, Long John Baldry, Lindsey Kemp, David Bowie, Johnny Cash and many others. However, Keith did seem to take to me. He came and went at the address with great rapidity depending on what show he was working on. Being Welsh he sang like a thing possessed and musicals were his game. Keith appears mostly in music hall, but is a Dame of great stature in pantomime, having picked up many skills of that art from Tommy Trafford with whom he worked for many seasons. When he is in London, Keith resides with me in Charing Cross Road and looks after much of my empire.

Deliveries of mail in Charing Cross Road have varied, both in time and enthusiasm, but for many years we were fortunate in having a postman with experience and personality. James had delivered mail at 132 Charing Cross Road for over thirty years since the moment when his mother decided he was not right for the church. He noticed everything, everyone, and could almost prophesy what the letter contained. He knew when one was behind with the license or rent, whether you have a medical appointment coming up, and even which party you were going to vote for in a forthcoming election. He was punctual to the minute each day, ten past eight (morning, I

323

fear, not evening) and was only late once when he was attacked by the doctor's wife in Number 6 for the non-delivery of a parcel. James was a reliable as Jessie Matthews was when playing Mrs Dale on the radio and as healthy as a monk at communion. He retired one Good Friday and was never seen again.

Noise in the Charing Cross Road has always been heavy. As the years passed the volume grew alarmingly, but on the whole was acceptable and not without an amusing interlude or two.

On the left at 132 Charing Cross Road we had a café which changed hands with great frequency. The waiters were mostly foreign talent, who acknowledged the early morning and one's presence by nodding their heads since they could only manage a couple of words in English, the rest of their chat being from whatever colony had produced them.

On the right was the 'bag' shop with bags of every description from handbags to large overnight bags, and, more often than not, a human bag to serve them. Residing over this establishment was an Indian gentleman by the name of Ashe. He was small in stature and bought his stock from all over. He disappeared for two visits each year to foreign parts and returned, rejuvenated and ready for some quick trade. His brother Kiran, was a different bird altogether. Good looking, tall and hung like a stallion, he had a contrasting outlook. He was most valuable as a salesman, his figure boasting strong assets of interest to the ladies. Many a maiden had hesitated before a purchase until Kiran flashed his muscles and wide smile whereon she bought the article in question immediately. With a wandering eye on a summer's day, he is a great additional attraction to the excellent wares of the establishment and could sell sand to an Arab. Though not as dedicated as his brother, Kiran forms a very successful team with Ashe.

Bringing tales of my abode up to date, people now come and go like a fortune teller's predictions. The house has changed out of all recognition, but my flat is still light, roomy and nestles as it does in Charing Cross Road. The world flashes by and you are part of life, London and the neon theatre signs advertising their delectable wares.

One could say Charing Cross Road belongs to me or that I belong to Charing Cross Road.

Chapter 22

Snow White and her Seasons with Hansel

As we wandered into the middle and later eighties my children's musical took off. 'Hansel & Gretel' started the craze, though there were doubts about Hansel's sexuality. 'Snow White' came into her own and mastered the seven little perverts. 'Pinocchio' proved he wasn't just made of wood. With 'The Wizard of Oz' there were doubts that the Yellow Brick Road was yellow at all the less said about Beauty and her affair with the Beast the better!

In those days the show would do a whole week, mostly at No 1 theatres. Venues we played in included The Theatre Royal in Edinburgh, The King's Theatre of Glasgow, The New Wimbledon Theatre, The Gordon Craig Theatre in Stevenage, The Wyvern at Swindon, The Beck Theatre in Hayes, The Octagon in Yeovil and many more. At The Theatre Royal , Newcastle, 'Hansel & Gretel'; broke records and stayed on a second week.

We did two matinee shows a day, mostly in front of the set of the evening's offering. Of course wages were quite low and £250 and £275 was the norm for a week. Russell Grant played in most of them, though it was considered that his performance at the title role in 'The Wizard of Oz' was the best of his repertoire and, as it turned out with his astrological predictions, he obviously knew a thing or two.

I was considered part of the older brigade, leader of the 'Fairy Stories' if you like, well before 'Sesame Street' and 'The Tweenies' came along.

My friends and colleagues governed the theatres we played in. Chris Potter still ran The King's in Edinburgh, Derek Coleman had the little Pomegranate Theatre in Chesterfield, Ronnie Scott-Dodd administered The New Wimbledon

Theatre while George Johnson managed The Theatre Royal, Newcastle.

Walt Disney dominated children's imaginations with Shirley Temple's 'Animal Crackers In My Soup' a vibrant memory for grandma only. Schools came in droves and when they got back to the classroom the teachers would set an essay on what the children had seen. One always knew if the show and the artistes had done well if the children listened intensely and did not even think of going to the toilet until the interval came up. If children chatter and are restless you know the piece is not going down satisfactorily.

Headmistresses were always in the first few rows and were on hand if they saw or heard anything they did not like. I remember one buxom lady, at least 6' tall, getting up when the witch in 'Hansel & Gretel' was valiantly shoving Russell Grant into the cage. "We'll fatten you up!" screamed the witch. The head of the school party bellowed back, "Certainly not! He's far too fat already!"

My off sales and other show merchandise, of course, were a major attraction before and after the show. These provide some of us producers with our main income if the box office receipts are lower than required. The industry has grown considerably from the eighties and nineties and now there are major companies who do nothing but specialise in manufacturing children's novelties to support the juvenile show on display.

Castings for these children's romps were always fun, though one always encountered grand madams and fussy sires who though touring in a children's entertainment was beneath them. They 'pooh-phooed' the idea vigorously, but if you looked through many an actor's resumé you would discover that a large number of the stars of today started in this realm. Some of the actors who thought the whole thing was beneath them will probably be serving in a supermarket to supplement the rent until the end of time.

As the hold of television progressed, school visits to the theatre lessened somewhat. Many schools started showing certain children's television programmes and films in class as alternatives instead. By the early 2000s, school parties were sadly much fewer and less regular in coming. Into each life a little rain must fall, but be there with a bucket just in case!

Chapter 23

These Changing Times Or 'Things Are Not What They Used To Be'

As with all forms of life, patterns are constantly changing and no more so than in the world of entertainment. What was the toast of the town twenty years ago is relegated to obscurity in this current period of activity.

We are now approaching the end of the nineties and looking forward. The world of theatre was changing. Many of the theatre managers were not there anymore. Some had retired, some were replaced by more youthful and enterprising talent (often lacking the former affection and care of their predecessor). Some had gone abroad to live by the sea and some had died. It was a different scene altogether from the seventies or early eighties.

Increasingly, tours of dramatic plays were few and far between. Producers such as David Kirk, Michael Codron, Vanessa Ford and Brian Hewitt-Jones have either retired, thought again or gone on to bigger and better things. Of course death has also taken one or two.

Producers nowadays, of course, cater to much more youthful tastes with rock and roll, jazz and pop concerts etc. Songs and concerts of yesteryear are mere period pieces in today's atmosphere. Theatres such as the Astoria in Charing Cross have become homes to the James Blunts of the world. As always though, star names come and go as quickly as the weather changes. Three years ago a fellow such as James Blunt was probably working in Sainsburys, but is now the wonder of the age, the pin-up of the moment. Two successes in the charts have made him a rich and eligible fellow. He does however seem a sensible chap and has recently bought a farm in Spain where the sun always shines and he counts pigs and rabbits amongst his constant companions.

Stars such as Madonna hold on to their popularity. She still admires her good looking husband, Guy Ritchie. But he has moved on to create movies for his own company. Clearly a talent to watch. Madonna makes her own movies when she is not singing like a lark and in her latest spotlight the late Duchess of Windsor.

Kylie Minogue, recovering from a tiresome bout of cancer, returns in glory and sells out stadia for her pop concerts at the end of the year and beyond. A girl of considerable charm and adorable looks, she obviously knows how many beans make five and sells out in a matter of twenty minutes some ten thousand seats. Either the girl is a wonder or her puppet master is a man to be admired.

Movies had likewise taken on a new meaning and action films displaying great feats of magic, mystery and daring, entice all ages into the cinema to grovel over their current wares. 'Stormbreaker', 'Pirates of the Caribbean' and the return of 'Superman' are strong examples of this genre. Gone is the age of stars, of people like Greta Garbo, Marlene Dietrich and Bette Davis, instead of ushering in artistes of much lesser calibre who will probably last only for a few moons and then disappear forever. As the great Garbo said, "Time is a-fleeting," and no words were ever truer.

Casting directors again came and went in the late eighties and nineties. Professionals such as Jill Pearce, Michael Barnes, Jessica James and others have vanished and a whole new set of casting directors have emerged such as Claire Toeman of Crocodile Casting, Lesley Beastall of Broad Casting, Belinda Norcliffe, Val Weyland, Nina Gold, Suzy Korel, Ali Fearnley. The moving staircase of this brigade comes and goes as the industry moves on.

On my own scene I was producing one nighters rather than several week nights of the same production. Some of my variety names had withered and died. Stadiums, marquees and larger theatres were screaming for newer favourites whose names were featuring more and more in the nascent DVD charts.

One can be unconscious of the teenager and youth market.

It is so easy to assume that everything is what it is in the world of entertainment. I chanced to go into Foyles to buy a copy of a new book on Bette Davis. The girl on the counter, chewing gum as she spoke, had no idea who Bette Davis was. She advised me to go to the biography counter, which I did. After a lengthy search I came up with the Bette Davis opus I required. I thrust the book under the nose of the gum-chewing wench and told her that if she didn't read up a little more in her present role she should retire to a mental home, if they would have her. Such is life.

Some stars are not forgotten as they are with us forever, Cliff Richard being one. Shirley Bassey is another looking madly good in her sixties while Sophia Loren is still dazzling at a mere 71 and advertising the latest face creams.

Drama schools were springing up like mushrooms by the river bank. Many had the most peculiar names, together with carrying numbers of students, advertising their wares with abandon. To my amazement, many did not teach newcomers the delights and potential rewards of being an assistant stage manager. So, when a prospective employer gently questioned the graduating student if they were interested in being an ASM, with an occasional small part to play, they did not know what the hell you were on about, and certainly could not recognise the opportunity you offered. Whereas years ago we would foam at the mouth for even an offer of an ASM position, now the only time a drama student would go wild was if they were offered a part in a TV soap. When interviewing, many a graduating student invariably ended up trying to interview you and often you would tell them to disappear, rather than bother to analyse their potential further.

Drama schools continue to flourish, turning out over three thousand new recruits every spring. One wonders where they will all go. A few, who are very talented indeed, delighting agents such as myself with their artistry, go and quickly make their mark claiming lead parts in theatres, cinema and television. The middle group is gradually absorbed by the world of tours, repertory theatres (there are a few left), children's shows and Theatre in Education or TIE. The remaining group who scream that they are only looking for film, TV and lead theatre parts, go into oblivion quicker than a knife through butter and are promptly never seen again. Two drama school I favour are the Bristol Old Vic and Guildford School of Acting. Both are major. They hardly ever turn out a dud and get more praises heaped upon them each year. Others worth mentioning are Mountview, the Academy Drama School and Webber Douglas. Some train for three years, which seems a long, long time, and some just for one year or at an evening course, which is much more practical.

In drama schools, for every male actor one has ten females. Why? How? I told one oldish harridan that women were put on Earth for three things, to cook... to sew... and to fuck. The poor dear in question said rather demurely, "Oh dear. I'm afraid I'm not very good at any of those things."

For singers and choristers of note there is only one tutor, Mary Hammond at the Royal College of Music. A charming lady, not at all grand, she turns out more nightingales than an aviary. She keeps up with the times, the songs and arias of note and is sought after by any singer or vocalist worth their salt.

Another new generation of theatregoers demand more daring plays. They want them more modern in style and approach. These appear and collect certain audiences as they go along. Many older groups fall back on playwrights who know their business and revive plays and musicals to delight a new crowd all over again. Terence Rattigan, Noel Coward, Tennessee Williams, Arthur Miller, Alan Ayckbourn, Alan Bennett hypnotise a second time. Other revivals do the works of Rodgers and Hammerstein, Jerry Herman, Stephen Sondheim, Jerome Kern, Cole Porter and George Gershwin. Their catchy and wonderful melodies are rediscovered and once again are in vogue.

Still though, notices can make or break the run of a show. However, critics are often proved wrong – take 'Les Misérables', for example, which has flouted their original judgements by recently celebrating its twenty-fifth anniversary.

Since the seventies and eighties it has also been the fashion to 'come out', with masses of male actors declaring for all who wished to hear that they were gay, merry or camp, whichever handle you prefer. Personally, I am not sure many people were bothered except for the middle-aged matron who previously thought she had a chance with such and such actor.

Shows such as 'La Cage aux Folles' did much to dispel any reservations even though they came at a time when a couple of butterflies caught AIDS and brought the disease into general circulation. Many of the actor-managers in days gone by would eye up a prospective actor and tell you which way he 'went' in the blinking of an eyelash.

With everything out in the open, people in the trade were so often propositioned that it was up to the person in question to say 'Not a chance, kind sir' or possibly, 'What a lovely idea'.

Over the years Equity has done its best to try and get a better deal for its members. Occasionally it has too, although I say it is up to the artiste himself to sort out the wolves from the lambs and to know whether in a certain job they are likely to get jam on their bread and butter.

Chapter 24

Variety... Snippets from the Wicker Basket

My dates with variety up and down the country were mostly good earners and great fun. I had a regular retinue of top artistes and dates were fairly easy to come by. Amongst my stars were John Hanson, Frankie Howerd, Don Maclean, Elizabeth Dawn, Bob Monkhouse and Ruby Murray.

John Hanson was with me for about twelve years. Probably the last of the musical comedy singers, his fame was remarkable and his fans ardent and faithful. He had enjoyed several runs in the West End, each one of two years. His shows included 'The Desert Song' and 'The Student Prince'. His tours were legendary. We toured most towns with one nighters (following up tours in the 1950s and 1960s when 'The Desert Song', 'Rose Marie' and others were poplar). On the tours, coach parties would book up months ahead to bring ladies aged from 50 to 80 to the nearest theatre in order to join in the adoration of John. They knew what he would sing, which arrangement from which musical and it didn't matter one jot.

He told a joke against himself. Once, at a matinee at the Grand Theatre in Wolverhampton, an old lady got so excited before the concert began that the attendant had to get her back out to her coach. As the man put his arms around her to help her get out of her seat she whispered, "Oh, I wish you were the Red Shadow!" (The Red Shadow was the lead John had played in 'The Desert Song').

He was the housewife's dream. His wife Barbara often came along with him. She would listen on the tannoy to the strength of his reception by the audience and sometimes look at me as if to say, 'He's still got it!' She was petite and terribly pretty and we all used to say that when John kicked the bucket she would be a widow most merry and probably marry a very rich elderly man immediately. Actually, it didn't turn out that way. She was taken very ill and had to endure constant nursing for the rest of her life in a wheelchair, and she eventually died very near to her John.

John would be quiet, look at the supporting cast with an assured eye, and smile at me. Occasionally he did look askance. One day at the New Theatre in Southport he noted that I had booked Elizabeth Dawn alias Vera Duckworth from 'Coronation Street'. He winked at me and said, "I hope you know what you are doing!" Of course I did! She was to close the first half. Elizabeth had a strange act, but she was a vibrant lass and the audience took to her well. However, her language was a bit strong. After a couple of 'fucks', John Hanson came steaming out of his dressing room and said, "Are my ears deceiving me or am I in the wrong theatre?"

John was a modest man in spite of his stardom. I felt that he was quite wealthy and had put loads aside for a rainy day (after all he was a star for 30 years), but he always brought sandwiches wrapped in silver paper for his gigs.

Opening the variety bills for John were Richard and Laura Beaumont, children of Sally Barnes in song and dance. Richard went on to act with his second sweetheart Lynn. Laura married Bill Oddie (after a stint in 'Sale Of The Century') and is often seen on television.

On most variety concerts I starred Monica Dell, a great friend of mine, whose rich soprano voice was perfect for the type of audience we attracted. Monica was born in Yorkshire, but married a Frenchman (she worked in Paris for many years). Then she divorced her Parisian husband and came back here to continue her career. Her stage dresses were a riot and her clothes offstage likewise. She is one of the few women I know who can wear trousers superbly. She has a rather tough manner, and will never suffer fools gladly, although underneath runs a lovely current of humour. She retired from the stage around eight years ago and lives with her second husband, Eric, a superb designer, in quiet bliss in Weybridge.

Chapter 25

Looking Back

As one passes through life, seemingly slowly, but in fact, very rapidly, one occasionally looks back and remembers little incidents.

One of my first acting jobs was in the army. Someone had the bright idea of doing a play (they probably saw an early Judy Garland/Mickey Rooney film on their day off) and all the men in my particular army camp came to see it. I was never much of an actor, but I am excellent at disguise and some of my impressions are not far behind. In my current Songbook productions, my Marlene Dietrich still brings down the house when I trill 'See what the boys in the backroom will have' (from her magic comeback movie: 'Destry Rides Again').

I can remember meeting Errol Flynn at the Rif Hotel in Tangier and thinking how friendly the chap was. Greeting Ingrid Bergman in her dressing room at the Cambridge Theatre was an event also. She looked quite plain until she smiled. Then her smile was like the heavens opening. Suddenly she looked radiant and beautiful and you felt you had known her forever. The visit was instigated by Jeremy Brett, then one of the most beautiful men in England (and he knew it). He had married Anna Massey. Whether he desired to belong to the royal Massey brigade or because he was madly and passionately in love with Anna I do not know, but he was gay when the tendency was frowned upon.

Charles Laughton, whom many regarded as our best actor, was a bit of an oddity. So was Elsa Lanchester whom he married. Charles wed Elsa at twelve noon on the dot one Sunday. By four p.m. had pleasured at least three young men and Elsa knew in a flash that her life would never be dull.

More lately, I was on 'Woman's Hour' with Anne Rogers (who was playing Jessie Matthews in a quickie of her life at the Jerymn Street Theatre in the West End for the impresario Richard Stirling). Anne came on the radio spot and told the interviewer she had never heard of Jessie Matthews before she was offered the show. I said, "You must be mad or telling lies." I was furious. Anne came out of the musical Billy Elliott when it was previewing at the Victoria Palace Theatre saying that her part had been made too small. Ann Emery (Dick's sister), whom I had featured many times in variety, took over the role and walked off with most of the notices. Ann without an 'e' curtain speech at the end of her variety act was always Thanks for having me – and for those who haven't have patience!"

Mandy Rice-Davies was a smashing lady. Stylish, her clothes were a delight. She had looks and a good dollop of talent. She came on board to do a play for me up in the little Georgian Theatre in Richmond in North Yorkshire. A unique northern beauty spot became instantly unique for having Mandy there in the play. During the Profumo Scandal, Mandy had the sense to turn the tables on the newspapers and the scurrilous hags who bayed for blood. Most men like a bit of skirt, but this lady was more than a match for the lads. She went on with her hopes and dreams as if nothing had ever happened. Not so for the girl who headed the scandal, Christine Keeler. She went into hiding, took up knitting and was never heard of again. When we were there, the Georgian Theatre was looked after by an enchanting couple in the autumn of their years, Mr and Mrs Fairbrother. They cared so much for their tiny theatre in the hills and the artistes fortunate enough to play it. We did over twelve other plays there over a period of time and when we went back it was always like going home. Mandy went on to marry extremely well and teach the world all about style and fashion. She was a strong actress also and measured up in the straight play well. Quite a star. Today she will be a much older lady, and a lesson to us all.

Marlene Dietrich was a woman I could have written three books about. She was an immense star and was adored by almost every Tom, Dick and Harry. Her striking looks when well past her prime provided hope for us all. She could launch a thousand ships, captivate and mesmerise an audience of thousands, but would go and sit by the beds of countless wounded soldiers three times weekly during moments of darkness. I don't think she was very prudent with money even though she earned truckloads of gold coins over the years. She never lost the common touch and wallowed in the adoration her fans gave her, from that of her fellow stars like Noel Coward, Tyrone Power, Charles Laughton, Dirk Bogarde and John Mills (and we all know how difficult Dirk Bogarde was to please) to the love offered by the little man on the street, the widow in the Midlands and the pensioners who never missed a show of hers. Marlene Dietrich was also very gracious to her fans in return. "May I have your glove?" enquired one lady from Lancashire.

"One will not do. You must have two," was Marlene's response. She removed both her gloves and kissed the woman on the cheek. I dare say that lady did not wash her face for a week.

The book on her daughter Maria Riva was strangely odd and cold and left many gaps to be answered, but then, as the bishop said, one candle was better than none.

As we pass along life's highway, many of the famous have proved so memorable – and so different from their pictures. But we are never really what we are painted (except perhaps Bette Davis) and it is left to the connoisseur to draw back the veil and illuminate what is on view and in discussion.

Already a fan of Wilde's novel, 'The Picture of Dorian Gray', I was accosted recently by an old friend who I had not seen for twenty years. She looked at me and said, "Goodness you don't look a day older than when I last saw you," but added, "How's the picture in the attic?"

As one passes through, we get glimpses of a face, a nod, shrug, as life takes us on our way… and then, there is just a quick flash of time and we are in another town, another place and another moment.

Chapter 26

An Unexpected Scene

After my summer seasons at the Hippodrome Theatre in Eastbourne (1991-2) I started to send out again my popular children's musicals. Although wanting very much to write and take out a play for the mature masses (I had been starting a play with the riveting title 'Murder in the Tarot Cards') my 'Tales from the Jungle Book', 'Snow White and the Seven Dwarfs', and 'The Wizard of Oz' were the proven successes and took enough money to show a reasonable profit wherever we went.

I was lucky to retain a talented company of players who knew the pieces and were mostly acquainted with the theatres they would play, which is always a bonus. One gets to know a theatre so that going back to it is like returning to an old friend with love and affection. If, in the interim anyone had altered the décor, stage or seating capacity, it would be noted and probably disapproved of accordingly. New administrators often would like to alter certain points as if to announce that someone new had arrived and things would change.

Around this time, my Songbooks were again proving popular, though some of the soloists would eventually go on to better things and longer runs in various musicals. But I knew my singers, my nightingales, and had a secret book where all was recorded, noted and if necessary revealed.

I still would take a well-known children's musical into a theatre and not a pantomime; I would leave pantomime to the bigger fish. As the years have rolled on, more and more theatres increasingly contract larger and larger companies to present pantomime, gradually cutting out the smaller producer – which is a real shame. I fear it is a sign of the times, almost akin to the supermarket cutting out the little greengrocer's on the corner.

In the early nineties, around thirty artistes wrote in on an average week requesting consideration for various projects. I tried to see them all, pointing out opportunities if they were ready to project their particular talents, be it in vocal skill, dramatic prowess or commercial filming. I auditioned every month, giving new talents the opportunity to sing, dance and illuminate a 'piece' with their own personalities. Every so often a person comes in who you can see is a natural and will light up the sky whenever he or she gets the chance. That makes our day (for I always have my choreographer and drama teacher, Madame Simone, with me). In general, I think artistes are not given the time and space to give their all and impress the producer or agent.

With such a busy office to administer, any personal illness is not to be tolerated. However, once, an unexpected thing happened. I was walking along and suddenly could not manage my steps. My head reeled and I was altogether not well at all. I had not been visiting box offices at any theatres I was shortly playing, which had, in the past, precipitated several seizures or palpitations. I was not really thinking about anything. I called a cab and managed to get home to my flat in Charing Cross Road, which, mercifully, is only on the second floor. I then rang a friend. She raced round, took one look at me, bundled me into a cab and we flew to University College Hospital as fast as the cab could manage.

The A&E department quickly perused me, laid me out and did some tests. A hospital sister arrived and declared that I must be admitted to a ward without delay. I could not quite gather if she was playing a part in a series or if it was real, but she insisted and I was admitted forthwith.

A few hours later I seemed to gather what was happening to me. I looked around and was in a corner of a ward. It gave me the impression of being high up, but was actually on the first floor. I seemed a little away from everyone else.

A nurse came. "Are you feeling a little better?" she ventured.

I didn't know. It was obvious I had been attended to... dealt with, if you like. Everything was a trifle strange, but it seemed that I was dangerously ill. I decided to court sleep and passed out until the morning.

Seven a.m. came, and it held no terrors for me. It was my usual waking hour. On the stroke I awoke.

"Ah," said the early morning nurse. "You are looking better." It was obvious I had gone from resembling Dracula to Boris Karloff. I smiled a weak smile. "Tea?"

"Yes, please. Three teabags and a smattering of sugar."

The nurse smiled. Three teabags indeed. She had never heard the like.

I managed to sit up and survey the scene. Being in the corner of a ward I could not really see the dramatis personae of this particular drama... but it seemed to be a mixed cast with men, old men, boys, girlies and old maids. It was an odd little comedy.

Time passed and the day unfolded. People came and went. Everyone was very kind. I had masses of flowers. My table looked like the Chelsea Flower Show. My view was only spoilt by the Hungarian in the next bed who had his pisspot on the table. I called the sister over.

"His exhibition is really spoiling my flower display."

The sister looked at him and then at my table. "Yes, I suppose it is."

These days flowers are not permitted, God knows why, they did so much to brighten up a ward.

I noticed after lunch that the bloke in the next bed had gone and we had a spinster of the parish in his old bed. She only had a bunch of primroses in a little vase. She smiled and I smiled back.

We all mattered to the nurses. They had never heard of me, but I began to think that I did interest them. Maybe it was because I lived on fruit, or that they gathered from my visitors that I belonged to the world of entertainment, especially as the parade of fruit and flowers that appeared would not have disgraced an opening night at Covent Garden. In these surroundings, I did feel that whatever had attacked me and caused my indisposition could be abating.

Later on that evening, after declining tea and supper, I

341

dozed off a little, just before a stream of friends arrived. The kindly sister must have let them in. They didn't encourage masses of visitors, especially at night.

The next day I was moved over to the centre of the ward. I felt much better and was sitting up. My stage manager, Tony Joseph, was staying at my flat and feeding my cat Maud, who was a massive size, I didn't approve of dieting. Tony brought me the mail over each morning so I could sift through and see if there was anything urgent.

The sister came over again the day after. I was feeling so much better I felt that they could let me out into the wide world. She was obviously in the mood for a chat and drew up a chair. Apparently my blood had clotted and this was the real problem. She emphasises that my age was a contributing factor and the same predicament could occur once more. Oh, calamity. But they had a cure. I was to take Warfarin tablets forever... and ever. She assured me it was a common complaint and masses of people took Warfarin as regularly as their cornflakes in the morning. The house doctor, who issued your tablets for the day, allocated you a number of pills. Of course my dosage would be higher than anyone else's, then or now. Nine!

Later that day, they let me out. My desk at the flat was littered with letters for interviews, requests for casting suggestions, several demands for money, and a few cheques. Life was back to normal... and bookings had to be arranged. Tony made two strong cups of tea and a good selection of biscuits. Life was indeed back to normal.

I cannot praise the University College enough. A benefit must be arranged!

Chapter 27

Impresarios

Very often, impresarios are not too familiar with the goods in their shop window, preferring to leave the actual mixing of the show to the producer. But they want to have their name on the top of the poster or programme, and be the boss.

One of my favourite impresarios is a man who has climbed the rusty stairs to some success – and is still climbing. His name is Paul Holman. He joined the throng many years ago and initially attracted attention at the St George's Theatre, Great Yarmouth, after it graduated from being a church with choristers of various talents to a theatre. It first started to achieve notoriety when a double act called Burdon and Moran bought some tabs and humbly asked the public to support their artistry. Pantomime performers of a fine standard, Maurice Moran was the boss of the outfit. Together with his colleague Roger Burdon, their ugly sisters in 'Cinderella' were really something to see. They became one of the best paid of the ugly sisters available; and were variety artistes of repute. They had toured the length and breadth of the land in music hall and revue etc. and knew how to captivate an older audience and how to make less attentive hags sit up and pay attention.

When Maurice Moran collapsed and died one spring a few years ago, his partner Roger called it a day and Paul Holman came into my realm. I had, with my own company, played many concerts and variety bills over the years in Great Yarmouth during Maurice's reign. Paul managed the running of the theatre from then onwards and took to the trade with gusto. He got the tills busy with paying customers and built up a following. Previously he had been a musical director of note. After a while, Great Yarmouth became too small for his endeavours. Mr Holman had quite a few bob by now and he started to make his name and face known to a much wider public up and down the country

Paul is a large man, with an enormous carriage that he controls with strong dexterity. He has a sense of humour second to none and laughs like a hyena regularly. He dwells in South Ruislip, a village not so far from London, and has a team of six to help him cast and regulate his empire.

Paul's mainstay and possibly the backroom boy is John, his partner. John is a demon with paperwork. His precision is faultless and he is rumoured to once have been a bank manager. Around sixty years of age, he moves stealthily in the background, attracting little attention until a catastrophe occurs and then he rectifies it with much skill and speed. Many artistes who work for the company are not aware of his dedication. John is what you would call laid back, which is not a bad thing, and keeps his trained eye on most of the pantomimes and revues under Paul Holman's banner.

Paul started with three pantomimes and quickly added more each year until now he boasts thirteen and is like a fox to the kill when a further date became vacant or possible. He exhausts quickly, driving his large Rolls Royce up and down the countryside. He has many ailments he shouldn't have, but, in spite of this, he never misses engagements, auditions, and discussion on how to make money and how to enchant a theatre owner long before the curtain rises. He is as stage struck now as he was at twenty years of age and would play a shithouse in Istanbul if it was going. He is never well and visits his GP more times than a nympho on heat, which is almost every day, with a new complaint or symptom. The GP is either a quack with the patience to charge high fees or a masochistic lunatic craving punishment. But that said, he received Paul at every visit, prescribes God knows what to each malady and is certainly a man of medicine whose details you ought to have listed in your address book. If you speak to Paul Holman in the morning, afternoon or evening, he is forever in avid negotiation for a new date for a concert or pantomime or is possibly looking for a cure for a current affliction. He is a tonic to know and a gentleman to boot. Pantomimes are his main dish, and he collects stars as one would do if posing as an astronomer. He is an unassuming businessman and sometimes asks an absurd and way out price for his goods that the astonished theatre manager agrees to, but, more usually, he starts high and finishes midway when arranging payments for his products.

Paul's executive producer is a young man called Adrian Jeckells, whom I started off on the road to success or complete contentment. He hails from Great Yarmouth, which was a cross to bear from the start. Whether religion was a help, or whether his ruthless ambition carried him along was never known, but Adrian was a good bet from the beginning. We found him early on when he was just a virgin on a camping weekend with boy scouts and he quickly joined my office as an assistant in my menagerie. Being a hoofer of quality with a smashing voice, we were able to offer him much work in our Songbook concerts plus some excellent touring engagements on the Number One circuit in such fables as 'Hansel and Gretel', 'Pinocchio', 'The wonderful Wizard of Oz' and 'Snow white'. He quickly learned about the birds and the bees (and possibly the butterflies) and enchanted many a maiden with his prowess. He starred and worked in many shows for me in the early nineties and was perfect for the clientele we attracted, being slim, boyish, with a cute grin, plus loads of personality allied to a strong baritone voice. He delighted the old girls, the maiden aunts, ambitious spinsters and nuns that make up most of my audiences for the Songbook concerts of rare distinction that we present up and down the land. He could learn a song in two shakes of a lamb's tail and be familiar with the whole programme (and several of the soloists it was rumoured) in no time at all. He remains a strong choreographer, plotting movement for many a charade and persuading lots of hoofers to dance like ferrets and give their all when the music plays. I like to think that Adrian picked up the rudiments of the business with me and, as a consequence, is now an executive producer for Paul Holman. He has lost some of his hair in the passage of time, but his older looks persuades most of the novices who sing for him that he is a producer of substance and experience and that they would benefit from joining his zoo, which indeed they would. Recently Adrian left the Paul Holman menagerie and bought a promising drama school known as The London School of Musical Theatre. He runs it superbly and the students all sing like things possessed. They leave fully fit for promising parts in top class musicals.

Adrian had the luck to meet and fall in love with a very talented chorine and choreographer, Helen, who, still looking like a child though in her late twenties, married the said Mr Jeckells without delay.

Lee Waddingham completes the Paul Holman team. A shrewd and quick young man, he is a wizard at publicity, as efficient as they come and will surely be a producer and impresario before many moons are out. He is in the right stable to form and nurture his talents. Lee has been around for more than a year and a day, flitting from working as a publicity associate for Colin Simmons at the Westminster Theatre before it closed to being the press officer for the Mountview Academy of Theatre Arts. Paul Holman advertised for an assistant of expertise and stability in a local paper and, out of all the hags that applied, Lee was selected as the best. A likeable lad of reasonable looks, he can fill in as a singer and tap like a thing possessed if anyone is ill and is a pursuer of power. One to keep your eye on, he falls in love much quicker than one could digest the 'Gay Times', but whether he favours the girls or the boys is the ten dollar question. I have nicknamed him Lee the Flea, which he accepts with a modicum of grace.

I should say here that many have come and gone in the wilderness which is the world of touring and producing. Those I am not going to comment on now. Let us instead deal with the producers who are still with us, some counting their gold almost nightly, some living in the grand mansion at the top of the hill, and some in a shop around the corner.

As the business is always in the throes of constant change, some impresarios fit in, some change and some disappear forever into oblivion.

Other I have worked with and held in high regard for their quality and class are Dick Ray, David Lee, Charles Vance (who is mentioned elsewhere), Colin McIntyre, Garth Harrison and Duggie Chapman.

Bill Kenwright, who started with us all in the nineteen seventies, was always an ambitious gentleman and an avid follower of football. Very handsome, he attracted ladies by the score and knew how to bat one off against another. He took chances that a lion tamer would be proud of and whimpered not when he fell into the mire of a theatre production gone wrong. Early on he saw the potential of 'Joseph and the Amazing Technicolour Dreamcoat' and 'Blood Brothers', acquired their rights and presented these two musicals in the West End for a number of years. Both shows have provided the mink, the lushness of luxury and the gold to front many splendid shows which rewards a top producer with courage.

A partner of mine, Keith Hopkins, the fine Welsh singer, caught the bug of presenting shows from me and from a very old friend Tommy Trafford. Tommy was a northern comic of great popularity, very similar to Les Dawson and equally as regarded. Tommy taught Keith much of his artistry, but was not always spot on when forecasting the takings of a new tour (but then few of us are, except Bill Kenwright). Tommy starred Keith Hopkins in numerous summer seasons and Old Time Music Hall galas so that nowadays there is no one more reliable for this medium. Many a time his booking has turned a so-so show into a sure hit. He first appeared as Dame at the little Princess Theatre in Hunstanton and was an instant star there, so much so in fact that he starred in pantomime there for over twelve years. Keith is a genius with the needle (the sewing type) and his designs for various shows have been outstanding successes. He is a Piscean, which does dampen his ambition and enthusiasm quite a bit, but he surely will be top of the bill before long.

I really cannot write a chapter on impresarios without mentioning Alexander Bridge. Known as 'Momma Bridge' in the trade, Peter was his real name. He introduced musical comedies to the masses, touring up and down the country for twenty years. He was also responsible for bringing back some of the old magic of the Ivor Novello musicals. He lured June

Bronhill from Australia. After she had completed a celebrated run of 'The Merry Widow' at the London Coliseum she was his star for four or five years. Musicals were Peter's delight and he could arrange, rehearse and stage a show in several days. He knew what he was going to do, when and how. No one knew the age of the musical like this man. He employed many stars on and off and was responsible for bringing back many, including Jessie Matthews and Evelyne Laye (not simultaneously, that would have been total war), Olive Gilbert, Jack Buchanan, John Hanson and, of course, June Bronhill. He toured No 1 theatres and smaller ones up and down the country and brought many a superb night of melody to those who might never have seen one in the theatre. He was generous, kind and a total idiot with money. Often debt collectors show up out of the blue. He pacified them, gave them tickets for his shows and sent them on their way. Somehow he survived and many are the memories of his wonderful nights in the theatre.

Amongst Alexander Bridge's team was a good young actor, Bruce James. We always felt that Alex was in love with Bruce, but we also could tell that Bruce was not at all gay. Of course Alex (Peter) certainly was. Once Peter had departed to the heavens, Bruce started his own company. After all those years with Alexander Bridge, he had learnt all the tricks of the trade and is now a most reputable and busy manager. He quickly stages, produces and sweeps around the provinces like a thing possessed. If Momma Bridge is looking down from the heavens, how pleased he would be to see that Bruce has built such a mighty career and alternatives between straight plays and musicals as a touring manager of class.

The Jarla Theatre in Stockholm became our home once more. We had previously played record seasons of plays there for the Danish impresario Neils Wenkens. I cast the company from my stable with the involvement of Terence Young, the film director. Terence was becoming a solitary figure in the entertainment business. It was some time since he had directed a film, even though his career until then had been impressive. He shot several of the early Bond films and he and Sean Connery got on like a house on fire.

Terence was a quiet man, still an attractive one, but I always felt something had saddened him and turned him into a recluse. Tommy Iwering found the key and gradually we got Terence interested in directing and mounting plays for a couple of seasons in Stockholm. We presented 'Don't Dress For Dinner', 'Anyone For Breakfast' and a couple of classic Agatha Christies.

John Redgrave, another impresario, presented shows here and there and it chanced he had the Hippodrome in Eastbourne for Sunday night shows for a season. He came to me and together we worked out a programme of songs from the pens of Jerome Kern, Cole Porter, Gershwin and many others to make an agreeable Sunday night concert. John was a middle-aged man with much panache, enthusiasm and wit. He was just my cup of tea and so was the show. We played the whole season with four nightingales singing and myself narrating and doing the occasional number such as 'Que Sera Sera'. We seemed not to have put a foot wrong as the whole season was full every Sunday night. My 'West End to Broadway Songbook' courtesy of John Redgrave was a great success in 1991 and 1992 and we never played to less than 90 per cent of the house on any week.

After this season in the nineties, an associate of John Redgrave, one Colin Matthew, saw the commercial magic of this concoction and quickly arranged a lease for the Hippodrome. John and I were down the Swanee, which was a shame. However, we started many concerts in other towns which were most popular and remunerative.

John was not related to the Redgrave dynasty, but quickly became a talent that was much in demand. His lighting might worry Nostradamus and his shows were regarded as the crème de la crème. We worked together again in the nineties when I asked him to produce and light my show at the London Palladium. It starred Jim Bailey, a high class drag artiste, who made his name with an impersonation of Judy Garland. He had achieved success for many years in the States and was not all that famous in this country, even though he had an English manager. I took an almighty chance for the Palladium engagement, risking some £18,000. But it came off (mainly thanks to the publicity campaign I created for Mr Bailey). On the night we were sold out. We were then booked for Brighton (some say there are more queens in this resort than many a Royal Ball, but no matter). That was okay, but Mr Bailey insisted in presenting his impersonation of one Barbara Streisand. Instead of saying now, no, no, I said, "Okay, do it your own way." That was my undoing. Brighton and the many queens residing there did not want to see Jim Bailey's impersonation of this Jewish superstar. They wanted Garland, and because they didn't get her, stayed away. However, fate did come to my assistance this time. A close friend, one Peter Tod, who was the then general manager of the Hippodrome in Birmingham, was an enormous fan of Jim Bailey. He booked the show for his venue for the following Sunday. Garland we did, and it was a great success. I picked up the loot I had dropped at on at the south coast. I have never played Brighton since.

Rainbow Theatre has been going quite a while and the ship is captained by a strong director by the name of Nic Young. Looked after by a coterie of most experienced females (including his lovely wife Alex), he entertains schools and art centres throughout the South East with snatches of Shakespeare and fine plays of his own creation. Nic was formerly the artistic director at the Connaught Theatre, Worthing, but tired of this and set up his own company where he hones the skills of many young actors who otherwise would have no opportunity to develop their talents through the virtually extinct repertory system. Sometimes mistaken for a fortune teller or other new age mystic, he works through each year with an amazing dexterity. Actors frequently ask to go back and do another season for him as they enjoy playing two to three schools a day and teaching the small babies all about Shakespeare.

Nic can be a bit Jewish regarding salaries, but we all have a cross to bear. Two protégés of his, Madame Hilary and Master Andy Long, run a company of similar excitement called Rainbow Theatre London East in Greenwich. They also skip around that area with their versions of various Shakespearean frolics. Rainbow's activities culminate each year in the early summer with outdoor productions of two Shakespearean classics. In the last couple of years they have established a feted season at the Royal Observatory Gardens in Greenwich Park that opens after their run finishes at Highdown Gardens outside Worthing. It is so popular that even the rabbits book early for a good view.

Ian Dickens first set eyes upon me during my brief sojourn running the lovely Lyceum Theatre at Crewe. He emerged as a producer with class in the early 1990s, touring major plays with stars and a few angels in all No 1 theatres. He works like a demon, directing one play whilst juggling another, and sometimes has as many as four or five plays on the go at any one time.

Ben West joined my merry crew several years ago, a lad from Ipswich (now there's a title for a play). An actor who had thoughts about being an agent. He came and tasted the agency wine and liked what he saw. His acting as Scarecrow in my touring production of 'The Wonderful Wizard Of Oz' and his playing of Baloo in 'Tales From The Jungle Book' have earned him many plaudits. He looks like a jockey some days (he loves wearing a cap) and a politician on others. With a telephone manner to be savoured, he is clearly a chap to keep your eye on.

Somewhere along the line I met one, Colin Simmons. A modest and attractive man, slowly approaching middle age but quite a character. He had been dabbling in the world of show business since the Second World War (I suspect he was something in ENSA then) but he booked my 'Tales From The Jungle Book' the moment he met me and we got on like a jungle on fire then and ever since. He had organised costume balls, regattas, charity star concerts and God knows what and I found the man quite captivating.

He had taken over the fading Westminster Theatre at Victoria and although this grand old building was almost on its last legs he managed to breathe magic into the building, and mounted some interesting and spellbinding shows before it caught fire and closed forever. Several mentions in the press have reported that a smaller theatre will be built on the site, but years have passed, and only a few bricks have been put in place to perhaps start this new venture. Time waits for no man and it certainly didn't have to wait for Colin Simmons who was on to many new ideas, adventures, and extravaganzas which make up the world of greasepaint. A very interesting and adventurous man.

Before I end my impresario ranting I must also tell you about Andy Smith (we call him Andy Pandy). He was in Norwich booking shows for the natives after spending his youth and early teens as a circus performer of quality. He rang me up one fine day and offered me a week's work at The Playhouse Theatre in Norwich. Although perhaps the poor relation to The Theatre Royal in that noble town it was nevertheless a building with a history of class. "How would Mowgli like to come and dazzle Norwich?" he enquired. I replied that Mowgli would be delighted, he mentioned an agreeable sum so we loaded the caravans and played The Playhouse. The marketing was magic, and Andy gave us a superb week of business and fun. Soon after Andy moved to London to market his expertise and charm in entertainment for the capital. He has created work, interest, and many superb productions since then and I believe guides many a would-be stage struck youngster onto the road to fame. Much more than an impresario Andy, is a man of remarkable energy and liable to pop up at any time.

Above, I have covered many of the gentlemen who are impresarios. They have provided lots of entertainment over the years, lost vast sums in doing so, yet still come back for more. Hungry they are they will never be any different.

Chapter 28

A Revival, Indeed!

As we entered January in the year of grace 2006 I suddenly came across my script for the musical 'Oh Camille!' I had first tried this out with some success in the late seventies at the Arts Theatre as I said in Chapter 9. The idea was to promote the classic film 'Camille' as a comedy with Marguerite Gautier played a la Mae West. It had a scintillating score by one David Aman which was quite remarkable. David was a tall Dickensian man, with a long, sharp nose and a most studious manner. He resembled a muddling professor on a good day. But music he could write and write well. We had used one or two of his efforts already in my touring children's musicals 'The Wonderful Wizard of Oz' and 'Pinocchio'.

For the 2006 run I was looking around for a West End theatre for a week's try-out. That January, The Arts was being run by a slip of a girl, vague as buggery on matters of the theatre, (probably a former waitress in McDonald's I should not wonder). She asked £11,000 for the week's rent and I told her I did not want to buy the place. I tried the Player's Theatre underneath the arches, which has changed hands more times than a second-hand bookshop. They asked for £9,000. After this I contacted the manager of the Duchess Theatre. Although he was familiar with my work (he had previously declared my Jessie Matthews Show at Shaftesbury Theatre in 1977 his best night in the theatre), he never even bothered to reply to my enquiry. So we looked further.

So there I was with a promising musical revival but without a theatre. Suddenly a nun out selling poppies reminded me that there was the Shaw Theatre near King's Cross in the Euston Road. I had formerly staged 'Tales from the Jungle Book' at the Shaw several years before. Then; with a box office guarantee from a fetching manageress, Madame Nina, it went extremely well. Several years on, when we had repainted the Yellow Brick Road, I staged my popular 'The Wonderful Wizard of Oz', which had also fared well. But Madame Nina had departed to other shores or other professions. The Shaw was then being run by a large and rotund fellow by the name of Tim Sayers. He had just arrived from several years at the Bridewell Theatre, a poor and struggling outpost possessing immense courage for staging interesting shows in the City. The Shaw Theatre had recently been acquired by Brian Daniels, an impresario who had been floating around for some time and achieving a ripple of success running the New End Theatre, a fringe venue with a future.

I arranged an interview with Messrs Sayers and Daniels. After discussion, it transpired these two gentlemen with aspirations were demanding £3,500 cash for a 9 day run. I pondered. After all, I had been all over town and if I did not get 'Oh, Camille!' back on stage now, I never would. I looked into my handbag, which, on a good day, can be deceptive, I decided to risk my lot. A contract was drawn up and we were in business. What I had not really reckoned on was the fact that the theatre had bugger all equipment, with hardly a weight and brace to its name. All the equipment needed to stage a good show had to be hired, or borrowed, and, to boot, there were no staff backstage, not even mice.

The Shaw Theatre had much to answer for. From the word go, my office and staff had to take charge of the publicity. The box office at the Shaw turned out to be a shambles, opening and closing as it chose.

I assembled a cast. I wanted several of the originals, but, of course, it did not occur to me that all of the cast of the original tryout were now twenty-seven years older. I, like many hags of my profession, am always conscious of my advancing years, but somehow I am of the opinion that everyone else remains the same.

I was warned of the many pitfalls and difficulties on staging 'Oh, Camille!' but I was positive that once the show was on and liked, the public would gradually catch on to the magic of the piece.

Some had doubts about 'Oh, Camille!' Not that they did not like the piece, for they did. But the Shaw Theatre did not entrance them and the management in control excited them even less. However, rehearsals were already arranged and an impact was extremely possible in this unfashionable venue in the Euston Road.

The fact was that I knew that I could count on a large number of friends and artistes I represented in this period to buy tickets. Up to a point, this ploy worked well. But selling tickets beyond this charmed and so so circus would be a time consuming adventure and newspapers did not exactly fall over themselves to mention the show. Keith Hopkins, my associate, directed, and, being a musical comedy star of the provinces, he had some excellent ideas. Some upgrading of the script was necessary though, as one-liners that were a sensation circa 1980, might not catch fire in 2006.

I must say that the new cast were very commendable, though our choice of leading lady, Jade Bradley, a most promising young filly from the Guildford School of Acting, was no Ruth Madoc. Ably supported by one Gareth McLeod, a wildly talented new lad, another girl, Leah Grayson, quickly caught all the comedy in an enchanting performance as Nanine. As always we could count a hundred per cent on an old friend and excellent pro, Simon Bashford. Simon worked constantly with me on the show and, apart from being a splendid actor, his choreography was a delight. We opened 'Oh, Camille!' to a mere sixty people. This we followed up with eighty on the second night. I set the gala performance for the third evening just in case everyone had not mastered their lines (I was never an enthusiast for rehearsals and thought five days a lifetime), but as it turned out, the cast were perfect in every way. The gala attracted three hundred and forty people, mostly friends and admirers of the cast and myself, plus a selection from my fan club. A few managements turned up out of interest to see what the hell I was up to.

The evening could not have gone better. The crowd that stayed after the show was a wonderful mix and provided an enjoyable finale. Jeanna L'Esty, who was in the original version, turned up out of the blue. Stunning in personality and appearance, she was a major delight for all. She looked no more than thirty years of age, when in fact she must have been forty-five.

As the week went on, the audiences were poor and patchy. By Friday I came to realise that I was not going to cover my running costs and it was going to be a grim spring. The management could not even be bothered to come and see the piece, not even on the gala night with its added allurement of free wine. They were either absent from the theatre and their offices or having a tipple in the hotel or some other secluded corner. The press stayed away as if we were staging an epidemic. Even the Camden News, usually primed to review a charade, an end of term frolic or gay revue of dubious intention, ignored us. I did get a mention on a BBC radio programme in the late night roundup starring my good friend Sadie Nine. However, as she was on from ten p.m. until two a.m. her audience were a little mixed to say the least, being on the way home from either a masquerade or a prayer meeting at the local tavern. Novotel, who owned the theatre and the hotel, could not be bothered with whatever fare was on at their premises and relied on conferences to keep the theatre financially afloat. They never came to see a show of any kind from a producer that was stupid enough to mount a production and pay for the privilege.

At the end of the run I had lost several thousand pounds quite easily, plus a lot of time and patience. This was the only time I had ever produced a profit share production and it would certainly be the last. I pawned a bit of jewellery to give the cast a little support. Confessions of my errors seemed to be the most appropriate move. The moral of the tale seems to be that a revival needs a lot of thought and a little testing of the water. A few months ago the composer of 'Oh, Camille!' David Aman, left us to go to the heavens. He had been ailing for a considerable time, and his eyes were failing him. A superb composer, he was never rewarded for the major talent he was. Perhaps in his next life he will be.

The year of 2006 was moving on however, and so was I.

We returned to the wonderful Broadway Theatre (formerly the Lewisham Theatre – why names of theatres are constantly changed I shall never know!) and played as we do every February to packed houses with much adulation for three superb days. This helped start fill up the handbag somewhat, but it still took the whole of March to finally pay everyone their dues.

Life upon the very wicked stage indeed...

The theatrical scene is constantly changing and currently there seem to be more and more productions and new companies. Moreover, there are so many new creatures running theatres. Many venues harbour lady managers, new to the game and, more critically, new to theatre. Producers like myself miss days gone by when they knew the manager backwards, a man who had probably run his theatre from the year dot. Some of these managers have now departed to the heavens to book different delights while other old friends have retired to catch creatures of a different kind in mountain streams or country meadows.

A new generation has taken over, lock, stock and barrel. A much more brash sound of entertainment is demanded. Shows such as 'We Will Rock You', 'Stomp' and 'Dancing In The Streets' sweep in with superb results and draw in teenagers and older hags in their twenties to scream, rock, dance in the aisles and generally treat the theatre as a dancehall. Ben Elton has been lucky with his show based on Queen's catalogue. His writing is dubious to say the least and it is Queen's music that rules the day, the dialogue being superfluous. True, there is still an audience for classic pieces and revivals of such authors of Peter Ustinov, Alan Bennett, Noel Coward, Terence Rattigan, Michael Frayn and others. Strong vehicles succeed such as 'Hay Fever', recently blessed with stars the calibre of Judi Dench and Peter Bowles, (artistes who know their stagecraft backwards whatever it may be), and they help draw in the town and the many tourists that flock to West End Theatre. But prices are still much too high. Sixty-seven pounds for a seat is enough to send critics into the church to preach a sermon on living today.

Newspapers introduce new reviewers regularly. Some are superb and some cannot review their own arses to save their lives. People like Sheridan Morley and Nicholas de Jongh were institutions and had a large following, dictating whether the play in question will be a hit, or not. Whatever age groups we impresarios are supplying shows for, all have learnt to read.

It is always a good thing if new producers choose more carefully the product they propose to tour. They have to be familiar with theatre managers and book shows one to two years ahead to maintain a long tour. Having stars to embellish the commercial nature of a production is quite a necessity, whether they are newcomers from some hit TV series or an older name who had been around for a year and a day and are now happy to find a living touring the provinces. Towns up and down the country are not what they were and, in many cases, television names have swollen the heads and are not prepared to keep traipsing around the country unless the play is right and the salary excessive. Stars' fees can be fair to outrageous, whether it be for taking part in a hot musical or in a pantomime as, for instance, Peter Pan duelling with Captain Hook. Finance is an issue that can make a show or sink it.

Life upon the very wicked stage can be most lucrative if you are a regular on the box or your work is repeated a dozen times a day in the advertisement of the moment. I think many dismiss radio as an inferior vocation and out-dated medium, but this is wrong as radio commands a massive band of listeners, building millions of converts that are the envy of the Salvation Army. Years ago, Jessie Matthews made her eponymous role in 'Mrs Dale's Diary' addictive listening and many a household was compelled to tune in to this long-running series about the daily life of a provincial lady.

Chapter 29

Finale

Having survived many tempestuous seas during my eighty year life, I am constantly asked how I look so young. (I shouldn't say 'so young', but rather younger than I should look). To be camp, I always murmur "Oil of Olay' of course!" But I deliberate madly on how you look, behave and operate.

In the theatre you strive, persevere and achieve, usually in that order. Most give up the battle, marry a rich fellow or filly, and piss off to open a tea house or a bookie's. A few do stay in the game and they are the ones that feed the newspapers, catch the critics and generally are available for TV programmes.

Joan Collins is a good example. She looks marvellous (though only her husband knows what she really looks like, a selection of many wigs helping enormously). The gal has spunk, courage and a small shade of talent. I knew her father well, he was on one of the same committees as me. An astute man, not at all grand, he must have had something special in the bedroom to have had two such enchanting daughters. Her sister, Jackie Collins is not likely to wind the Booker Prize, but every housewife in the land looks forward to her books for a liberal helping of fornication, scheming and how to handle a divorce well. Escapism, I think, is what it is called.

I have been on several radio programmes recently and am often asked what I attribute to a long life. Some old hags, especially soldiers, reply, "Sex, whisky and wild women" – that's a story in itself. The main thing is to be aware of life, progress, changing moods and ideals. Always have an agile brain. Think, take in and be part of life as it is today without reminiscing all the time. A little reminiscing is delightful... a lot is totally damaging.

A lady who knew the essence of growing old gracefully was Barbara Cartland. She wrote like a thing possessed, laced wit with some grandeur and awareness, was always in the headlines and the libraries. A gossip columnist once asked Gina Lollobrigida how she felt when compared with Sophia Loren. The lady replied, "It is like comparing the racehorse with the donkey." You can take that anyway you like.

Staying power is a commodity that comes early in life. Either from one parent or both, but it is a jewel to be treasured. My thoughts are constantly turning to new adventures, schemes and possibly avenues that I have never explored before, or perhaps not even thought of.

Nostradamus told us that the world will end in this part of the century, early in the 2000s he decreed. If one looks around at the state of the world, the resurgence of mass murder, robbery, violence and weak governing, he could be right. With disease, the other killer that stalks all of us night and day, perhaps we have come to the end of the line on the train that leads us who knows where.

I think someone should start a college of reissue, where people could start to reassess and live again. I am sure ladies of mature age would crowd in to join such a venture. It would insist they re-valued their life so far so that they became aware of their disappointments and it would urge them to make up for all the things they had not done and should do.

Mrs Thatcher, whatever you thought of her politics, was a winner in many ways. She ruled instead of embroidering and knew that women could always master men, whatever their creed, religion or profession. She did not do so well with her son, Mark Thatcher, but her daughter Carol shows a little of the spunk her mother embodied. I always personally hail Jane Austen's Lady Catherine de Burgh as my pilot, a woman who dominated all others and was an interesting mortal to boot.

Anything can happen and everything is possible. One example is very encouraging. Ten years ago, the writer J K Rowling had not a bean to bless herself with. She sat down, probably with a strong brandy, and mapped out a campaign as a writer and storyteller. Her love affair with Harry Potter has made her woman of the year, if not the decade.

The great thing is that each day dawns with a new

beginning, an epic of its own. One should always look as good as possible without resorting to Elizabeth Arden and other make-up too much as it might make the natives pause and ponder and declare to themselves, "What a funny creature!"

Those of us with a theatrical streak, a talent to amuse or an enchanting episode to relate, view a new day with excitement. The telephone could ring. It could be an offer for an appearance on a television show, a load of crap deciding who and what is talented with a chance to win thousands, yet go away with fuck all if you are hopeless. It might herald the possibility you will meet someone who will change your views, your life or create a new strong affection of passion. There may be an announcement or email to inform you of riches beyond comprehension that you have been awarded, won by pure magic, which will change your circumstances forever. (Incidentally, those that inherit the earth yet change nothing, doing the same mundane things they have always done, are obviously mental, deranged and should be put in a hatbox at the top of a cupboard for all eternity, or at least until the mice get them.)

Temperament is a commodity, we all have, endure, or measure out according to whim. There is always the threat of war, or isolation, or complete obliteration of our existence brought on by man, dealt with by man, and at the end of the little comedy, completed by man. But never let that put you off from buying a new hat, taking a new lover or creating a tempting new dish for supper, be it your last or one of many.

Entertainment has been with us for centuries in one form or other, and always will be. There will always be creatures who fuss, impersonate and yearn for the adoration of others. Make sure you are ready if you come into the fold, as it is always such a joy to have something to rehearse. Those that haven't, become sticks in a matchbox – always on the mantelpiece, but never used to ignite a fire.

Some people go ignominiously to their grave or cremation or whatever they have decreed and get meted out. Others have their dream realised, and sparkle all the way to the Golden City regardless of their creed. I believe they are all treated equally,

361

ready to be reborn as God knows what. There's something to think about.

In your career, pastime or ordinary existence you probably have come across someone you have seen before, a creature who resembles or is a double of a past disciple or relative. You have probably both been reincarnated. You may have been on a train to paradise, or a jungle adventure. That previous world, life or period you imagined suddenly becomes real. Just make sure you are looking your best, for you never know who is taking you in, assessing your worth for a future casting.

To a lasting star of many, many moons or to an ageing chorine, the question of sex, whether before, during or after confession, becomes a talking point. For some it is always present, perhaps when wearing a particular gown or suit, or cufflinks and possibly a brooch, but it is always there. We are told that sex is a three-letter word, but it so often registers as one of four letters. To many, a performance will always contain a hint of sex (Marlene Dietrich's, for example), where in other artistes' hands or could be the mainspring for creating artistic perfection.

All through the years and beyond, sex has been a way of life, a creed, a passion and a must. Men do revel in this contagious scene and rarely turn the tap off, whereas women go along with men for the ride. Centuries later we have learnt how potent it has been throughout the ages.

Legendary idols of far gone days are reported to have been sexually active when all along we had believed them sterile. Newspapers tell us that certain names that have held sway in the public eye copulated like rattlesnakes, and sometimes evidence of activity with the same sex emerges, which is a little alarming and surprising. We are assured in print that Sir Laurence Olivier had a strong and constant sexual affair with Danny Kaye. This was a revelation, although many of Sir Laurence's supporters maintain that if one had lived with Vivien Leigh for years anything was possible. When it comes to the autumn of one's existence, things and attitudes change and on a summer day in a heat wave one can always imagine that Mae West never went in for sex or its delights. It was all an illusion… now there's a thought.

The sun has come up, the day is starting and the doorbell rings. It could be Mother Superior, Joan of Arc, the tax collector, Basil Brush or Simon Cowell.

It is time to go. Have a good day.